DEMOCRATIC DEFICITS: ADDRESSING CHALLENGES TO SUSTAINABILITY AND CONSOLIDATION AROUND THE WORLD

DEMOCRATIC DEFICITS: ADDRESSING CHALLENGES TO SUSTAINABILITY AND CONSOLIDATION AROUND THE WORLD

Gary Bland and Cynthia J. Arnson, editors

January 2009

Woodrow Wilson
International
Center
for Scholars

INTERNATIONAL

Available from the Latin American Program
and RTI International

Latin American Program
Woodrow Wilson International
Center for Scholars
One Woodrow Wilson Plaza
1300 Pennsylvania Avenue NW
Washington, DC 20004-3027

www.wilsoncenter.org/lap

RTI International
701 13th Street, NW, Suite 750
Washington, DC 20005

www.rti.org

ISBN 1-933549-46-7
Cover photo: David Silverman

The Woodrow Wilson International Center for Scholars, established by Congress in 1968 and headquartered in Washington, D.C., is a living national memorial to President Wilson. The Center's mission is to commemorate the ideals and concerns of Woodrow Wilson by providing a link between the worlds of ideas and policy, while fostering research, study, discussion, and collaboration among a broad spectrum of individuals concerned with policy and scholarship in national and international affairs. Supported by public and private funds, the Center is a nonpartisan institution engaged in the study of national and world affairs. It establishes and maintains a neutral forum for free, open, and informed dialogue. Conclusions or opinions expressed in Center publications and programs are those of the authors and speakers and do not necessarily reflect the views of the Center staff, fellows, trustees, advisory groups, or any individuals or organizations that provide financial support to the Center.

The Center is the publisher of *The Wilson Quarterly* and home of Woodrow Wilson Center Press, *dialogue* radio and television, and the monthly newsletter "Centerpoint." For more information about the Center's activities and publications, please visit us on the web at **www.wilsoncenter.org**.

About RTI International

RTI is one of the world's leading independent, nonprofit research and development organizations, dedicated to improving the human condition by turning knowledge into practice. Headquartered in Research Triangle Park, N.C., RTI pursues its mission through cutting-edge study and analysis in health and pharmaceuticals, education and training, surveys and statistics, advanced technology, democratic governance, economic and social development, energy, and the environment. RTI's specific work in democratic governance includes anticorruption, conflict mitigation, crime reduction, elections, legislative strengthening, and decentralization and local governance.

Growing from a handful of scientists in central North Carolina over the past fifty years, RTI today has more than 3,800 professionals providing research and technical services to governments and businesses in more than 40 countries. RTI is an affiliate of three North Carolina universities—Duke University in Durham, the University of North Carolina at Chapel Hill, and North Carolina State University in Raleigh, which together founded RTI in 1958—but operates separately with its own offices and staff. RTI works with their scientists and faculty on research programs and projects and, likewise, currently collaborates with some 70 U.S. and international universities overall.

Home to RTI Press, RTI supports education, charities, and service groups through a generous philanthropy program and other community initiatives. For more information about RTI and our work, please visit us on the web at **www.rti.org**.

RTI International is a trade name of Research Triangle Institute.

CONTENTS

III. LIMITATIONS AND THREATS PRESENTED BY CONFLICT

How are democracies around the world addressing the deficits they face today? What cases are viewed as particularly successful in addressing poverty or social services? Have institutional reforms—anticorruption measures, participatory mechanisms, judicial or ministerial reform, and decentralization, among others—been successful or even useful? Does ethnic or religious division prevent progress, and how can it be best addressed?

These are among the central issues addressed in this compilation of essays prepared for the policy forum, "Democratic Deficits: Addressing Challenges to Sustainability and Consolidation Around the World," cosponsored by RTI International and the Woodrow Wilson International Center for Scholars. The day-long event, held at the Wilson Center in Washington, D.C., on September 18, 2007, brought together scholars, journalists, and development practitioners for three purposes: first, to highlight three core areas of democratic development—social services, poverty, and inequality; institutions; and the management of conflict. Second, we intended to explore government policy and development practices that have shown mixed results with respect to improving the quality of life of citizens in democratic regimes. Finally, we sought to identify and analyze case studies that can be utilized regionally or even globally to support the progress of democratic government and the improvement of U.S. foreign and development assistance policy. The quality and stability of democratic governance, in short, was the focus of our attention for the day.

This volume delves into the difficult challenges facing democracies today. Through an examination of a diverse set of countries, the authors help advance the state of knowledge and the policy debate among scholars, policymakers, and development practitioners alike on the obstacles facing countries seeking to sustain and eventually consolidate their democracies. Our hope is that these pages contribute to the ongoing debate among scholars and practitioners about democratic development—how it comes about, why it collapses or survives, and whether or not it is sustained and then consolidated.

We would like to thank all of the staff at RTI who made this publication possible. Derick Brinkerhoff and Sara Vande Kappelle were especially important to the success of the policy forum. Other RTI staff provided ideas and support, including Debbie Cavalier, John Fieno, Barbara Friday, Nicole Gerber, Margaret Pinard, and Gayle Schwartz. We express gratitude to Adam Stubits and Nikki

Nichols of the Latin American Program for their assistance with the conference and this publication. We also thank Lynda Grahill for her editorial assistance and Michelle Furman for the cover design and publication layout.

—Gary Bland
Cynthia Arnson
January 2009

INTRODUCTION
Gary Bland[1]

The establishment or return of democratic government is invariably greeted in the home country and abroad with great enthusiasm. The various "revolutions" in Eastern Europe and Lebanon in recent years are some of the latest examples. The widely studied transitions to democracy of the 1980s and 1990s in Latin America were also accompanied by well-deserved, hemispheric-wide congratulations for the historic progress of political democracy in the region.[2] Even slight progress in places like Iraq and elsewhere in the Middle East is, for obvious reasons, accorded major international significance.

Unfortunately, the emergence of political democracy in these and other cases is often encumbered by unrealistic expectations. Such expectations are in large part generated by a tendency to highlight democratic process—elections in particular—to the neglect of the difficult and long-term work of consolidating democratic practice and culture in the face of continued challenges to its legitimacy. As the fundamental socioeconomic and institutional weaknesses of the system invariably return to the fore and a public backlash emerges, the threat to democratic legitimacy can be severe.

The inability of democratic governments to address deep-seated poverty or systemic inequality especially weakens them. Social inequality can abruptly undermine a democratic regime and lead to political instability, increased criminal activity, and eventual erosion of the rule of law.[3] When large and increasing numbers of children cannot attend school or when much of the public cannot access even basic health care, the long-term stability of any political democracy is certainly at issue.

Institutional reform does matter for democracy. The rules by which institutions operate reflect the motivations of designers; generate fundamental incentives, favorable or otherwise; and can shape the prospects for the institutionalization of democratic practice. Well-designed institutions can increase official accountability to the public; poorly designed institutions can be anti-democratic or a wasteful drain on state resources. Corruption in particular (or the belief that it exists or is increasing in serious measure) can corrode public faith in the system.

Deep-seated societal divisions or open conflict can be resolved only after years of effort domestically and internationally to generate some kind of consensus upon which a democratically elected regime can be sustained and strengthened. Be it through diplomatic and economic pressure, military occupation, foreign assistance programming, or any number of other possibilities, international involvement in conflict and its resolution can have both positive and negative consequences for the eventual democratic maturation of the regime. Close examination of the impact of international factors is critical in each case.

Our examination of democratic deficits is, if nothing else, a reminder that democracy is an ideal, one that can have little to do with the reality or rhetoric on the ground in any country. We are reminded that the regimes we study in this book and see around the world today are destined to be imperfect approximations of the notion of government by and for the people. Indeed, to make this point, Dahl famously called these imperfect institutional arrangements "polyarchies" rather than democracies.[5] Democratization, then, is about establishing and improving a system of governance in which citizens select their leaders by popular vote as a *first step*—a step in many instances to be celebrated, to be sure, but a first step nonetheless. If we are serious about adding quality to democracy, we need not just to recognize, but to anticipate and appreciate that any country striving to democratize is on an extended, multifaceted, and difficult journey to perfect the imperfect that can never really be concluded.

In addressing the question of achieving democratic quality (and so as not to delve into, here, the definitional and other debates around transition and consolidation), I posit that the concept that most completely captures our concerns is "legitimacy"—and the value of maintaining or strengthening it. Democratic legitimacy provides the foundation for democratic stability. Legitimacy requires the belief with some intensity by at least a majority of a country's citizens that "no other type of regime could assure a more successful pursuit of collective goals."[6] Legitimacy implies that a democratic regime is working well enough to maintain for the long term the confidence and support of the population, and the public respects the system because it cannot envision a better alternative. Conversely, if the deficits in the functioning of a regime grow severe enough, the public's faith may begin to erode, elected officials faced with political and economic crises may turn increasingly arbitrary, and the populace may demonstrate increased interest in more authoritarian alternatives.

The process of building democratic legitimacy involves three highly interrelated state functions: administrative effectiveness, political responsiveness, and security.[7] Administrative effectiveness refers to the ability of the state to provide basic services, economic opportunity, and socioeconomic advancement. Effectiveness implies rules-driven and transparent development of public policy and corruption-free operation of the apparatus of government. It encompasses functions that most directly influence the quality of life and social equality. Michael Bratton (Chapter 2) assesses through his survey research in Africa, for example, the impact of public experience with and perceptions of delivery of services such as health and education on the public's view of democracy. Evelyne Huber (Chapter 3) demonstrates a link between some leftist, reform-minded governments in Latin America and strong reductions in poverty and social inequality.[8]

Political responsiveness involves the ability of the institutions of government to reflect public preferences, translate them effectively into policy, and be held accountable for the outcomes. Responsiveness requires the appropriate design of institutions (elections, separation of powers, local autonomy, basic rights, etc.) for effective representation, citizen participation, and accountability. Concerns about institutional design acquire particular salience when a country is engaged in negotiations for the settlement of a conflict or following long periods of authoritarian rule. The divergent paths to the development of responsive local governance in India are detailed by Patrick Heller (Chapter 4), for example, while Luis Chirinos (Chapter 5) describes the role of civil society in generating improved public accountability at the regional level in Peru.

Security—the protection of life, liberty, and property through effective functioning of the rule of law—is the most fundamental of the three components of legitimacy. Where security is weak, the functions of effectiveness and responsiveness are of relatively little consequence. Security encompasses issues of crime, the security forces, the reintroduction of ex-combatants, and other activities that fall under rubric of the state's monopoly over the use of force. The four country cases examined in this volume can be included among the most deep-seated or protracted conflicts in the world, and the severity of the challenges in these cases moves us beyond the question of democratic quality and well into the realm of democratic regime stability.[9] In Afghanistan, Larry Goodson (Chapter 9) explains that the issue is whether any type of transition to stable democracy can take place given the conflict and given the other factors—narcotrafficking, corruption, the weak state, etc.—that fuel the violence. Afghanistan's deep and multifaceted cleavages tend to be reinforcing. As Tim Judah (Chapter 8) points out, management of the continuing potential for conflict in Kosovo has raised the stakes for the world's newest nation-state, and the incentive of EU membership may be the only practical resolution.

COMMON THREADS

Four common or frequent themes appear throughout the volume and warrant highlighting. These include concern with democratic stability as well as quality, the link between decentralization or local governance and the growth of civil society, the conspicuous role in some cases of external actors on democratic development, and the variety of policy options and more general recommendations for improving the prospects for democracy.

Democratic Quality and Stability. The extensive literature on the various types and subtypes of democracy aims to account for the diversity of democratic regimes, be they quasi-authoritarian, predatory, and socially unequal or pluralistic, participatory, and regularly accountable to citizen demands.[10] The authors concentrate on a variety of the core issues as they relate to quality and stability.

In a book about countries with democratic traditions as divergent as India and Afghanistan, one cannot neglect the distinction between democratic quality and democratic stability. Once the deterioration of a democratic regime becomes so severe that a large and increasing number of citizens question its legitimacy, stability becomes the primary concern. The downward spiral can begin through the failure of the democratic political process (fraudulent elections being the most obvious), a persistent decline in social and economic development, or any number of other factors—many of which are addressed in the following pages—that can spark widespread political opposition.

Conversely, as Philippe Schmitter (Chapter 1) argues, wide acceptance of the political rules of the democratic game can bring about quality and stability, and the emergence of political democracy since the mid-1970s testifies to this point. It is widely held, moreover, that democracy endures when a government's economic performance leads to broad-based improvement in living standards and poverty reduction. Socioeconomic progress can also produce social and other changes—increased literacy, the growth of new social organizations, for example—that can, under the right circumstances, facilitate democratization.[11]

One should not to draw too fine a distinction between quality and stability, however, because an apparent element of quality, such as rising crime or widespread anti-government mobilization, can become an actual threat to stability.[12] The distinction proves slippery in the reverse, as well, when destabilizing circumstances appear ready to topple a regime, but ultimately work out well and serve to strengthen the quality of the democracy.

Schmitter addresses directly the debate over the definition of democratic quality, objecting to the "ever-expanding set of criteria" used to assess it. He draws a fundamental distinction between contemporary political democracy and a democratic regime's ability to meet a long list of citizen desires, the absence of which has subjected governments to continuing criticism. Demands include, for example, economic prosperity, civic culture, social equality, and crime reduction. Schmitter challenges "the presumption that these [expectations] can or even should be produced by the advent of political democracy and should, therefore, be used as defining elements of its quality." Rather, the three active ingredients of a democracy are citizens with equal political status, elected and selected representatives, and "rulers who are empowered by citizens and their representatives to take binding decisions on everyone."

"The challenge for the quality of democracy," Schmitter writes, "is to find, establish, and sustain institutions that embody these three active ingredients and do so in a way that best fulfills the [available] potential." To Schmitter, concerns about stability have been exaggerated, as the political democracies that have emerged since 1974 have done quite well.

In her discussion of corruption, Phyllis Dininio (Chapter 7) draws critical linkages between institutional strengthening, social inequality, and democracy. "Corruption hurts the poor disproportionately and further skews the distribution of wealth and power in a society," she argues. "Bribes demanded by public officials," for example, "can be considered a regressive tax because they constitute a greater share of poor households' and small firms' income than of wealthier households' and larger firms'." Corrupt activity undermines the public's trust in government. Likewise, examining mass policy preferences, questions of accessibility, and corruption, among other issues, Bratton concludes that factors such as the poverty status of service users and their experiences with service providers have important implications for satisfaction with a democratic regime.

In the case studies captured in this volume, the stability of political democracy is the central issue in Afghanistan, Lebanon, and Kosovo, and cannot be discounted in Bolivia. Goodson argues that the indicators for democratic transition in Afghanistan are bad. "This is not a place," he adds, "that will embrace democracy enthusiastically, and the difficulties will be exacerbated by resistance from increasingly enriched and entrenched elites." "The confessional system upon which the Lebanese system rests has reached its limits," argues Rami Khouri (Chapter 11). "[The] dominance of group rights over individual rights degrades the quality of public life and any attempt to have a functioning democracy or an efficient government system."

In Kosovo, as Judah illustrates, the democratic process is being called upon to accommodate a deep and ancient, but freshly recharged societal cleavage—

centuries old ethnic tensions and conflict between the Kosovar Albanians and Serbs. The potential threat to the progress of the Balkans made over the past eight years remains. Kosovo's opaque patronage-based system is, moreover, heavily influenced by business tycoons and mafia-bosses; democratic culture will not easily blossom. The question of quality and stability is highly pertinent in Bolivia as well, given the recent years of popular unrest and political and territorial division. As Brooke Larson (Chapter 10) points out, the overarching, vexing question for Bolivia is: How can an internally fractured, desperately poor nation build a sustainable democratic order capable of addressing those endemic social problems? The country's recent experiences with neoliberalism and democratic reform, she argues, provide a rich context for understanding the daunting challenges facing President Evo Morales and his ethnopopulist party today. "In light of Bolivia's ongoing social tensions and the constitutional meltdown," Larson explains, "the cohesion and viability of the nation now seem to be more at risk."[13]

Decentralization and Local Governance. Like most institutional reform, decentralization and the development of local governance are closely related and highly political processes involving a transfer of power to the local level. To ensure success, which is difficult to achieve under any circumstances, the two processes are ideally characterized by clear objectives, well-designed reforms to meet those objectives, and consistent, effective implementation. Decentralization and the development of local governance are also invariably characterized by considerable political dispute—decentralization does involve, after all, the redistribution of power—and continued adjustment as lessons are learned over a period of not just years, but decades. Decentralization is a means to some end, therefore, not an end in itself. The extent to which decentralization and the progress of local governance actually supports or weakens democracy remains a question that must be closely examined in all its aspects on a case-by-case basis.

Michael Malley (Chapter 6) traces the origins of Indonesia's decentralization to Indonesia's transition to democracy from 1998–99 and seeks to identify the key processes that reshaped the balance of power between national and subnational government. He illustrates how broadening our notions of decentralization and its causes can reshape our view of its impact and of appropriate policy to address its less-than-positive effects. Examining the origins and the political aspects as opposed to just the legal and administrative aspects of Indonesia's reform improves our understanding and provides a more favorable view of the impact of decentralization. The "overwhelming concern [of the reformers] was to maintain national unity, and on that point the record is in their favor," he explains.

We also discover that the new participatory mechanisms that accompany decentralization reform can, in fact, work, and do produce positive change in the way local citizens interact with traditional local power structures. The critical ingredient to such success is the intergovernmental shift of power, particularly the transfer of financial resources, and the authority to manage them, to the local level. For Heller, "better policy or more enlightened attitudes will do little to change inequality until the question of power is addressed," which is why the decentralization (Panchayati Raj reform) in Kerala and Madhya Pradesh—where the transfer of financial resources has been "very significant"—is so important. By creating new points and opportunities for contact with the state, he writes, decentralization helps address the institutional and associational problems. Larson describes how the "mushrooming of grassroots politics and networks in Bolivia during the 1990s also reflected the growing pressure on the central government to shift revenues (and slough off the intractable problems of development and governance) to Bolivia's regional and municipal governments." Under the 1994 Popular Participation Law, 20 percent of national tax revenues and a new array of functions were transferred to municipalities.[14] Given the current tensions over regional autonomy and territorial integrity, the final word on the impact of Bolivia's decentralization on its democracy has yet to be written.

Chirinos provides an extraordinary account of how, in the post-Fujimori period, a newly active Peruvian civil society took advantage of isolated but significant allies domestically and internationally (through aid programs) and among more reform-minded regional administrations to provide a model of effective citizen oversight of new regional government budgets. Civil society organizations, Chirinos argues, were able to exercise a newly created legal right and overcome organizational and representational problems they had faced in the past. In Kosovo, decentralization and municipal governance are seen as the core mechanisms for resolving the ethnic conflict surrounding the demand of Albanian Kosovars for national determination. Establishing new and relatively autonomous, majority-Serb municipalities, Judah reminds us, is another reflection of the effective creation of "two parallel societies." How do we account for democracy under this situation?

The Impact of International Influence. The cases in this volume, especially the four presented in the section on conflict, provide more than enough justification for the argument that a democratic nation-state, by definition, must be self-governing and unconstrained by the actions of some other, external political system.[15] For good and for ill, the policies of regional and international powers, demonstration effects, advances in telecommunications, and especially economic globalization are among the many factors pressuring the world's new democracies. The impact of external influences is generally more indirect or discrete, however, for most of the developing world than we see in, say, the case of Afghanistan.

Khouri argues that it is impossible to speak of democracy in Lebanon without considering such major international factors as the struggle between Lebanon and Syria, notions of territory and destiny in the Arab world, and pan-Islamic identity. In Kosovo, the United Nations Mission (UNMIK), the European Union, and the United States continue to exert considerable influence over the world's now-newest nation-state. Judah notes that Kosovo, which he describes as a political football in the international arena, has the potential to derail the progress which has been made in the Balkans since about 2000. Kosovo's future democratic stability is directly linked to EU accession because "it is the only tool we have."

In Bolivia, external influence is less visible but highly significant because, as Larson explains, historically the country "has occupied a critical place in the shifting geopolitics of Latin America." Neoliberalism—a reference to the market-based structural adjustment and reform programs pushed by the United States and multilateral financial institutions in Washington during the 1980s and 1990s—initially deepened poverty and generated social dislocations that have undermined the structures of governance, she adds. Finally, according to Goodson, "Afghanistan's future is most likely one that will be shaped more by actors other than the U.S.," yet U.S. engagement is crucial to the future stability of the country. Goodson concludes that the international community is making too much of elections as the solution and that the difficult situation in Afghanistan makes the prospects for a stable democratic transition unlikely. The continuing influence of Islamic fundamentalism on the future of Afghanistan is no less consequential.

Policy Choices. The authors were asked to consider the policy implications of their findings, and some policy options we see in the following pages are more explicit than others. Bratton finds that Africans judge health, education, and other social services largely in terms of the user friendliness of service agencies. Government officials should look to be as open and accessible as possible, because responsiveness, perceived corruption, and customer service do make a difference. Khouri makes a similar point indirectly in explaining the strength of Hezbollah in Lebanon, where the group "delivers key social services and meets other needs of their constituents: medical care, vocational training, and unemployment insurance;" it also "fights corruption and inefficiency, and provides a model of non-corrupt, efficient service delivery." Dininio likewise makes the convincing connection between democratic legitimacy and corruption, and the evidence that practitioners should be focusing on this area, as many are, seems clear.

Huber finds that more liberalized economies performed better with respect to economic growth and improvements in democratic quality than less liberalized economies. However, they suffered higher volatility, saw greater increases in inequality, and experienced higher levels of poverty. Pointing to successful programs in Mexico and Brazil, she argues strongly for the redirection of resources from social insurance to social assistance in an effort to address inequality. Heller and, more implicitly, Chirinos, meanwhile, argue for the proper design of institutions, particularly the establishment of mechanisms for citizen participation in governance in India and Peru, respectively. Heller points out that "participation is more plastic than we assume," and so participatory reform "can change the transaction costs that the poor and marginalized face in engaging the state." The creation of participatory institutional mechanisms at the local level also paved the way for more a more participatory civil society and democracy in Bolivia, as Larson illustrates.

Have we identified all the major democratic deficits in the developing world? Hardly. Do we now know how to address these deficits and thereby better sustain and consolidate new democracies? To a limited extent, at best. The country cases and topics discussed in this volume do provide us, however, with a better understanding of the complex concept of democracy and of the difficult practical reality surrounding attempts to improve democratic regimes facing deep poverty, social inequality, weak institutions, and many years of societal conflict. Elections, clearly, are not enough. It is the insights like those found in these chapters that provide the foundation for continued democratic progress.

REFERENCES

Bland, G. 1999. "Bolivia's Popular Participation Law and the Emergence of Local Accountability." *Bolivia Institutional Governance Review*. World Bank: Washington, DC.

Brinkerhoff, D., ed. 2007. "Introduction: Governance Challenges in Fragile States." *Governance in Post-Conflict Societies: Rebuilding Fragile States*. New York: Routledge Press.

Dahl, R. A. 1971. *Polyarchy: Participation and Opposition*. New Haven: Yale University Press.

Dahl, R. A. 1982. *Dilemmas of Pluralist Democracy: Autonomy vs. Control*. New Haven: Yale University Press.

Carothers, T. 2002. "The End of the Transition Paradigm." *Journal of Democracy* 13, no. 1 (January).

Collier, D., and S. Levitsky. 1997. "Democracy with Adjectives: Conceptual Innovation in Comparative Research." *World Politics* 49 (April).

Diamond, L. 1999. *Developing Democracy: Toward Consolidation.* Baltimore: Johns Hopkins University Press.

Diamond, L., J. Hartlyn, J. J. Linz, and S. M. Lipset, eds. 1999. *Democracy in Developing Countries: Latin America.* Bolder, CO: Lynne Rienner.

Lamounier, B. 2002. "Introduction: Globalization, Social Inequality, and Democracy." J. S. Tulchin with A. Brown, eds. *Democratic Governance & Social Inequality.* Boulder: Lynne Rienner.

Linz, J. J. 1978. *The Breakdown of Democratic Regimes: Crisis, Breakdown, and Reequilibrium.* Baltimore: Johns Hopkins University Press.

O'Donnell, G., P.C. Schmitter, and L. Whitehead, eds. 1986. *Transitions from Authoritarian Rule: Prospects for Democracy.* Baltimore: Johns Hopkins University Press.

Schmitter, P. C., and T. L. Karl. 1991. "What Democracy Is ... And Is Not." *Journal of Democracy* 2, no. 3 (Summer).

ENDNOTES

1. I would like to thank Cynthia Arnson for her helpful comments on this chapter.
2. See, for example, O'Donnell, Schmitter, and Whitehead 1986; and Diamond, Hartlyn, Linz, and Lipset 1999.
3. Lamounier, p. 5.
4. The authors were not asked to prepare formal papers but, rather, "think pieces." The chapters in this volume are their written products or transcriptions of presentations.
5. Dahl 1971.
6. Linz 1978, pp. 17–18.
7. This analytical framework is drawn, in modified form, from Brinkerhoff 2007, pp. 4–7.
8. For a supporting argument on the link between social democratic government and the reduction of inequality, see Dahl 1982, pp. 174–175.
9. On quality and stability of democratic regimes, see Lamounier 2002, pp. 4–5.
10. See Collier and Levitsky 1997. For a dissenting definitional view, see Carothers 2002.
11. Diamond 1999, pp. 78–80; and Diamond, Hartlyn et.al. 1999, pp. 44–48.
12. Lamounier 2002, pp. 4–5.
13. At the time of publication, the Morales government and opposition had just finally come to agreement on the terms of the draft of the new constitutional, and the referendum on its approval was slated for January 2009.

14. For a study of the impact of the Popular Participation Law on local government and participation, see Bland 1999.
15. Schmitter and Karl 1991, pp. 81–82. See also, Diamond, Hartlyn et.al. 1999, pp. 57–60.

I. SOCIAL DEFICITS, POVERTY, AND INEQUALITY

DEFECTS AND DEFICITS IN THE QUALITY OF NEO-DEMOCRACY

Philippe C. Schmitter

The quality of democracy has become the flavor of the year or perhaps of the decade among students of democratization. They seem to be competing among themselves to find the most negative or the most diminutive qualifier they can place in front of the word "democracy," in order to detract from the accomplishments of those democracies that have emerged roughly since 1974. This negativity seems especially widespread among Latin Americanists.

We are led to believe that these neo-democracies are flawed-, façade-, pseudo-, partial-, semi-, ersatz-, stalled-, or of low intensity, just to cite a few examples. In Washington, D.C., the favorite descriptor among pundits seems to be "illiberal." "Delegative," "defective," and "deficitary" are more commonly found among academics. In our 1986 book *Transitions from Authoritarian Rule: Tentative Conclusions about Uncertain Democracies*, Guillermo O'Donnell and I may have anticipated this reaction by coming up with the contrast between so-called "*dictablandas*" and "*democraduras*." We had already, in some sense, anticipated the game of trying to identify different hybrid forms of inferior democracy, although we did not think of the qualifiers as adjectives but, rather, as distinctive sub-types.

ONE POSSIBLE EXPLANATION

I think I can explain why this proliferation of negative descriptors has emerged. Quite unexpectedly—and quite contrary to previous experience in Latin America—the countries that have democratized since 1974 have been successful in installing and even in sustaining the basic institutions of so-called formal or electoral democracy. I earlier made the crude calculation that of every three attempts to democratize in Latin America between 1900 and 1970, two had failed. This time, however, none has failed, at least not by reverting to autocracy. There has been some back-sliding, but (so far) no emergence of overtly dictatorial or authoritarian regimes. These countries all have impeccably democratic constitutions in terms both of their proclaimed rights and purposes and of their rule and institutions. They even have an impressive array of constitutional courts, ombudsmen, independent electoral commissions, general auditing authorities, specialized human rights monitors and anticorruption agencies—instruments that many well-established democracies do not have. In short, they have all the "bells and whistles," not just of vertical accountability in the classic democratic sense, but also of this newly touted horizontal accountability.

In formal terms, therefore, the neo-democracies—such as the ones in Latin America, those in Southern Europe, and so far, those in Central and Eastern Europe—all deserve the title of RED, meaning "real existing democracies." One can call then polyarchies, to use Robert Dahl's term, while noting the serious limits that this implies: government by representatives elected by mass publics, in territorial constituents under pre-established constitutional and legal constraints, within a predictable and narrow range of uncertainty concerning who will win and what they will do once they are in office. In short, they respect the two hidden rules of real existing democracy, namely *contingent consent*—that is, you can afford to lose, with the expectation that you will be allowed sufficient resources and sufficient opportunity to get back into power—and *bounded uncertainty*— meaning that if you lose, you have reasonable expectations that whoever takes power will not take unpredictable actions that would deprive you of your resources to compete in the future. This is the implicit shared understanding that lies behind all real existing, i.e., liberal, representative, political, democracies.

Some neo-democracies have even settled into such predictable patterns of mass and elite behavior, that they are as boring to themselves and to outside observers as their archeo-democratic predecessors in Western Europe. I was once asked very early on in my thinking about democratization: "But how would I know when a democracy was consolidated?" My response was: "It's simple. As soon as your politics becomes boring, your democracy is consolidated. As soon as you can predict reasonably well who is going to win and what kinds of subjects are going to be on the agenda, your democracy is probably consolidated."

This state of affairs has been profoundly unsettling to most students of democratization, especially those like me who went through the exciting days of regime changes under conditions of high uncertainty and even higher expectations about what these changes in regime would produce. I was first pulled into this field of study because of Portugal. Portugal's transition, in retrospect, was the most uncertain and tumultuous of all of the changes from autocracy to democracy. Not only do we feel disenchanted with the results, but so do many, if not most, of the citizens in these neo-democracies—if one is to judge by the admittedly primitive questions that are posed to them by instruments such as Eurobarometer, Latinobarómetero, Afrobarometer, and other specialized mass surveys in Eastern Europe, the former Soviet Union, and Asia.

The dirty secret, then, is that **democratization and the consolidation of democracy have been so successful because democracy has been so much less consequential than its proponents wished and than its opponents feared**. We in the Woodrow Wilson Center's "Transitions" project in the early 1980s were wrong to presume that the previous supporters and beneficiaries of autocracy would strongly oppose democratization. Now, in retrospect, we have learned that those elites of the *ancien régime* learned rather quickly that such changes do not necessarily threaten their existence or their vital resources. They can agree to relinquish power, even to tolerate a substantial transformation in the rules of the game, and still return to power within a relatively short period of time.

For example, in Central and Eastern Europe, with only two exceptions, every government is now headed by a party that was formed from the individual cadres and organizational structures of its previous Communist Party. This is a dramatic example of how fortunes can change, but also how the initial losers very quickly learn not merely how to play the new game, but also that it is not necessarily detrimental to their material resources and personal situations. In Portugal, one of the few cases where the process of regime change did manifestly challenge and transform the resources of classes, sectors, and persons supporting the former autocracy, these effects proved to be momentary. That wonderful clause in the second paragraph of the Portuguese Constitution of 1975 that dedicated the new democratic government to the abolition of all differences between social classes was discreetly removed and never taken seriously.

Commenting on why disenchantment with democracy has been the norm is outside the scope of this chapter. However, the strategy of not demanding "too much" socioeconomic change has begun, belatedly, to pay off. Countries have foregone, for one reason or another, the temptation to produce more than political democracy *tutto e subito* (right away). This has helped politicians to agree among themselves that "real-existing democracy" has become the only game in town, as Juan Linz likes to put it, even when they do not agree on the precise rules for playing that game and, therefore, are incapable of consolidating a specific type of democracy. They have tricked each other into playing according to those rules of contingent consent and bounded uncertainty. They can now look forward to the perpetual struggle over who gets what, when, and how. Hopefully, this will gradually and erratically satisfy some of those displaced, frustrated expectations that democratization has brought with it.

ONE MINOR COMPLAINT

The literature in recent years that has examined the quality of democracies needs some redirection. First, one preliminary and relatively minor criticism is that we really should not be talking about the **quality** of democracy. We should be talking about **qualities** of democracy. The presumption that all that is good and all that is bad with democracy somehow cluster together and therefore can be monitored or scored by a single number or by a single adjective, and therefore understood as part of a single continuum, is wrong.

Democracy is composed of many different qualities, not all of which may be compatible with each other and certainly not all are attainable within the same time-frame. We should, therefore, be careful not to try to arrange the quality of democracy along this imagined continuum. Which means, above all, we should not be using aggregated indicators to measure "it" (whatever it may be).

One such indicator, which has been used frequently in quantitative analysis is the Freedom House rankings. It is especially useless since it is "an aggregation of aggregated data"—and the criteria for performing the aggregations are not transparent. Two countries could get exactly the same score and be utterly different in terms of the detailed scorings on the particular items or qualities that contribute to those scores—not to mention the rather obvious point that by simply adding together scores, one is assuming that every source of variation is equally important in determining the quality of democracy. Even the most cursory glance at normative democratic theory would reveal that some items are a lot more important than others. If aggregation into a single score is so desirable (a dubious assumption, in my view), they should be weighted in some explicitly defensible way. What these weightings should be is a matter of dispute, and they are likely to vary in the opinion of different publics and from the perspective of different theorists. More attention should be focused on the problem found in the literature of over-aggregation and its underlying theoretical assumption, which is not sustainable.

THREE MORE SUBSTANTIAL COMPLAINTS

My first is the impression one can get that neo-democracies are intrinsically and uniquely defective. **All REDs are defective**. Old democracies and new democracies may have their own specific deficiencies, but all real existing democracies are based on compromises. They are "mixed regimes" with many non-democratic components and many heavily circumscribed democratic mechanisms, not the least of which involve different forms of representation. They are all, in other words, works in progress moving in dubious directions that fail to live up to the potential embedded in the core semantic notion of "rule by the people."

If this were not confusing enough, the standards we apply to evaluate the performance of democracies keep changing. It is true that, for many more countries today, the only game in town has become RED. But its goalposts are constantly moving further apart. It has become increasingly difficult to identify a high-quality democracy, even when judged by one's own citizens, since those citizens will inevitably be looking across the pitch at other players playing a similarly labeled game. People now assess the quality of their own democracy not just by what is going on in their country, but by how it performs in relation to what is going on in other countries.

The central message of a White Paper on "The Future of Democracy in Europe," which I have written with a group of other scholars and politicians for the Council of Europe, concerns the increasingly defective performance of these democracies and, consequently, widespread and growing public dissatisfaction with them.[1] We assemble a good deal of aggregate and survey data to support this claim over the last 30 years and then project them forward for another 20 years in order to draw inferences about what RED might look like unless some serious effort at reform is made in the meantime. We also suggest what sort of reforms might intervene to improve the quality of "future existing democracy" in Europe.

The time series evidence seems compelling to us that the quality of real existing democracy has been diminishing—at least in Europe (we do not evaluate its performance elsewhere). The inescapable conclusion is that new democracies and old democracies do not form two separate clusters or distinct trajectories; they overlap. Depending on the scoring and weighting system one applies, it is not clear at all that **neo**-democracies are necessarily doing worse than **archeo**-democracies, especially if one takes into consideration differences in their respective points of departure.

The second general problem with the literature is that of inserting an ever-expanding set of criteria into the assessment of the quality of democracy. The most obvious way to ensure that neo-democracies will be found defective is to extend the criteria for their evaluation in substance and/or time to include dimensions that old democracies did not satisfy for many, many decades, in some cases for centuries. These criteria also have no theoretical relationship to a strictly **political** definition of what democracy is. Those who write about the quality of democracy should be reminded to specify not merely what democracy is, but also what democracy is not.[2] They should also be differentiating between what democracy is not necessarily capable of producing and what it can produce but only over a very long period of time. I remember a debate in Buenos Aires in the late 1980s in which one famous sociologist declared—in response to my observation that the problem there was no longer democracy but its consolidation—that how could I suppose that Argentina was democratic when there were still children in it who are underfed? I am sure there were underfed children in Argentina—then and now—but the per capita consumption of calories in Argentina was and still is among the highest in the world! What I find theoretically disputable is that the level and distribution of child nourishment should be considered a major indicator of the quality of political democracy in Argentina—or, for that matter, of the quality of the previous autocracy there. Not only is that the outcome of a much more complex set of factor endowments, but the country had only changed its regime some five years previously!

Democracies can be criticized for many reasons: for not always respecting the rule of law and human rights or not according justice equally to everyone and in every place; for not increasing economic development and prosperity; for not bringing about greater social equality; for not reducing gender discrimination; for not eliminating poverty; for not improving ethno-religious tolerance; for not having or fostering a civic culture; for not reducing criminality or internal violence; for not improving state capacity and policy effectiveness. The list could go on. No one denies that these are all things that most of the citizens of newly democratized polities would like and may even expect to enjoy as the result of regime change. What I challenge is the presumption that these can or even should be produced by the advent of political democracy and should, therefore, be used as defining elements of its quality. Many old democracies would still not meet all the conditions on this list.

A third general problem with the literature rests on its reliance on fixed rather than relative measures for measuring the quality of democracy. I personally do not find it enlightening or useful to be informed that the quality of democracy in Brazil—however measured—is less than that of Sweden, or even that the quality of democracy in Honduras is less than that of Hungary. The concept should convey—if it is to be both analytically valid and politically useful—an estimate of where any specific polity is relative to its potential, i.e., relative to where it could be given the human and material resources that it has to work with.

The mechanisms for RED are multiple (and not just electoral), and they can be specified in universalistic terms. Every democratizing polity seeks to implant the same generic processes of citizenship, representation, and accountability of rulers, even though their institutional expressions differ a great deal. If nothing else, the comparative study of REDs in Europe and North America demonstrates this deeply entrenched similarity in processes and diversity in rules and practices. It is the "goodness of fit" between the two, relative to a specific setting (level of economic development, degree of cultural/ethnic/religious diversity, extent of class and sectoral conflict, and so forth) that one is trying to assess when referring to the quality of democracy. How one performs or what one can do to improve that performance depends on where the country starts and what resources are available at the time it undertakes its experiment in democratization.

There is a famous story in which an Irish priest is approached by someone in the countryside, who asks, "Father, how do you get to heaven?" He thinks for a minute and responds, "Son, there are many ways to heaven, but none will get you there from here." Some countries may have a more difficult time getting to that democratic heaven than others, and this difference should be incorporated into our understanding of the quality of democracy.

TWO POTENTIAL PITFALLS

I see two problems with the relativistic position that I have staked out above. First, what determines the **potential** for democracy in a given setting is uncertain and may even be unknowable. There is extensive research on this subject, mainly focusing on such variables as level of economic development, religious or cultural values, and colonial heritage, but it is hardly conclusive. And, the evolution of regime persistence since 1974 suggests that some of these variables may have subsequently lost their potency. What is it, today, that produces the famous "structured contingency," that Terry Karl has referred to and that presumably determines the relative favorability of a given context?[3]

I have explored this issue in my recent work concerning the impact of democracy promotion upon political liberalization in the Middle East, North Africa, and democratization in Central and Eastern Europe, where I created a statistical formula to predict, as of 1985, how well different countries in these regions would have advanced in both dimensions 12 years later. The same three variables proved valuable in both cases. The first, and by far the most important, was the Human Development Index of the United Nations. It predicted most of the subsequent variance. The second was the openness of the economy at the time that democratization began, and the third was the distance to Brussels. Using these three, I was able to predict about three-quarters of the variation in how well different countries in North Africa, the Middle East, and Central and Eastern Europe, would perform. I am not saying this is some magical and universalistic formula and that, in the case of Latin America, for example, we could substitute the distance to Washington, D.C., for the distance to Brussels. Nevertheless, there is an obvious potential for at least using such information to evaluate how well particular polities have done with democracy relative to what we might expect given their economic, social, and geo-strategic attributes.

A second problem—that of **diffusion**—is much more serious in its impact upon evaluation. I presume that people (and, certainly, elites) in Brazil have some idea of what is going on in Sweden, for example. Therefore, they may not evaluate the quality of democracy in their country simply based on what is going on in it. They may do so relative to what has already been accomplished in Sweden and they may even discount their own progress accordingly. Diffusion, in other words, can lead some Brazilians to imagining themselves as the future Swedes of South America. When I started out as a student of this world region, Uruguay was often referred to as "the Switzerland of South America." I do not know whether the Uruguayans still compare themselves to the Swiss, but—if so—this could seriously bias the evaluation of the quality of their democracy. Obviously, this becomes especially problematic when one shifts from an objective/analytical perspective, to one based on subjective/normative perceptions. Perhaps, this is one reason why so many mass surveys in neo-democracies show widespread *desencanto* (disenchantment) with their performance. The respondents may not be reflecting only on the conditions existing at the moment or during the transition itself; but on their unsatisfied expectations at not having becoming "Swedish" or "North American."

THREE POTENTIAL SHORTCUTS

There are three potential shortcuts for those who choose to continue to grapple with these questions. The first is to evaluate the quality of democracy only among groups of countries that are democratizing more or less within the same timeframe, because, as I have noted above, questions about the standards for evaluating democracy and expectations about democracy have changed greatly over time. If we consider the successful wave of democracy following the end of World War II, the quality of their democracies cannot really be compared with that of the new ones that have emerged after 1970, partly because of the difference in time lapsed, but mainly because the latter have already internalized the accomplishments of the former.

A second suggestion is to compare the quality of democracies only across countries within the same cultural area or geo-political region, as one can assume that there are certain commonalities at the point of departure. This was relatively easy to do when studying Central and Eastern Europe, due to the simple fact that these countries previously had all been living under roughly the same kind of autocracy and their levels of economic development and sometimes even the degree of relative openness to foreign trade and investment, among other features, fit within a fairly narrow range. We could treat them as equivalent at a point of departure, as having had the same potential—excluding, of course, those post-communist societies in the former Republic of Yugoslavia that rapidly descended into ethnic warfare, thereby radically changing the entire equation for evaluation.

As a third and final suggestion, all countries that have been REDs for 20 or more years—regardless of where they are today—could be considered to have the same potential for attaining the quality of their democracy, now and in the future. If a country has been able to sustain this form of rule for such a length of time, it seems reasonable to presume that their expectations and criteria for evaluation of performance will have converged. For example, using identical measures to compare the performance of Costa Rican or Uruguayan democratic institutions with those of Western European countries should be valid because these countries have had (with a brief interruption in the case of Uruguay), long-term democratic regimes and have pursued more or less analogous welfare goals —albeit with different resources.

SEVERAL "REALISTIC AND RELATIVISTIC" COMPLICATIONS

Shifting to a realistic or relativistic basis for evaluating the quality of democracy has important theoretical and practical policy implications. Chief among them is that this approach excludes the common assumption that similar or identical institutions will produce similar or identical effects across countries or across time periods. It is this assumption that leads to the peddling of panaceas to neo-democracies. We find three or so such panaceas in the literature.

One of them is that parliamentarism is better than presidentialism for the consolidation of democracy, and, some people even claim, for the quality of democracy. I see absolutely no reason to believe this, as the data emerging from Central and Eastern Europe and the former Soviet Union republics seem (so far) to demonstrate. This conclusion simply rests on the accumulated result of the lengthy (and largely unsuccessful) Latin American experience with presidentialism and may have little or no relevance for contemporary experiences—there or elsewhere. In other words, the deficiency with this form of executive power could have had more to do with the regional context in which it was most frequently applied than with its intrinsic impact upon regime stability. The fact that, even in Latin America, presidential regimes since the 1980s have yet to collapse into autocracy or to perform noticeably worse should give pause for reflection on the initial assumptions.

Second, there is the widespread notion that democracies with two-party systems based on majoritarian ("first-past-the-post") electoral systems will be of a higher quality because there is a greater possibility for the electorate to hold elected officials directly accountable. I see no compelling evidence among neo-democracies for this conclusion, and, hence, no reason to believe that those systems, assuming different points of departure, would produce the same effects.

Finally and perhaps most controversially, is the notion—strongly promoted by many international financial institutions in Washington—that the quality of neo-democracy will be improved if its institutions are decentralized or even federalized. Some regard decentralization as simply desirable on its own on the grounds that placing decision-making institutions closer to their subjects/ objects (known as "subsidiarity" in Europe) is more functionally efficient or administratively effective, but also sometimes included among the indicators of the quality of democracy on the grounds that citizens will accord them greater legitimacy. I see no reason for this to be the case. Almost every Latin American country that has democratized since 1970 has, at some point, decentralized some layer of its governmental structure—and I have yet to see any evidence to support the conclusion that those that did it the most have actually have produced better democracies. Decentralization certainly can produce good effects; and it also can create bad effects.

ONE GENERIC DEFINITION

To get to the heart of the matter, I will provide a definition of democracy that furnishes a generic basis for then exploring the question of the quality of democracy. "Modern political democracy is a regime or system of government in which rulers are held accountable for their actions in the public realm by citizens acting indirectly through the competition and cooperation of their representatives."[4] This definition has three components, which together provide certain ideas about democracy's mechanisms. (1) Citizens, all persons with an equal political status, are the central and most distinctive component of democracy. (2) Representatives—elected and selected—are another essential component; although one must keep in mind that there can be various direct channels of citizen action depending on the type of democracy. (3) The final "mechanism" consists of a set of rulers who are empowered by citizens and their representatives to take binding decisions on everyone. These three somehow interact to produce an outcome: "accountability for actions in the public realm" that presumably ensures (in the long run) responsiveness to citizen preferences for public goods and the (eventual) legitimacy to govern.

The challenge for the quality of democracy is to find, establish, and sustain institutions that both embody these three active ingredients and do so in a way that best fulfills the potential that is available in that particular setting. Granted that, in the longer run, one can hope that the practice of such apposite institutions will serve to enlarge—even to transform—that potential, but initially the challenge is to exploit the unit's "structured contingency" to the fullest possible extent. The founders and consolidators of a neo-democracy have to choose rules that bind themselves to each other and to the citizens and their representatives in a process that produces accountability. And, as Karl Marx put it some time ago, they have to do so "under conditions which are not of their choosing."

A MULTITUDE OF PARTIAL REGIMES AND POTENTIAL INDICATORS

What are the mechanisms—hopefully, institutionalized—that connect the three sets of actors to produce such an outcome? I begin with the notion that all democracies are composed of a number of "partial regimes" that function relatively independently to make these connections. In the scholarly literature and in popular imagery, the most prominent and, hence, indispensable one connects citizens as voters in territorial constituencies to elected representatives in parliament via competing political parties according to electoral systems that predictably translate votes into seats. The rules configuring this partial regime differ a great deal, but without some such mechanism no polity could plausibly claim to be democratic. But this by no means exhausts the potential. REDs also usually have partial regimes regulating the interaction between different levels of territorial authority; setting the conditions under which associations and movements can form, recruit members, and interact with government; prescribing how governments will be formed and disbanded; influencing how capital and labor will bargain with each other; allocating checks and balances among public powers; controlling the relation between civil and military actors; specifying the rights of citizens—and more.

In some preliminary thinking about them, I have deduced thirty-three different potential mechanisms involving the interaction between citizens, their representatives, and their rulers. All I can do in the present context is to provide some examples of my proposed approach to evaluating their contribution to the quality of democracy in a "realistic and relativistic" way. I will concentrate on those involving citizens, their role and their participation in the political process since this constitutes the bedrock upon which the entire edifice of RED rests. Autocracies usually have some forms of representation, and except for the most despotic, they have prescribed rules for making decisions among a privileged few. What they do not have are citizens in the sense I am using. It follows that evaluating the forms, conditions, opportunities, meanings—i.e., the mechanisms—of citizenship is the place to start when evaluating the quality of democracy.

I am convinced that research on the quality of democracy needs a new system of measurement, based on explicit theoretical foundations. Ironically, if that system is eventually to be "realistic and relativistic," it must begin by being "idealistic and absolute." Let me explain.

Assume for a minute that through comparative analysis political scientists are capable of specifying that which is, at any moment in time, the best practice for ensuring citizen participation in parliamentary or presidential elections. "Best" in this case would mean that set of existing rules that comes closest to fulfilling the normative expectations ("ideals") of democratic theory.[5] In this example, these rules should ensure the highest voter turnout, the least skewed distribution among non-voters, the most accurate tallying of votes cast, the most even weighting of these votes according to constituencies, the highest level of information about candidates and their parties, the most equal distribution of resources among candidates and parties, and the participation of citizens in elections at all levels of public authority. Needless to say, no RED has a set of rules that perfectly satisfies all these ideals, but virtually no theorist of democracy could deny their validity. One needs the ideal and absolute specifications in order to measure the real and relative performance and, thereby, to assess how close any given polity comes to reaching these "best practices." One also may need to compensate (i.e., "to relativize") for the fact that some of these standards may be impossible to reach in a newly democratizing country with more limited material resources or more pressing immediate security preoccupations.

Let us give each political democracy one hundred points to start with. If it perfectly satisfies expectations by having the rules that best satisfy the above norms, it would keep all of those points—at least, with regard to the 'partial regime' of citizen participation in elections. However, for each rule or practice that fails to do so, points would be deducted. For example, twenty points could be subtracted if citizens can only vote in national elections and only ten points if they can vote only in national and local/provincial elections—provided, of course, that such multiple levels exist in the polity being assessed. In short, what is important is that elections exist for the choice of public officials at each level with some degree of independence and authority. A more disputable principle would be to reward a polity simply for having the most layers of government and detracting points from those with more concentrated or centralized systems.

Any RED would suffer a large deduction in points—say, forty—if its voting rules excluded adult minority populations on ethnic, religious, gender, ideological, or other grounds.[6] The question of voting rights for legally resident foreign citizens ("denizens") is a particularly sensitive one. In Europe, one of the most serious issues involving decline in the quality of democracy focuses on the increasing proportion of legal residents who have no formal voting rights. Some countries have begun to respond to this, especially by enfranchising denizens at the local level. Hence, it would seem justifiable to punish a RED—say, by losing one point for each percentile of the age-eligible legally resident population that is not registered to vote at the local level—for ignoring this problem. Since no RED has yet to extend full voting rights at the national level to this population, none of them would suffer a corresponding depreciation in their measured quality of democracy.

Other points should be awarded or deducted according to the system of voter registration. Best practice would be compulsory, uniform, permanent, and complete registration, at a specified age irrespective of place or length of residence. Practice in the United States RED satisfies none of these criteria and there are many persons there who have never registered to vote or who are ineligible to do so because they have moved recently. Virtually all European REDs would score higher—although not all of them would reach the coveted 100 points.

There is another interesting 'quality' comparison between democracy in Europe and the United States. In at least some American states, if an individual has been convicted of a felony he or she is denied civic rights—even after serving the sentence. Since these convicts hardly constitute a random sample of the population, it would seem justified to deduct additional points on grounds of ethnic and/or class discrimination.

A more controversial principle involves the notion that every vote cast should count in the sense that it should contribute to the election of a representative.

Votes should not be "thrown away" either because they were not cast for the winner in single candidate, majoritarian constituencies or because they went to parties that failed to cross the minimal threshold in proportional representation systems. Poorer quality democracies would lose, say, a one-half point deduction for each percentile of the total votes cast that did not contribute to the election of any candidate. This, of course, would discriminate systematically against Anglo-American "first-past-the-post" electoral systems and those Continental PR systems with higher thresholds for national representation. In a recent Polish parliamentary election, for example, there were more than fifty parties competing, and 53 percent of the electorate voted for parties that did not get a single seat. That, according to the principle enunciated above would be an indication of a poor quality democracy.

A country would also receive a one-point deduction for each percentile decline in voting turnout compared to its moving average over the three previous elections. Many scholars have argued simply that the lower the turnout, the lower the quality of democracy. But that is based on a disputable assumption. Some countries have different and quite persistent habits related to abstention, some of which stem from registration procedures and electoral rules, others from quite rational and independent voter calculations. My favorite case is Switzerland, which has the lowest voter turnout in Europe. Swiss turnout is regularly at 30–35 percent, and hardly changes in any significant way. But if one asks the Swiss about the quality of their political system, over 80 percent will tell you they have the best political system in the world. The absolute standard would be simply to measure citizen electoral participation and deduct for any performance other than the highest one observed. The relative approach would not only use REDs of comparable historical experience to set the standard, but also to measure rise or fall in the quality of democracy in terms of a polity's own previous behavior.

I could continue further, just in evaluating the partial regime of citizen participation in elections—not to mention in exploring how one should calibrate the "**Best Practice**" in other domains relative to democratic accountability. But this cannot be the work of a single person. What is required is a joint venture—analogous to that assembled by the Bertelsmann Foundation—that would collectively review the "idealistic and absolute" standards in the normative literature and try to agree upon some consistent system for deducting points for "**Less Than Best Practice.**"[7]

Accomplishing this would also have two other ancillary benefits. On the one hand, it should help to identify marginal "trade-offs," if not outright "contradictions," between democratic norms, i.e., practical situations in which satisfying one criterion of excellence (say, equality or representativeness) might make it more difficult or even impossible to satisfy another (say, freedom or effective government). On the other hand, it would also provide us with something that has heretofore proven rather difficult—especially in the post-1974 era of democratization when so many new regimes have managed to sustain their electoral credentials—namely, an agreed-upon standard for identifying those polities whose practices fall below a prescribed minimal standard. For example, any polity receiving a score of less than 70 on major partial regimes of democracy would deserve some adjectival condemnation (say, "defective") and those receiving less than 30 should be banished from the category altogether.

A HURRIED CONCLUSION

The quality of democracy depends on the functioning of political mechanisms that predictably and systematically link citizens, representatives, and rulers to produce accountability in the use of legitimate public authority. Certainly, no one would deny that having free and fair competitive elections with citizens participating on equal footing is one of those mechanisms. But there are lots of other ones having to do with the intervention of organizations in civil society and the direct activity of citizens in demonstrations, referendums, initiatives, recall measures, letters to representatives, and communications by e-mail.

In the "classical" version, this accountability is "vertical," i.e., from citizens up to representatives and then to rulers. More recently, emphasis has shifted to so-called "horizontal" accountability involving checks and balances between ruling state institutions.[8] Reference has even been made to "oblique" accountability in which social organizations in civil society mobilize, outside or alongside the party system, to influence the behavior of rulers. Evaluating the first two spatial dimensions is a relatively easy matter since their practices are usually embedded in formal rules—constitutional or other—and this ensures a relatively public record concerning their performance. Oblique accountability, however, is exercised in a much more informal and episodic fashion and this implies the need for a quite different set of measuring devices if we are to capture its contribution to the quality of democracy.

I have argued that even the longest-established REDs in Europe are not doing very well, especially in the traditional vertical dimension. If this is the case, then, it may not be the case that new REDs are doing as badly as many have claimed. Their electoral and party systems are, admittedly, defective as evidenced by rapidly declining turnout, very low levels of partisan membership and identification, and high volatility in voting preferences. Conversely, however, they have been overloaded with an unprecedented multiplicity of institutions for horizontal accountability and invaded by an impressive variety of civil society organizations coming from older REDs. And they all face the additional burden that their citizens have already internalized the same substantive expectations as their more developed neighbors.

I have also argued that, if one is to evaluate the quality of either new or old democracy, one should begin by applying political criteria to the task— normative ideals drawn from democratic theory and institutional standards derived from "best practice." Which does not mean that one should stop there. Democracy may bring its own intrinsic rewards, but most of those who struggle for it and learn to live with its eventual compromises do so because they expect it to reward them extrinsically with such things as more dignified treatment by authorities, fairer administration of justice, more regular application of the rule of law, greater social equality, more economic prosperity, stricter respect for human rights, greater tolerance for cultural diversity, and, of course, greater freedom of choice. Now, 20 to 30 years after having made this collective choice, it may still be too early to judge whether neo-democracy was worth it. Western Europe took much longer than this to realize most of these substantive benefits—and suffered two horrendous international wars and many authoritarian reversals on the way to getting there.[9] The risk that these countries in Southern and Eastern Europe and in Southern and Central America have taken is to assume that consolidating some form of democracy, even one of poor quality, will eventually satisfy their citizens' aspirations for justice, prosperity, dignity, and freedom. That they will be able to do so immediately, given both the less favorable points of departure and the greater burden of meeting higher expectations, seems to me very unlikely. Seen from this "realistic and relativistic" perspective, I would argue that they have (so far) been doing astonishingly well—much better than I thought when I began my inquiry into *Transitions from Authoritarian Rule* at the Woodrow Wilson Center in the early 1980s.

REFERENCES

Bertelsmann Stiftung (ed.). *Bertelsmann Transformation Index 2006.* 2006. Gütersloh: Verlag Bertelsmann.

Karl, T. L., "Dilemmas of Democratization in Latin America." *Comparative Politics*, 23, no.1 (October 1990): 1–21.

Schedler, A., Diamond, L., and Plattner, M. (eds.). 1999. *The Self-Restraining State: Power and Accountability in New Democracies.* Boulder: Lynn Rienner.

Schmitter, P., with Trechsel, A. 2004. *The Future of Democracy in Europe. Trends, Analyses and Reforms.* Strasburg: Council of Europe Publishing.

———, with Karl, T. "What Democracy Is ... and Is Not." *Journal of Democracy* 2, no. 3 (Summer 1991): 75–88. Reprinted in: L. Diamond and M. F. Plattner (eds.). *The Global Resurgence of Democracy.* 1993. Baltimore: Johns Hopkins University Press: 39–52; *ibid.*, 2nd ed., 1996: 49–62.

ENDNOTES

1. Schmitter 2004
2. Schmitter 1991.
3. Karl 1990.
4. This definition can be found and is further explicated in the article cited in FN 2.
5. I doubt if specialists in comparative politics at this stage would easily agree on which are the best practices in REDs—even in such a well-examined arena as that of elections. Only by setting up such a system of evaluation for each partial regime and engaging in extensive deliberation about the effects of different rules might such an agreement emerge and be converted into a valid instrument for measuring the quality of democracy.
6. Or, if its rules prevented political parties from competing that claimed to represent such interests.
7. The Bertelsmann Stiftung has assembled an impressive and comprehensive group of scholars to produce its "Transformation Index." Not only are its procedures fully transparent, but they are based on an extensive conceptual discussion and a large number of independently scored indicators. Cf. Bertelsmann Stiftung 2006.
8. For an extensive (if inconclusive) debate about the significance of horizontal accountability, see the essays in Schedler 1999.
9. Western Europe also had the great advantage that the rule of law and, in many cases, even constitutional government preceded rather than succeeded RED.

ARE YOU BEING SERVED?: POPULAR SATISFACTION WITH HEALTH AND EDUCATION SERVICES IN AFRICA

Michael Bratton

Are you being served? This inquiry always greets the well-heeled customers in the fictional department store in the classic British television comedy series. But it is rarely asked of the ordinary men and women who consume basic public services in Africa. This paper seeks to remedy the situation.

The 2004 *World Development Report* frames the debate. Its authors seek to "put poor people at the center of service provision: by enabling them to monitor and discipline service providers, by amplifying their voice in policy making, and by strengthening incentives for providers to serve the poor" (World Bank 2004, p.1). We already possess extensive narrative testimonies of poor people's demands for socioeconomic development (Narayan 2000; Narayan et al. 2001, Institute for Policy Alternatives 2005). We also have macro-level evidence from India that responsive governance—the public sector analogue of customer service—depends on the free flow of information in the context of electoral competition (Besley and Burgess 2002; Keefer and Khemani 2003 and 2004). Yet research from the same perspective in Latin America suggests that democratic elections and public spending alone are insufficient to guarantee high quality social services or equitable service delivery (Nelson 2005; Kauffman and Nelson 2005; World Bank 2004, p. 36).

This chapter builds on these foundations by exploring the determinants of public satisfaction (or dissatisfaction) with health and education services in Africa. I select these basic services because of their intimate links to economic growth and human welfare. And, I show at the end that factors like the users' poverty status and their experiences with service providers have implications for satisfaction with the governing regime.

RESEARCH QUESTIONS

The following research questions guide the study:

- How important are basic social services among Africans' development priorities?
- How satisfied are Africans with government performance in the health and education sectors?

- For users, which aspects of service delivery matter more: quantity or quality?
- If quality matters, which aspects of users' experiences with service providers are decisive?
- Does official corruption always undermine popular satisfaction with services?
- Is there a link between satisfaction with service delivery and satisfaction with democracy?

The chapter proceeds in three parts: contextual, descriptive, and analytic.

Part One describes the context of service delivery. It begins by asking whether (and where) concerns about health and education appear on a "popular development agenda." It also probes the questions "who should provide?" and "who should pay?"

Part Two conceives and measures the main dependent and independent variables. The object of explanation—popular satisfaction with service provision—is measured in alternate ways. We then theorize that service satisfaction will be determined principally by users' perception of the quality of services rendered. Various measures of service quality—ranging from the general ease of access to services, to specific encounters with maladministration and corruption—are reviewed for both health and education sectors.

Part Three is analytical, testing a full range of prospective determinants of service satisfaction in multivariate models. We find that "user-friendliness" in service access is essential, especially to poorer clients. But the low quality of daily service provision undermines client contentment, and corruption has unexpectedly mixed effects. The analysis ends by demonstrating that public satisfaction with basic social services is also part of the instrumental calculus that Africans employ to arrive at judgments about new regimes of electoral democracy.

DATA SOURCE

Data are drawn from the Afrobarometer, a comparative series of public attitude surveys on democracy, governance, markets, and living conditions.[1] The series is based on randomly selected national probability samples ranging in size from 1200 to 3600 respondents per country and representing cross-sections of adult citizens age 18 years or older. Samples are selected from the best available census frames and yield a margin of sampling error of no more than plus or minus 3 percentage points at a 95 percent confidence level. All interviews are conducted face-to-face by trained fieldworkers in the language of the respondent's choice. Response rates average above 80 percent. Because a standard questionnaire is used with identical or functionally equivalent items, comparisons of results are possible across countries and over time.

Analysis is based mainly on Round 3 of the Afrobarometer, which covers 18 African countries during March 2005 to February 2006. Recent coverage includes 12 anglophone, four francophone, and two lusophone countries.[2] Because survey research is most feasible in open societies, the Afrobarometer over-represents stable democracies, although some unstable and undemocratic countries—such as Uganda and Zimbabwe—are included. While the survey results can be generalized to people who live in Africa's new multiparty electoral regimes, they should not be taken, without due caution, to refer to all Africans.

PART ONE

The Popular Development Agenda

Given difficult life circumstances, Africans demand health and education services. But what priority do they attach to various felt needs? The best way to find out is to ask ordinary people, as with the following Afrobarometer question: "In your opinion, what are the most important problems facing this country that the government should address?" Respondents are encouraged to offer up to three answers. Overall, the distribution of answers can be regarded as a popular agenda for development.

Table 1 shows the top ten problems identified by over 25,000 respondents in Afrobarometer Round 3 surveys in 18 African countries circa 2005.[3] Unemployment is the biggest concern, mentioned by 39 percent of all respondents. Problems of economic livelihood dominate the list; in priority order, these are unemployment, food shortage, poverty, transport infrastructure, agricultural production and marketing, and the management of the national economy. Together, economic problems account for two-thirds of the top ten items, suggesting that Africans conceive of development primarily as a matter of economic survival or material advancement.

Social development has a lower profile on the popular development agenda, though health care, especially for malaria and HIV/AIDS, is the second most frequently cited problem, mentioned by 30 percent of respondents. Education (ranked fifth) and household water supply (ranked sixth) round out the list of frequently mentioned social service priorities.

Table 1: The Popular Development Agenda, 18 African Countries, 2005

Most Important Problems	Percent of Responses	Percent of Respondents
Unemployment	13	39
Health	10	30
Food Shortage	8	25
Poverty	8	24
Education	7	22
Water	6	20
Transport Infrastructure	5	16
Agriculture	4	13
Management of the Economy	4	11
Crime and Insecurity	4	11

Source: Afrobarameter Round 3 (N of responses = 69,095).

Total in last column exceeds 100 percent due to multiple responses.

Unless crime and insecurity are classified as political problems, there are no issues of good governance on the popular development agenda. Not shown in Table 1 is the fact that official corruption ranks eleventh, suggesting that, unlike international aid agencies, ordinary people attach limited importance to this obstacle to development: just 8 percent ever mention it.

In other respects, however, the popular agenda converges with official development priorities. Mass preferences are broadly consistent, for example, with the United Nations' Millennium Development Goals to "eradicate extreme poverty and hunger," "reduce child mortality," "improve maternal health," and "achieve universal primary education" (United Nations 2006).

How has this popular development agenda evolved over time? Several trends are evident when selected results are compared from three rounds of Afrobarometer data, 2000 to 2005 (see Figure 1).[4] First, unemployment is the top preoccupation at every moment, reflecting the central role that cash income plays in individual and household welfare. Moreover, popular concern about joblessness is rising, from one in three Africans in 2000, to four in ten by 2005. Second, food shortages are the fastest growing problem, with the proportion mentioning hunger more than tripling between 2000 and 2005, a period when drought hit East and Southern Africa. Third, access to health care is always the leading social problem, rising by a significant 10 percentage points and being mentioned by more than a quarter of all persons interviewed in 2005, an upsurge that coincides with the acceleration of deaths related to HIV/AIDS.

Figure 1: Trends in the Popular Development Agenda: Most Important Problems, 12 African Countries, 2000–2005

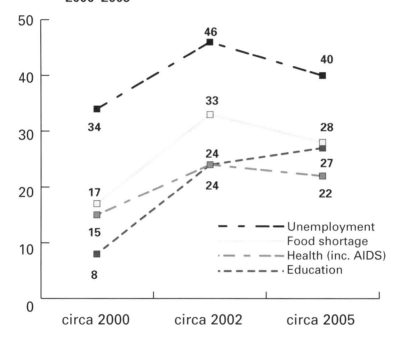

Mass Policy Preferences

How will demands for health and education be addressed? Whom do Africans hold responsible for providing these basic social services? Is it the state, the private sector, or the individual?

We find strong evidence of popular support for state intervention. Asked in 2000, "Who is responsible for providing schools and clinics?" a majority of 59 percent across 11 countries said "the government" (see Figure 2). Only 4 percent chose "private companies" or "individuals," but some 28 percent were willing to countenance "a combination of these providers."

Thus, public opinion clearly holds that the national government has an obligation to provide education and health care for all. This position is not inconsistent with the international policy consensus that "no country has achieved significant improvement in child mortality and primary education without government involvement" (World Bank 2004, p.11).

Figure 2: Preferred Provider of Health and Education Services, 11 African Countries, 2000

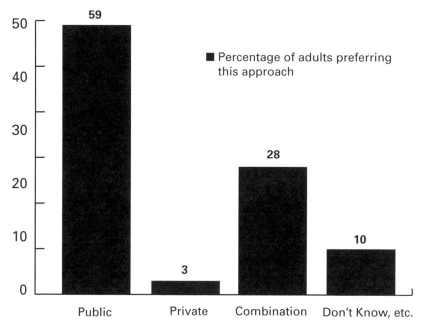

I am going to read out a list of things that are important for the development of our country. In your opinion, who is responsible for providing (schools and clinics)? The government, private businesses, or the people themselves? Or some combination of these providers?

But who should pay? African governments have taken a range of policy stances with regard to financing basic social services. Whereas the governments of Cameroon,

Kenya, Malawi, Tanzania, Uganda, and Zambia have introduced free universal primary education (UPE), governments in countries like Ethiopia and South Africa, among others, continue to require payments for tuition (Development Committee 2001; Boyle et al. 2002; Bentaouet-Kattan and Burnett 2004; Stasavage 2005). Moreover, even where education is ostensibly free, parents may still have to cover uniform, book, exam, or activity fees. And parents also support community schools in the rural regions of countries—like Chad, Mali, and Togo—where the state has been unable to deliver public education.

African governments have adopted a similar gamut of financing policies in the health sector (WHO 2004; Thiede et al. 2004). At one extreme, South Africa's extensive health care system provides free primary care at public clinics for anyone who is uninsured. By contrast, patients in countries like Benin pay for consultations with medical personnel and cover up to two-thirds of total costs through out-of-pocket payments (Wadee et al. 2003; Dieninger and Mpuga 2005).

The bold introduction of universal free access to social services invariably involves a massive expansion in the number of users and a concomitant decline in service quality. Over three rounds of surveys, the Afrobarometer has asked citizens to weigh the pros and cons of this trade-off. For example, is it better "to have free education for our children, even if the quality of education is low?" Or is it better "to raise educational standards, even if we have to pay school fees?" One might predict that poor populations with limited previous access to schooling would be enticed by the prospect of gratis provision and would discount the issue of educational quality. But, most Africans we have interviewed have always shown commitment to high educational standards, even if fee payments are required. But the majority preferring this policy has declined over time—from 62 percent circa 2000, to 60 percent circa 2002, to 53 percent circa 2005 (see Figure 3)—perhaps as people have come to appreciate the equalizing benefits of primary school provision to the poor.

As might be expected, support for a policy of tuition fees is highest in countries where people are accustomed to paying for education, as in Ghana (74 percent in 2005), Mali (69 percent) and South Africa (67 percent). By contrast, a majority of people prefers universal free education in those countries wherever this policy prevails: for example in Tanzania (56 percent), Zambia (55 percent), and Kenya (51 percent). It is noticeable, however, that mass endorsement of free education is lukewarm in the latter group of countries. And Uganda constitutes an intriguing exception: despite the availability of free primary education since 1996, a barely changing minimum of 55 percent of Ugandans—whether in

1999, 2002, or 2005—has repeatedly sided with a policy of school fees and high educational standards. Because primary school enrolment doubled in five years, Ugandans are perhaps weighing the costs of overcrowded classrooms, low academic achievement, and rising dropout rates (World Bank 2002).

Figure 3: Trends in Education Policy Preferences, 11 African Countries, 2000–2005

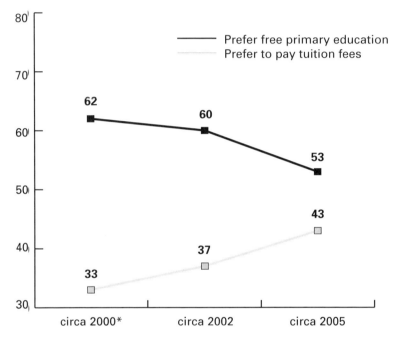

Please choose A or B:

A. It is better to have free education for our children, even if the quality of education is low

B. It is better to raise educational standards, even if we have to pay school fees

* In 2000, the question for Southern African countries referred to clinic fees

PART TWO

Within this context, we now address the central research question: What explains popular satisfaction with health and education services? Our thesis is that the people arrive at evaluations of government performance through a learning process: Popular satisfaction (or dissatisfaction) is shaped by individual experiences with access to services.

Popular Service Satisfaction

In this paper, we measure popular service satisfaction with survey responses to questions about "How well or badly would you say the current government is handling the following matters, or haven't you heard enough to say?" The relevant sub-items are "improving basic health services" and "addressing educational needs."[5]

Average results across 18 countries are given in Figure 4. Wide variations in positive popular evaluations suggest that Africans can readily distinguish among policy domains and arrive at separate and divergent judgments about each. With this indicator, a sharp differentiation emerges between social and economic sectors, as does a somewhat more cautious mood overall.

Figure 4: Satisfaction with Government Performance, 18 African Countries, 2005

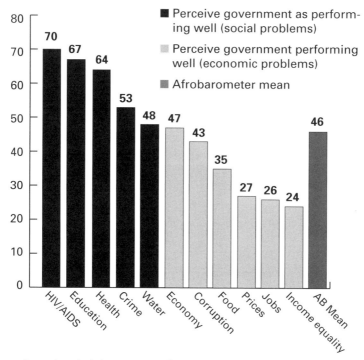

Percentage of respondents who think government is performing well or very well in this service sector: "How well or badly would you say the current government is handling the following matters?"

In the social sectors—health, education, crime, and domestic water supply—people consider that governments are performing well rather than badly. Two-thirds or more approve of government performance in the education and health sectors (67 and 74 percent respectively). It is notable that, government performance on every social service is seen to exceed the Afrobarometer mean (46 percent) for all policy domains.

Oddly, given the spreading ravages of AIDS deaths, people seem to be especially pleased with government performance at combating HIV/AIDS. This result (70 percent approval) may be skewed, however, by psychological denial

Figure 5: Trends in Satisfaction with Government Performance, 2000–2005

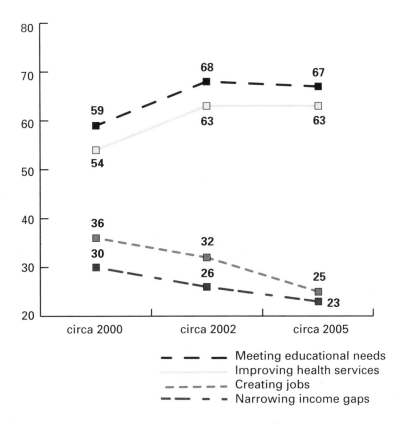

among respondents (just one-third admit that they know anyone who has died of AIDS), popular ignorance about policy programs (7 percent "don't know" how well government is doing), or the influence within the sample of the large numbers of interviews conducted in West African states (where infection rates—and therefore the salience of the AIDS issue—remain relatively low).

A contrasting picture emerges in the economic policy sectors (see Figure 4). The Africans we consulted were evenly split on the management of the national economy: 47 percent thought that governments were doing well, 48 percent badly. Otherwise, with reference to all other economic policies—from controlling corruption to closing income gaps—more people scored governments as doing badly rather than well. Moreover, performance at all economic tasks was evaluated as falling below the Afrobarometer average for government performance. At the extreme, only about one-quarter of respondents gave a positive rating to African governments' performance at inflation control, job creation, and closing the gap between rich and poor.

In addition, the gap in popular satisfaction with government performance between social and economic sectors is widening over time. As Figure 5 shows, satisfaction with education services was 29 points higher in 2000 than satisfaction with income redistribution. But by 2005, this difference had grown to a gap of 44 percentage points.

In sum, while people are reasonably satisfied with social sector policy performance, they are increasingly disturbed that their governments have made little progress at addressing challenges of economic management.

But it is still necessary to probe the sources of the unexpectedly high levels of popular satisfaction with government performance in health and education. Perhaps some elements within the national population—say poor, rural people—are easily satisfied with low-quality performance. We test this hypothesis with a simple statistical model that regresses policy satisfaction on a standard array of demographic predictors. As shown in Table 2, we get some confirmatory results. It is true that living in a rural habitat induces people to be more satisfied with health and education policies, and older people are more tolerant of existing levels of performance in the education sector.

On the other hand, education improves people's knowledge of policy outcomes, raises expectations for service quality, and therefore is negative for policy satisfaction.

Moreover, poverty pulls even more strongly in the same direction: Poorer people are decidedly less likely to approve of policy performance in both social sectors. The Afrobarometer employs a lived poverty index to measure poverty that is based on an individual's experience with shortages of basic human needs (Afrobarometer 2003). Since the index includes "medicines or medical treatment" and "school expenses for your children," it is hardly surprising that people who are deprived of these needs also feel that the government is underperforming in these domains. So, among demographic considerations, poverty will probably always be a strong (negative) influence on satisfaction, a proposition that we will test further.

Table 2: Demographic Sources of Service Satisfaction Health and Education Sectors, 2005

	Satisfaction with Health Sector Performance		Satisfaction with Education Sector Performance	
	B (S.E)	Beta (sig.)	B (S.E)	Beta (sig)
Constant	2.860 (.041)		2.731 (.042)	
Gender (Female)	-.015 (.012)	-.009 (.216)	.004 (.013)	.002 (.729)
Habitat (Rural)	.077 (.013)	**.042** (.000)	.109 (.014)	**.058** (.000)
Age	.001 (.000)	.009 (.214)	.003 (.000)	**.045** (.000)
Education	-.019 (.003)	**-.043** (.000)	-.014 (.004)	**-.030** (.000)
Poverty	-1.99 (.007)	**-.213** (.000)	-.153 (.007)	**-.161** (.000)

Cell entries in bold identify statistically significant relationships

"How well or badly would you say the current government is handling the following matters?"

In the analysis that follows, we employ three versions of the dependent variable: "satisfaction with health services," "satisfaction with education services," and "overall satisfaction with basic social services," which is an average construct of both (health and education) indicators. The construct is permissible because the first two variables are highly correlated.[6] Stated differently, the people who are satisfied with health services tend to also be satisfied with education services, and vice versa.

But what are the main determinants of popular service satisfaction? In the sections below, we define, measure, and describe the structure and processes of service access.

Accessibility of Services: Infrastructure

One possible source of public satisfaction is the physical proximity of service infrastructure in the towns and villages where people live. After all, the prospect of gaining access to a social service would seem to start from the

Figure 6: The Availability of Service Infrastructure: 18 African Countries, 2005

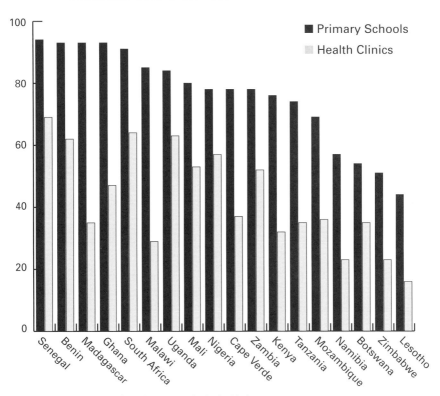

Percent of adults living in a locality with a primary school or health clinic.
Based on interviewer observations, confirmed by field team supervisors.

convenient availability of a nearby service outlet (World Bank 2004, p. 22). The Afrobarometer measures service infrastructure in a distinctive way. Apart from interviews with randomly selected individuals, the surveys include contextual observations by interviewers and supervisors for every primary sampling unit. Among other things, the field teams record the presence or absence of post offices, police stations, electrical grids, and—with relevance to the present inquiry—primary schools and health clinics.

As measured by this method, Figure 6 shows the percentages of adults in 2005 living in a locality with a primary school or health clinic in each of 18 African countries. According to our field observations, countries like Benin, Senegal, South Africa, and Uganda have a more physically accessible social service infrastructure than countries like Botswana, Namibia, Lesotho, and Zimbabwe.[7] The density of service infrastructure is everywhere greater for schools than clinics. More than three-quarters of adults live in areas with access to a local primary school compared to less than half with ready access to a local health clinic (on average, 76 percent versus 42 percent).

Accessibility of Services: User-Friendliness

Quite apart from proximity, the accessibility of services depends upon the organizational feature of "user-friendliness." From a user's perspective, a service may be simple, transparent, and inclusive or it may be formal, complex, and exclusionary. For poor or illiterate people, especially if they feel they lack the skills and status to engage with the agencies of a bureaucratic state, the approachability of the service transaction may be a prime consideration.

In short, do would-be clients find health and education services in Africa easy or difficult to use? The relevant survey questions are direct: "In your experience, how easy or difficult is it to obtain the following services: A place in a primary school for a child? How about medical treatment at a nearby clinic? Or do you never try to get these services from the government?"

Figure 7 suggests that people find it easier to get a child into school than to get medical attention. Whereas, in 2005, 67 percent reported that it is easy to gain access to a basic educational service, some 56 percent said the same about a basic medical service. But we reconfirm that, for both services, more people report a positive level of approachability than a negative one. And we note that the main difference between sectors lies in the proportions that find it "very easy" to obtain the service (21 percent for education versus 13 percent for health).

**Figure 7: Ease of Access to Education and Health Services;
Popular Estimates, 18 African Countries, 2005**

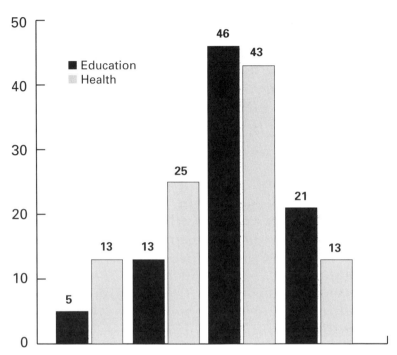

"In your experience, how easy or difficult is it to obtain the following services: A place in a primary school for a child? Medical treatment at a nearby clinic? Or do you ever try to get these services from government?

Service Experiences: Education

We now further disassemble the general concept of service accessibility by probing specific aspects of the service experience as seen from a user's perspective. Which obstacles—of service availability, quality, and cost—arise most frequently? For education, the survey asked, "Have you encountered any of these problems with your local public schools during the past 12 months?" A list of seven problems was then read out, ranging from "overcrowded classrooms" to "demands for illegal payments."[8]

Figure 8 compares the reported frequency of problems arising with education services. In this case, we count only those persons who have had contact with primary schools during the previous 12 months.

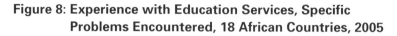

Figure 8: Experience with Education Services, Specific Problems Encountered, 18 African Countries, 2005

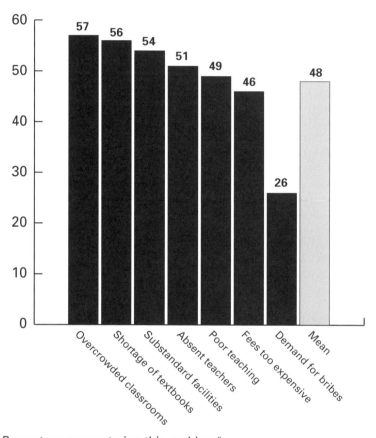

■ Percentage encountering this problem*
▨ Mean percentage encountering a problem

"Have you encountered any of these problems with your local public schools during the past 12 months?"
* Excludes those who say they don't know or have no recent experience with a public school.

Because popular demand for education exceeds the supply of school facilities, overcrowded classrooms are the most common specific problem, reported by 57 percent of users. This problem arises significantly more often for Africans in countries with universal free primary education,[9] but classroom overcrowding is widespread too in Benin and Nigeria. The related problem of shortages of textbooks and other classroom supplies arises with similar frequency (56 percent). A stunning 95 percent of Zimbabweans report textbook shortages, which reflects the desperate scarcity of foreign exchange in that country and the virtual collapse of routine functions within the Ministry of Education.

Is public schooling "too expensive?" Are users "unable to pay?" In the litany of user problems, the costs of primary schooling actually assume somewhat low priority. Fewer than half of all respondents say that the expense of required fees inhibits them from sending children to school. In this instance, the provision of UPE hardly makes a difference: In 2005, over 80 percent of Zambians still complain about school fees, as do about half of Kenyans, Malawians, and Ugandans. Only in Tanzania, where fewer than one third of adults see financial obstacles to school access, does free education have a large positive effect in reducing the problem of fees. Presumably, in the other UPE countries, parents still face a bevy of unofficial charges and expenses.

Finally, about one-quarter of users (26 percent) say they confront demands for illegal payments from teachers or school administrators. These may range from bribes in return for school placement to side-payments for private lessons. Such corruption reportedly hardly ever happens in Botswana and Lesotho (say under 10 percent), but it is said to be common in Namibia (over 40 percent) and rife in Nigeria (over 60 percent). Interestingly, educators are slightly but significantly more likely to report facing demands for bribes in countries with UPE than in countries without this policy.[10] Perhaps because teachers and administrators feel overstretched by the influx of waves of new pupils, they are more likely to feel justified in seeking illicit rents.

Service Experiences: Health Care

A parallel set of questions was asked about health care: "Have you encountered any of these problems with your local public clinic or hospital during the past 12 months?" A list of seven problems was offered, ranging from "long waiting times" to "demands for illegal payments."[11]

Figure 9 breaks down the recent experiences of persons who attempted to use clinics and hospitals. On average, slightly more users report a specific problem with health services (51 percent) than with education services (48 percent, see Figure 8).

This discrepancy is most evident in relation to overcrowded facilities, where three-quarters (73 percent) of clinic users complain about "long waiting times" (compared to 53 percent who see "overcrowded classrooms" in schools). By a clear margin, delays in delivery at the point of service are the biggest problem.

On any given day, urban hospitals are typically unable to accommodate all patients; long lines of applicants regularly assemble outside rural clinics; and, too often, some people are turned away at the end of the day without consultation or treatment. Relative to effective levels of client demand, health services are in even shorter supply than education services.[12]

Figure 9: Experience with Health Services, Specific Problems Encountered, 18 African Countries, 2005

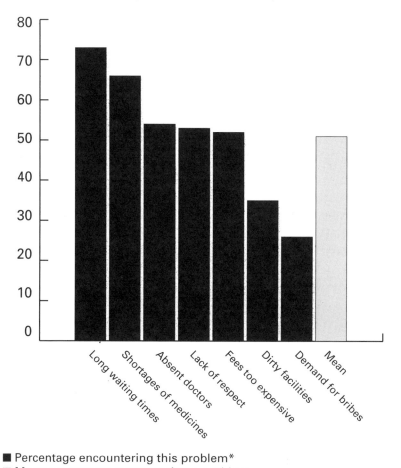

■ Percentage encountering this problem*
▨ Mean percentage encountering a problem

"Have you encountered any of these problems with your local public clinic or hospital during the past 12 months?"
* Excludes those who say they don't know or have no recent experience with a public medical facility.

Two-thirds of health care clients also report shortages of medicines and other medical supplies. Once again, users confront supply deficits with greater frequency in the health sector (66 percent) than in the education sector (where 56 percent see shortages of textbooks, see Figure 8). Regardless of whether a sound health infrastructure has been built, local clinics may lack the basic commodities needed for routine preventative care. Over 80 percent of Kenyans, Ugandans, Zambians, and Zimbabweans express concern about the under-provisioning of health care facilities.

Across all countries, however, health service problems are significantly more common in rural than urban areas. Waiting times are longer at rural clinics in part because of the sparser coverage of health infrastructure in remote areas; medicines are less readily available at clinics due partly to long supply lines from the capital city; and doctors are more often absent, in part because professionals are reluctant to serve at distant outposts. In the only exception to this general tendency, clients claim that medical staff—nurses, technicians, and clerks—are more likely to treat them rudely and without due respect at urban hospitals and clinics.

Across the health and education sectors, equal proportions of survey respondents say they receive corrupt proposals from service providers (that is, about one-quarter). Once again, citizens of Botswana and Lesotho report the fewest attempts at such extortion by health workers (under 5 percent). The South African health system also scores well in terms of the reported probity of its front-line officials. But Uganda now displaces Nigeria as the country where demands for bribes are reportedly most common: In 2005, almost half of all adults who use health services in Uganda say they faced a request for an illegal payment from a health care worker in the previous 12 months (48 percent). Again, in Uganda and elsewhere, demands for bribes tend to be more common at rural clinics, perhaps because Ministry officials find it difficult to supervise field staff in outlying areas.

Corruption

Popular encounters with official corruption are expected to corrode service satisfaction. As a key component of bad governance, the multifaceted concept of corruption is worth measuring from various angles.

On perceptions of the prevalence of graft, the Afrobarometer asks, "How many of the following people do you think are involved in corruption: (a) teachers and school administrators (b) health workers?" This question taps the popular reputation of service providers quite independently of whether an individual respondent has ever been directly approached for a bribe. In absolute terms, health and education workers in Africa have yet to win reputations for complete honesty. On average, 20 percent of the Africans we interviewed perceive that "most" or "almost all" health workers are corrupt. The equivalent figure for teachers and school administrators is 16 percent. In relative terms, however, these estimates are lower than for any other category of public official, especially customs agents (35 percent) and the police (43 percent).

On citizen behavior, the Afrobarometer asks whether, during the past year, individuals actually "had to pay a bribe, give a gift, or do a favor to a government official in order to: (a) get a child into school or (b) get medicine or medical attention from a health worker." These questions emphasize the distinction between being asked for a bribe and actually paying one.

A gulf exists between perceptions of corruption and the act of handing over a bribe. Some six in ten citizens think that at least "some" public officials are corrupt (62 percent). Yet only one in ten reports that they made any type of extra-legal side-payment to obtain a service during the previous year (10 percent). As such, people either over-estimate the extent to which corruption pervades their society, or they under-report their own involvement in the socially disapproved act of paying a bribe. Or, most likely, both these biases are present in the data. As such, the real level of illegal exchanges of public goods for private gain probably lies somewhere between these extreme estimates.

Importantly, illicit payments are reportedly almost twice as common for health care than for schooling (13 versus 7 percent), a result that confirms a relationship between the scarcity of a service and the likelihood that it will be traded on a parallel market.

PART THREE

This explanatory section of the paper aims at a comprehensive multivariate explanation of popular satisfaction with public services in a cross-section of Africa's new democracies.

Explaining Service Satisfaction

Regardless of the way that satisfaction is measured—with health services, with education services, or with both—the regression models in Table 3 tell a similar story. The strongest and most statistically significant relationships are highlighted in bold in the table and their explanatory power is ranked in parentheses.[13]

The most important consideration—consistently ranked first—is the **accessibility of services**. Across both health and education—and for these social services generally—what matters most is whether clients consider services to be "easy to use" or, in other words, "user-friendly." This quality captures whether citizens regard public services as being open to all types of clientele and as being uncomplicated to operate. It is a quality pertinent to low income, non-literate, peasant populations who seek to draw social services from the agencies of a bureaucratic state. They wish to avoid formal entanglements in administrative red tape and interactions with officials whom they feel to be socially distant. If ordinary people can get a child into school or receive primary health care with a minimum of such hassles, they are likely to be satisfied with service delivery.

It is important to note that this subjective element of service accessibility is much more critical than the objective one. As Table 3 shows, physical infrastructure—whether there is a school or clinic in the locality—remains largely unimportant to service satisfaction. For social services generally, the scope of infrastructure has absolutely no effect on satisfaction (beta = .000!), and a nearby school is actually negative (though statistically insignificant) for satisfaction, which again suggests that, for parents with school-age children, the quality of educational services trumps mere quantity.

The relative superiority of subjective over objective criteria raises a challenge for government ministries responsible for health and education in Africa. Success at service delivery is not simply a matter of building more clinics and schools. Instead, it requires an organizational commitment to an ethic of customer service by which the client comes to feel that his or her needs are being considered and addressed.

The second most important consideration for service satisfaction is the position of the user in the **social structure**. Several dimensions of social identity are relevant, including gender, habitat, education and, especially, poverty.

The poverty status of users remains the key social consideration. The connection of poverty to service (dis)satisfaction is at least three times as strong as the average for other societal influences. And poverty's impact is consistent for both health and education services, and therefore for these social services together. Notably, the impact is negative. The poorer a person, the less likely it is he or she will be satisfied with government performance at social delivery. This strong effect persists even after the physical proximity and the user-friendliness of services—among other factors yet to be discussed—are taken into account.

Table 3: Sources of Service Satisfaction, 18 African Countries, 2005

	Education Services	Health Services	Both Services
Constant	2.766***	2.662***	2.621***
Social Structure			
Gender (female)	-.008	-.018*	-.016*
Habitat (rural)	.037***	.033***	.033***
Education	-.027**	-.032***	-.030***
Poverty	-.098*** (2)	-.103*** (2)	-.100*** (3)
Service Accessibility			
School in locality	-.013		.013
Clinic in locality		.033***	.000
Ease of access to education	.129*** (1)		.061***
Ease of access to health care		.178*** (1)	.159*** (1)
Service Experiences			
Fees too expensive	-.045***	-.070*** (4)	
Shortages of supplies	-.048***	-.049***	
Poor quality of teaching/ treatment	-.090*** (3)	-.046***	
Absent staff	.007	-.039***	
Overcrowded facilities	-.016	.028**	
Substandard facilities	-.012	-.034***	
Service experiences (education)			-.079***
Service experiences (health)			-.108*** (2)
Corruption			
Demands for bribes	-.030***	.016	
Perception of corruption	-.080*** (4)	-.101*** (3)	-.092*** (4)
Experience of corruption	.008	.016*	.040***
Adjusted R square	.091	.126	.133

The regression method is Ordinary Least Squares (OLS). Cell entries are standardized regression coefficients (beta).
The strongest and most significant relationships are in **bold** (explanatory ranks are in parentheses).
Constants are unstandardized regression coefficients (B). Significance: ***p =<.001, **p =<.01, *p =<.05

This robust result indicates that existing services embody an anti-poor bias, at least in the opinion of the poor themselves. To the extent that poverty is more prevalent in the rural areas of Africa (as it is in *every* Afrobarometer country), this bias in accessibility is offset and obscured by the apparent willingness of rural residents to accept lower-quality services. This combination of facts suggests that, given a goal to boost popular satisfaction with service delivery, African governments would be well advised to design pro-poor health and education policies and to direct these services initially to urban populations.

Service experiences—that is, the quality of users' encounters with providers—are also part of a complete explanation.

For education services, only three out of six experiences seemingly matter. Leading the way is the poor quality of teaching, which may arise from the rapid introduction of UPE without enough qualified teachers. Shortages of textbooks (and related school supplies) and the expense of fees (including residual or ancillary charges even under UPE) also significantly depress popular satisfaction with primary education.

By contrast, every user experience is relevant to the popular evaluation of health services. Among all problem areas, the cost of services ("fees too expensive") is the principal source of dissatisfaction, markedly lowering popular approval. This outcome is consistent with the slower pace of "de-liberalization" (that is, removal of user fees) in the health sector as compared to the education sector in Africa. As expected, all other experiences—from shortages of medicines to substandard facilities ("dirty clinics")—also remain negative and significant for mass satisfaction.

But we discover an interesting anomaly: Even though users of health services cite overcrowded facilities ("long waiting times") as their most frequent problem (see Figure 9), this experience has an unexpectedly positive effect on satisfaction. In other words, would-be patients are apparently willing to overlook the inconvenience of lengthy lines, or even of being turned away from a hospital or clinic and being told return at another time. Users value health care so highly that they have resigned themselves to putting up with overcrowding as an unavoidable cost of accessing this scarce service.

Finally, what is the impact of corruption? Table 3 indicates that general perceptions of official corruption (that is, the popular wisdom that "all" or "most" service workers are dishonest) have predictably strong, consistent, and negative effects on service satisfaction. Whether with reference to the health or education sectors, or both, such perceptions are deeply corrosive to public confidence in service institutions. And it does not matter whether these perceptions are accurate or not; the mere popular belief that officialdom is an arena of corruption is enough to drive down mass satisfaction.

Table 3 also shows that, if people encounter demands for bribes from teachers and school officials, their satisfaction with educational services drops by a significant margin. In other words, the impact of actually encountering a bribery attempt from a school official, which may be unlikely, has an additional negative effect. But this relationship does not hold for health services, which raises questions about whether there are distinctive consequences to concrete experiences with bribery across the two service sectors.

The results for experience with corruption certainly suggest so. Recall that this concept is measured by the frequency with which *users actually* "pay a bribe, give a gift, or do a favor to a government official." When users themselves engage in corruption, their satisfaction with social services *rises* rather than falls. This positive effect may be miniscule and insignificant for education, and small but significant for health, but it is larger and clearly significant for both services combined.

This result is unexpected and counter-intuitive. Why would the payment of a bribe, in a context where corruption is generally associated with service failure, lead users to feel more satisfied with service delivery? One possible interpretation is that bribe paying opens the door to services that are otherwise scarce and inaccessible. Supporting statistical evidence can be found in the larger positive effects for health services (which are very scarce) than for educational services (which are less scarce). And positive effects are largest for *simultaneous* access to *both* sets of scarce services, a combination that is presumably harder to attain than access to either service alone.

Substantively, this suggests that corruption is a double-edged sword that cuts both ways. When ordinary people think that officials or other users are benefiting unduly from the corrupt service distribution, they feel dissatisfied. When, however, they occasionally make a side-payment themselves in order to gain preferential access to a scarce service, their satisfaction rises. The acquisition of the service, by fair means or foul, is the decisive factor.

The implications are far-reaching. Theoretically, we are reminded that official corruption is not an attribute of political elites alone. It is a dyadic relationship that involves both a bribe-giver and a bribe-taker. As such, ordinary citizens, as users of social services may sometimes be complicit in corrupt relationships. Moreover, such encounters do not have universally negative impacts on their satisfaction with government performance. Practically, the participation of some citizens in bribery greatly increases the challenge of rooting out corruption. If the problem has social foundations, it cannot be counteracted by punishment of state officials alone. A solution to the problem requires that governments enforce the broad and equitable distribution of valued social services so that citizens have fewer incentives to seek preferential access by illicit means.

Implications for Democracy

Does service satisfaction play a role in the consolidation of new democracies in Africa? After all, many scholars believe that, unless elected governments are able to widely deliver the benefits of socioeconomic development, citizens—notably poorer Africans—will lose confidence in democracy (Przeworski 1991; Inglehart and Welzel 2005).

As a means of exploring these extended ramifications, we employ a standard indicator that asks, "How satisfied are you with the way democracy works in (this country)?"

As a first step, it is worth noting that satisfaction with democracy is quite well predicted by a model with the same structure as satisfaction with social services (see Table 4, Model 1). The leading (negative) factor is now a summary measure of service experiences, but ease of service access remains positive and significant. Both poverty and perceptions of corruption are consistently negative, and carry much the same weight as before. Even the experience of corruption ("paying a bribe") is positive and significant for satisfaction with democracy just as it is for satisfaction with health and education services combined.

In other words, Africans seem to use similar processes of reasoning in evaluating *both* service delivery *and* democracy. One possible calculus is that people use their felt satisfaction with social services to inform their evaluations of the political regime writ large.

But the model has a glaring weakness. It explains only a limited amount of variance: just 9 percent for education services, 13 percent for health services, and only slightly more for both services (see Table 3). And it explains even less variance in satisfaction with democracy: just 7 percent (see Table 4, Model 1).

The model is therefore underspecified. Apparently, social and political satisfaction are also driven by other, unmeasured factors. What might these be? Based on earlier Afrobarometer research, we propose that satisfaction with democracy is driven by core instrumental considerations, such as the performance of the economy and polity (Bratton, Mattes, and Gyimah-Boadi 2005, Chs. 9 and 11). Economic performance is represented by an index of "how well" citizens regard the government's handling of a range of economic policies, namely "managing the economy," "creating jobs," "controlling inflation," and "narrowing gaps between the rich and the poor." Political performance is measured by a simple indicator: To what degree do citizens think that the country's last presidential or legislative election was "free and fair"?

Table 4: Sources of Satisfaction with Democracy, 18 African Countries, 2005

	Satisfaction with Democracy	
	Model 1	Model 2
Constant	*2.791******	*.734******
Social Structure		
Gender (female)	-.038******	-.022****
Habitat (rural)	.041******	.022****
Education	-.078******	-.040******
Poverty	-.132****** (2)	-.064****** (4)
Service Accessibility		
School in locality	.021*	
Clinic in locality	.031******	
Ease of access to education	.040******	
Ease of access to health care	.044******	
Service Experiences (combined)	-.138****** (1)	
Corruption		
Demands for bribes (education)	.008	
Demands for bribes (health)	.042******	
Perception of corruption	-.066****** (3)	
Experience of corruption	.040******	
Performance Evaluations		
Political performance		.298****** (1)
Economic performance		.268****** (2)
Social Service satisfaction		.086****** (3)
Adjusted R square	.066	.280

The regression method is Ordinary Least Squares (OLS). Cell entries are standardized regression coefficients (beta). The strongest and most significant relationships are in **bold** (explanatory ranks are in parentheses).
Constants are unstandardized regression coefficients (B). Significance: ***p =<.001, **p =<.01, *p =<.05

But our task is to determine whether government performance at *social service* delivery has implications for satisfaction with democracy. Hence we now treat our composite measure of satisfaction with both health and education services—formerly a dependent variable—as an independent variable. It is entered alongside political and economic performance as a predictor in Table 4, Model 2.

By adding performance evaluations to the standard battery of demographic predictors, we arrive at a much more powerful result. Model 2 explains 28 percent of the variance in satisfaction with democracy. To be sure, public estimates of the quality of elections and the government's capacity at economic management are the driving forces in the explanation. But, importantly, *satisfaction with basic social services also contributes to building a mass constituency for democracy*. Indeed, the positive effect of service satisfaction more than offsets the negative effect of poverty. In this regard, we can expect targeted, pro-poor social service policies will have a particularly salubrious effect on the survival and consolidation of new democracies.

Political and Policy Implications

By way of conclusion, this last section draws out political and policy implications.

- Africans now attach higher value to health care services than to education. Yet health services are in scarcer supply than educational services. Democratic governments that seek reelection in Africa would do well to attend to these expressed needs and popular priorities.
- Responsiveness matters. People judge the quality of basic social services principally in terms of user-friendliness of service agencies. Governments, especially those in electoral democracies, can gain political and development capital by aligning services to users' needs and organizing delivery in open and accessible forms.
- Users frequently encounter specific problems with different service providers. Ministries of education should give priority to raising the quality of teachers and instruction, especially in the context of UPE. Ministries of health should apply most efforts to reducing (but never eliminating) the cost of primary services, if only for the poor.
- Some forms of corruption can also have perverse effects. At the margins, users who pay bribes gain increased access to services and thereby express more service satisfaction. Anticorruption initiatives are required at the point of service and for local society as well as the political class.

- Corruption corrodes. But popular perceptions of corruption have more influence on service satisfaction than first-hand experiences. Thus, to counteract misinformation and establish grounds for accountability, rules and procedures for equitable service delivery should be made transparent and widely publicized.

All told, the delivery of basic education and health care in Africa would benefit from a healthy dose of customer service. But, in rural health clinics as much as in high-end department stores, customers are served principally when they pay. If public responsiveness is to be achieved in Africa, then users must make some contribution, however nominal, to the cost of service provision. And our research shows that most people are not averse to paying for high quality services, especially in education. Some, especially in health, are even willing to make illegal payments.

At the same time, the open exchange of information and democratic electoral contests can inject additional measures of disciplinary control over public officials. Only when real political and economic resources are at stake are citizens likely to succeed in bending social services to their needs.

REFERENCES

Afrobarometer. 2003. "Poverty, Poverty Measurement, and Democracy in Southern Africa." *Afrobarometer Briefing Paper No. 4*, www.afrobarometer.org.

Bentaouet-Kattan, R. B., and N. Burnett. 2004. *User Fees in Primary Education*. Washington, DC: World Bank

Besley, T., and R. Burgess. 2002. "The Political Economy of Government Responsiveness: Theory and Evidence from India," *The Quarterly Journal of Economics*, November: 1415–51.

Boyle, S., A. Brock, J. Mace, and M. Simmons. 2002. *The Costs of Sending Children to School*. London: Department for International Development.

Bratton, M., R. Mattes, and E. Gyimah-Boadi. 2005. *Public Opinion, Democracy, and Market Reform in Africa*. New York: Cambridge University Press.

Development Committee. 2001. *Education for Dynamic Economies: Accelerating Progress Toward Education for All*. Organization for Cooperation and Development.

Dieninger, K. and P. Mpuga. 2005. "Economic and Welfare Impact of the Abolition of Health User Fees: Evidence from Uganda." *Journal of African Economies*, 14 (1): 55–91.

Inglehart, R., and C. Welzel. 2005. *Modernization, Cultural Change and Democracy: The Human Development Sequence*. New York: Cambridge University Press.

Institute for Policy Alternatives. 2005. "Community Voices in Civil Society Assessment of Pro-Poor Policies and Programs in Ghana's Poverty Reduction Strategy (GPRS)." Accra: IPA-Ghana: 26pp.

Kaufmann, D., A. Kraay, and M. Mastruzzi. 2006. "Governance Matters V: Governance Indicators for 1996–2005." Social Science Research Network (SSRN): http://ssrn.com/abstract=929549.

Kauffman, R., and J. Nelson (eds.). 2005. *Crucial Needs, Weak Incentives: Social Sector Reform, Democratization and Globalization in Latin America*. Baltimore: Johns Hopkins University Press.

Keefer, P., and S. Khemani. 2003. "Democracy, Public Expenditures and the Poor." The World Bank Policy Research Paper No. 3164, November: 34pp.

———. 2004. "Why Do the Poor Receive Poor Services?" *Economic and Political Weekly* (New Delhi), February 28: 935–943.

Narayan, D. 2000. *Voices of the Poor: Can Anyone Hear Us?* Washington, DC: The World Bank, Volume 1.

Narayan, D., R. Chambers, M. Shah, and P. Petesch. 2001. *Voices of the Poor: Crying Out for Change*. Washington, DC: The World Bank, Volume 2.

Przeworski, A. 1991. *Democracy and the Market: Political and Economic Reforms in Eastern Europe and Latin America*. New York: Cambridge University Press.

Rotberg, R. (ed.). 2004. *When States Fail: Causes and Consequences*. Princeton, NJ: Princeton University Press.

Stasavage, D. 2005. "Democracy and Education Spending in Africa." *American Journal of Political Science,* 49 (2): 343–58.

United Nations. 2006. *Millennium Development Goals Report, 2006.* New York: United Nations.

Van de Walle, N. 2003. *African Economies and the Politics of Permanent Crisis, 1979–1999.* New York: Cambridge University Press.

Wadee, H., L. Gilson, M. Thiede, O. Okorafor, and D. McIntyre. 2003. *Health Care Inequity in South Africa and the Public /Private Mix*. Geneva: UNRISD.

World Bank. 2002. "Achieving Universal Primary Education in Uganda: The 'Big Bang' Approach." Washington, DC: The World Bank.

———. 2004. *World Development Report, 2004: Making Services Work for Poor People.* Washington, DC: The World Bank.

World Health Organization. 2004. "Health System Financing, Expenditure and Resource Allocation." *Technical Brief for Policy, No.1*. Geneva: WHO.

ENDNOTES

1. The Afrobarometer is a joint enterprise of the Institute for Democracy in South Africa (Idasa), the Center for Democratic Governance in Ghana (CDG), and Michigan State University (MSU).
2. Benin, Botswana, Cape Verde, Ghana, Kenya, Lesotho, Madagascar, Malawi, Mali, Mozambique, Namibia, Nigeria, Senegal, South Africa, Tanzania, Uganda, Zambia, and Zimbabwe.
3. Surveys in South Africa and Namibia were conducted in early 2006.
4. For this trend analysis, the sample is restricted to the original 12 countries covered by the Afrobarometer since these are the only cases for which we have three observations over time.
5. In both cases, responses are scored on a four-point scale from "very badly" to "fairly badly" to "fairly well" to "very well." The full scale is used for all inferential statistics, with "don't know" and "haven't heard enough" treated as missing data. For descriptive purposes, we commonly collapse the "very" and "fairly" categories together to create a simple two point scale of "badly" and well." For descriptive statistics, we calculate and report frequencies inclusive of "don't know" and "haven't heard enough."
6. Pearson's r = .606, p<.001.
7. We concede, however, that variations across countries in the size of primary sampling units and in the quality of field observations make these data less than completely reliable and comparable. They are best treated as estimates rather than definitive data points.
8. All were scored on the same four-point scale from "never" through "once or twice" and "a few times" and "often." Descriptive statistics are calculated against a base that excludes those who "don't know" or who had had "no experience with public schools in the past 12 months." To avoid losing cases, the latter respondents were assigned the mean value for the distribution on each sub-item when calculating all inferential statistics.
9. 66 percent versus 54 percent: Pearson's r = .153, p<.001
10. Pearson's r = .046, p<.001.
11. See endnote 11 (check).
12. This general finding holds for 15 of the 18 countries in the Afrobarometer. The only exceptions, where overcrowding is reportedly more common in schools than clinics, are Benin, Madagascar, and Mali.
13. Explanatory rank is derived from the relative size of the standardized OLS regression coefficient (beta).

THE NEW LEFT VERSUS NEOLIBERALISM IN LATIN AMERICA

Evelyne Huber

NEOLIBERALISM

The title of this chapter suggests an explicit comparison or a contrast between neoliberalism and new left politics, so I will begin by sketching how neoliberal reforms in Latin America affected poverty and inequality. For this purpose, I shall briefly summarize some key arguments of an article I wrote on the topic with Fred Solt, which was published in the *Latin American Research Review* in 2004 (Vol. 39, No. 3).

In the article we looked at five indicators, including growth, economic stability or absence of volatility, and quality of democracy, but this chapter presents our findings on poverty and inequality only. Since all Latin American and Caribbean countries embarked on some kind of neoliberal reform course in the 1980s and/or 1990s, we can begin by looking at the overall trajectory of our indicators in Latin America, assuming that overall performance was shaped by the debt crisis and then the thrust of the reforms.

If we look at poverty, we see a severe deterioration in the 1980s and an improvement in the 1990s; poverty fell from 48.3 percent of the population in 1990 to 43.8 percent in 1999, but still remained above the 1980 level of 40.5 percent (estimate for 19 countries; ECLAC 2002: 14). Arguably, this is a result of a combination of the changing class structure in Latin America and the failure of governments to include in their reforms the construction of solid social safety nets. The growing informalization and decline of formal sector employment, together with other reforms, have led to growing income concentration, as outlined by Portes and Hoffman (2003).

In looking at inequality, we find that it rose in all Latin American and Caribbean countries for which data are available in the 1980s, except for Jamaica and Uruguay, and it rose again or remained constant in the 1990s except for El Salvador, Honduras, Jamaica, Peru, and Uruguay. So, overall we saw a clear increase in the 1980s and a slight continued upward trend in the 1990s (Morley 2001).

Overall, the picture is not particularly encouraging. Proponents of neoliberal reforms are quick to argue that the problem has been insufficient commitment to reforms. If governments had been less cautious, less intimidated by political opposition, and instead more aggressive in pushing through a broad reform program, the outcomes would have been better. In their view, bold actions by politically insulated technocrats, including shock therapies, are indicated to overcome resistance.

In order to subject these claims to empirical scrutiny, we performed some simple comparisons. We compared countries that ranked higher on neoliberal reforms in the mid-1990s to those that ranked lower, and we compared more radical to more cautious reformers over the period 1982–95. We used the best available data on neoliberal reform in Latin America, the General Reform Index (GRI) constructed by Morley, Machado, and Pettinato (1999). The GRI has five components: commercial, financial, capital account, privatization, and tax reform.

The index confirms that all of the countries underwent neoliberal reforms in the years after the onset of the debt crisis; in fact, the 1995 GRI scores for all countries except Jamaica (.767) and Venezuela (.667) exceeded those of the most neoliberal country of 1982, Uruguay (.776). We first divide the countries into two groups, those above the median value of the GRI in 1995, and those below.

In order to better gauge the successes and failures of radical, that is, fast and extensive, neoliberal reform processes, we then classify the countries on the basis of the extent of these reforms from 1982 to 1995, measured as the change in GRI scores. We further include a measure for the magnitude of any drastic reform episodes their governments may have imposed during that period. We calculated the magnitude of drastic reform episodes for each country as its largest one-year change on the GRI. Again, both classifications are simple dichotomies, above and below the median of the measure in question. The three classifications overlap considerably. Costa Rica, the Dominican Republic, El Salvador, Guatemala, Peru, and Paraguay are above the median in all three classifications; Colombia, Honduras, Mexico, and Venezuela are consistently below the median. Despite these similarities, the three classifications yield different results that are useful for evaluating the claims made on behalf of neoliberal reform against its actual record in Latin America.

Our attempt to gauge the performance of more and less liberalized economies, and more and less radical reformers in the areas of poverty and inequality is somewhat hampered by the availability of data that are comparable over time and across countries. Income inequality data at the national level for Argentina, Bolivia, Ecuador, Paraguay, and Uruguay are unavailable; for the remaining countries, data for the closest available year was used. Poverty data at the national level for Bolivia and Uruguay are unavailable. Ideally, one would want poverty data for the period before the onset of the reforms, to measure change, but problems of comparability are serious. Nevertheless, even with restricted data availability, the picture emerging is clear and consistent.

Higher levels of liberalization and more radical processes of liberalization are associated with higher levels of inequality and poverty. The changes in inequality are impressive: The countries with the more liberalized economies as of 1995 started out around 1982 with lower levels of inequality than the countries with the less liberalized economies as of 1995, but the two sets of countries switched position, with the more liberalized economies ending up with higher levels of inequality around 1995 than the less liberalized economies. Looking at the process of reform, we see that the more radical reformers started out and ended up with lower levels of inequality than the more moderate reformers, as both sets of countries saw an increase in inequality. However, the gap between the two sets of countries narrowed considerably, as the more radical reformers increased their gini index twice as much as the more moderate reformers. The greatest costs in terms of inequality were incurred by drastic reform episodes; countries that had more drastic reform episodes increased their gini index nine times more than countries that avoided them. There is no doubt, then, that higher levels of neoliberalism and more aggressive tactics of liberalization are associated with rising inequality.

The picture on poverty is equally consistent. More liberalized economies and more radical reform approaches are associated with higher levels of poverty. Since we do not have comparable data for the period before the onset of reforms, proponents of neoliberalism will argue that this must be a result of initially higher levels of poverty in the radical reformers. However, we need to remember that the more liberalized economies started out with a higher level of GDP per capita in 1982, had higher economic growth in the period 1982–1998, and ended up with a level of GDP per capita in 1998 roughly a third higher than the less liberalized economies. So, the very least we can say is that economic growth certainly did not trickle down and did nothing to relieve the higher levels of poverty in the more liberalized economies. If we consider the poverty data in conjunction with the inequality data, this seems to be a great understatement.

So, what is the bottom line on the performance of more versus less liberalized economies and radical versus cautious reformers? In the Latin American context of the last two decades of the twentieth century, more liberalized economies performed better in economic growth and in improvements in the quality of democracy than less liberalized economies. However, they suffered higher volatility, saw greater increases in inequality, and experienced higher levels of poverty. The increases in inequality and the higher levels of poverty highlight the failures in linking economic neoliberalism to the construction of strong social safety nets. So, we are clearly far from a ringing endorsement of liberalized economies, even before taking into account the Argentine and Uruguayan crises. Given how few countries we are dealing with, the deterioration in those countries would clearly affect the picture in growth and poverty for the worse for the liberalized economies.

To counter our assessment of the extremely limited success of neoliberalism and the high costs of radical neoliberal reform processes, the proponents of neoliberalism might argue that these two decades are just too short a time span to assess the effects of the reforms, particularly since in some countries the bulk of the reforms was only implemented in the 1990s. To respond to this argument we need to ask whether the neoliberal reforms that have been implemented have put into place policies that will have beneficial effects in the long run on poverty and inequality. In this context we need to look beyond economic liberalization to accompanying reforms of social policies. Here, the picture appears equally unfavorable.

SOCIAL POLICY AND REDISTRIBUTION

Neoliberal reforms of social policy have done little to rectify the lack of a safety net for the working age population, and less to stem the decline of the value of the safety net for the elderly. Altogether, nine Latin American countries have implemented and a tenth has legislated full or partial privatization of their pension system. In five cases, privatization was total and the public system was closed down; in five cases it was partial and the private system remained a supplementary or a parallel option (Müller 2003). Now, it is well known that several Latin American countries had or still have excessively generous pension systems for privileged categories of workers, which clearly have to be changed. However, privatization of the public system as a whole is not the answer. Even in the best functioning privatized systems, such as Chile's, there are very serious problems with coverage, contributions, regressive structures of fees, high administrative costs, and cohort and individual risk of investments. Maintenance of a basic public pension is crucial, and given that about half of the workforce is in the informal sector, it should be a citizenship-based pension, not one based on employment. (For an elaboration of these issues, see Huber and Stephens 2000.)

Reforms in health care have been more heterogeneous, though in general the private sector has expanded its role, sometimes by design as part of a neoliberal reform project and sometimes by default as a result of serious underfunding of the public system. Certainly, the increase of the role of the private sector in health care is most likely to increase the price of health care and inequality of access in the longer run. We know from the OECD that the countries with the greatest reliance on private insurance and private providers have the most expensive and inegalitarian health care systems.

In the 1990s, most countries raised their social expenditures, so that they increased from 10.4 percent of GDP to 13.1 percent (ECLAC 2002), slightly above the level of 1980. Growth in the various categories of social expenditure, that is, education, health care and nutrition, social security, and housing and sanitation was roughly similar, with social security continuing to absorb the bulk of social expenditure, at 4.8 percent of GDP in 1998–99, followed by education with 3.9 percent, and health care and nutrition with 2.9 percent (ECLAC 2002: 26). Clearly, these levels of expenditure remained far below what would be needed for a concerted and successful attack on poverty and improvement of the human capital base. Also, the distribution on average is not as progressive as it could be. In a study of eight countries, ECLAC found that on average lower-income strata receive transfers and free or subsidized services, including social security, equivalent to 43 percent of total household income, compared to 13 percent and 7 percent for the fourth and fifth income quintiles. Nevertheless, the distributional profile of social expenditures varies greatly between countries, and in some of these countries the actual amount of the transfers to the richest stratum was twice as much as that going to the poorest stratum (ECLAC 2002: 28).

The reality of social security spending in Latin America at the beginning of the 21st century is that it is still regressive. The bulk of social security spending goes to pensions, and the remainder to a few other kinds of transfers such as family allowances and maternity benefits. In the great majority of countries social security coverage remains confined to formal sector employees, which means that often 20 percent to 60 percent of the economically active population remain excluded. De Ferranti, et al., (2004: 268–72), in a study for the World Bank, reviewed a range of studies and found that in most countries the regressive components of social security spending outweigh progressive components. Lindert, et al., (2005) confirm this assessment on the basis of their analysis of micro-data.

There are a number of cash transfer programs that are not employment-based and earnings-related and are progressive, such as non-contributory pensions and some conditional cash transfers. They generally are highly progressive and have additional beneficial effects insofar as the conditions for receipt are school attendance and primary health care visits of children. With the exception of *Oportunidades* in Mexico and *Bolsa Familia* in Brazil, however, they tend to be highly restricted in coverage and expenditures. Non-contributory, means-tested social assistance pensions are still relatively scarce and poorly funded as well (Muller 2005). However, it is on these types of programs that the emphasis needs to be put by governments that want to have a real impact on poverty and inequality. In the past few years, under the left-wing governments in Brazil, Chile , and Uruguay, such programs have been expanded considerably (but also in Mexico under the right-of-center governments of Zedillo and Fox). They are clearly a highly effective means to redistribute income and reduce poverty. Still, actual outlays on social assistance remain a small proportion of social expenditures, though they have been on the rise among left governments. In Argentina in 2003 social assistance accounted for 7.1 percent of total social spending and 1.4 percent of GDP, compared to social insurance with 43.2 percent of social expenditures and 8.3 percent of GDP. The corresponding figures for Chile in the same year were 4.4 percent and 0.7 percent for social assistance and 43.1 percent and 6.9 percent for social insurance (Lindert et al. 2005). In other words, Chile still spent ten times more on social insurance than on social assistance.

The development of health care systems in Latin America is linked to the development of social security schemes. In many cases, health care insurance has paralleled social security in the sense that part of employer and employee social security contributions have gone to health insurance. In some cases, care has been provided by social security clinics and hospitals, in other cases by private clinics and hospitals under contract with the social security system, and in still others by public clinics and hospitals. Public health expenditures have sometimes subsidized social security health care and always supported public clinics and hospitals and preventive health campaigns. In general, in line with the interests of their constituencies, left parties have favored an improvement of the public health care system and right parties have favored private provision and private or social security financing. However, where formal sector employment was high (before the debt crisis) and social security financing of health care had been established for some sectors of the work force, left-of-center parties supported expansion of employment-based insurance linked to private non-profit provision of care to reach virtually universal coverage (as in Argentina and Uruguay).

The educational system in Latin America shows a similar combination of private and public provision. At the primary and secondary level, private school attendance, heavily in Catholic schools, has been the norm rather than the exception for the middle and upper classes. At the university level, public universities played a prominent role. Catholic universities have a long tradition, but the proliferation of other private universities is a fairly recent phenomenon. Improvements in public education have been a consistent program point of the left, whereas the right has supported parents' choice between private and public schools—a choice heavily contingent on income.

There are regressive components of health and education expenditures, but in general the progressive components tend to outweigh the regressive ones (de Ferranti et al. 2004: 263-4). Studies of different programs show that expenditures on tertiary education are regressive, whereas basic education and health services provided by the public sector for the uninsured and school nutritional programs have a progressive incidence (e.g., Scott 2003 for Mexico; Wodon et al. 2003). ECLAC data for eight countries in the region show that the most progressive types of expenditures are spending on primary and secondary education, and that public spending on health care and nutrition is the second most progressive category (2002: 26). Lindert, et al., (2005) conclude that the bulk of education spending has a generally progressive profile and health spending has a slightly progressive or neutral profile.

One of the main arguments of neoliberal reformers, of course, has been that social expenditures should be targeted on the poor and poorest. In principle, this is reasonable, but it raises at least two fundamental problems: (1) how large a group is to be targeted and how? and (2) what will this do to the political support for these programs? We know from the experience of advanced industrial countries that programs targeted on small groups are politically most vulnerable, whereas programs that benefit most of the population are very popular. What would such an alternative system look like? Given that over 40 percent of the population is poor in Latin America, it would not be difficult to construct a needy target population that is a clear majority of the population. A coalition of the poor and the working class, or the informal and the manual formal proletariat, accounts for 60–70 percent of the population in Latin American countries (Portes and Hoffman 2003: 52). Basic but quality health care, nutrition, education, and a minimum income in case of illness, unemployment, or old age, targeted at this population, with entitlement based on citizenship (not formal sector employment) and financed out of general tax revenue, would be an effective and politically sustainable approach. These are fundamental principles of social democratic welfare state policies adapted for countries at low to medium levels of development. These principles contain a heavy emphasis on the development of the human capital base, which in turn is crucial for sustainable economic growth in a globalizing economy. (These ideas are elaborated in my chapter "Un nuevo enfoque para la seguridad social en la región," and in the other contributions to Carlos Gerardo Molina (ed.) *Universalismo básico: Una nueva política social para América Latina.* Washington, DC: Banco Interamericano de Desarrollo, Editorial Planeta. 2006: 169–187.)

Improvement of the human capital base requires not only higher investment in primary health care and education, but also a broader attack on poverty and inequality. We now have compelling evidence from a study by the OECD and Statistics Canada that investment in education alone is an ineffective tool to improve the quality of human capital at the bottom. Representative samples of the population in OECD countries were given literacy tests designed to assess to what extent people could understand documents and directions (OECD/ Statistics Canada 2000). There is no correlation between the achievements of the bottom quartile of the populations with overall expenditure on education, public and private, but there are strong negative correlations with the levels of poverty and inequality in the respective societies (Huber and Stephens 2002).

THE LEFT AND SOCIAL POLICY

If we look at the initiatives taken by left governments in Latin America in the past five years or so, we see some movement in the direction of more citizenship-based rights, linked to means testing. There is considerable variation in the allocation of social security and welfare expenditures between countries, and indeed we have demonstrated that a left-of-center balance of power in the legislature over the longer run is associated with lower income inequality in Latin American and Caribbean countries, controlling for other factors potentially associated with levels of inequality (see *American Sociological Review* ,Vol. 71, No. 6, December 2006). We have a companion piece still under review that demonstrates that a left-leaning balance of power in the legislature over the longer run is associated with lower poverty rates as well. By the same token, we demonstrate in these papers that strong records of democracy are associated with lower poverty and inequality in Latin America.

Other authors (e.g., Ross 2006) find that democracy is not associated with lower poverty. There are two main reasons for the differences in our and their findings: (1) They use worldwide samples, and we use only Latin America. In the worldwide samples, the alternatives to democracy have more frequently been left-wing dictatorships than in Latin America, where by far the dominant alternative has been right-wing authoritarianism. (2) They use democracy in the year of the observation or with a short lag, whereas we look at the accumulated record of democracy in the second half of the 20th century. Clearly, it takes time for democracy to work. The way that democracy makes poverty reduction possible is by giving the underprivileged and those promoting their interests the chance to organize, form parties, win elections, gain a share of legislative power, and implement policies conducive to poverty reduction. For parties to form, establish roots in society, and win a large enough share of seats consistently to be influential on policy and be able to sustain policies to reduce poverty effectively, takes years. Poverty reduction through transfers can be achieved comparatively rapidly, once the political power balance is favorable, but poverty reduction through improvements in human capital takes a generation. In other words, it takes a long record of democracy and of influence of left-of-center parties for effective anti-poverty policies to show sustained effects.

So, what are the main contours of social policies pursued by left-of-center governments in Latin America? Clearly, I cannot offer a comprehensive overview, so let me concentrate on Chile, Costa Rica, Uruguay (here we are dealing not so much with new initiatives but legacies of long-term left-of-center incumbency and social policy), and make some references to Brazil. I shall highlight some of the most significant initiatives in income transfers and in health care, where the emphasis has been on expanding access to quality health care for low income sectors.

Chile has a relatively large number of programs directed at the poor, in the form of both subsidies and goods and services. The value of cash transfers is low, though. All of these programs have strict eligibility rules, and throughout the 1990s there was little coordination between them. Chile Solidario was launched in 2002 under Ricardo Lagos with the purpose of targeting the 225,000 poorest families in the country and assigning them to a social worker who would coordinate for them access to all the transfers and services they are entitled to under the condition that they comply with certain requirements. These requirements are designed to keep the most vulnerable members of the households, primarily children, healthy and in school (Serrano and Raczynski 2004).

Targeting does work in Chile, and it has become more concentrated since 2000. In 2000, 37.1 percent of all monetary subsidies went to the bottom quintile of income earners; in 2006 this was the case for 47.9 percent of all monetary subsidies. In 2006, monetary subsidies accounted for 26 percent of the household income of the bottom decile (all figures from MIDEPLAN, CASEN, 2007). Between 2003 and 2006 real expenditures on health and education increased by 36 percent and 14 percent, respectively, and they are also progressive, though more so in health than in education. Of all the expenditures on pre-school, primary, secondary, and adult education, 33 percent benefited the lowest quintile of income earners (note that expenditures on university education are not included in these figures). Of all public health expenditures, 51.8 percent went to the bottom quintile. The highly progressive profile of health expenditures is at least in part due to the innovations of Plan AUGE.

The government of Ricardo Lagos undertook a major reform by introducing the plan AUGE (Acceso Universal con Garantías Explícitas). This plan was to offer protection to all Chileans for 56 major illnesses, with equal quality of care and financial protection, regardless of income. In order to make this possible, it specifies maximum waiting times, prices to be charged for treatment by all providers, and the right to access to private clinics or hospitals if public ones are not available. The legislation was to create a compensation fund that would redistribute the costs between members of the public and private systems, financed by part of the mandatory contributions, and state funding was to cover indigents. After two years of intense negotiations during which Lagos had to withdraw the compensation fund and reduce the number of illnesses covered initially to 25, the legislation was passed and the program began operating in July of 2005. Treatment is free for FONASA (the public health insurance system) members in the lower income categories and for the uninsured poor and requires a 20 percent copay from higher income members. The number of illnesses covered was to increase to 56 by 2007. New financing would come from a 0.5 percent increase in the value added tax; other tax increases were rejected by parliament. Essentially, the right opposed the provisions that would have increased equity and solidarity and infringed on the interests of the private sector, and they managed to get support from some members of the governing coalition from the Christian Democratic Party and thus to force modifications of the legislation (Dávila 2005).

Costa Rica, like Chile, maintains a register of poor families, categorized into four priority groups to receive support. The main programs to combat poverty and their effective coverage in the lowest income quintile in 2003 were school feeding programs (68 percent coverage), social assistance (54 percent), and housing support (43 percent) (Estado de la Nación 2004: 110). As this report makes clear, funding for these programs is pro-cyclical because it comes from a proportion of the sales tax, and the programs do not regularly receive the 20 percent of the sales tax that they should according to the law.

Costa Rica's unified public health system, arguably the best in terms of access and quality of care for the poor in the region, began experiencing the problems of long lines and long waits for major treatments as a result of the economic austerity policies implemented in the 1980s, with the result that higher income earners began to leave the system for the private sector and the private share of health expenditures rose from 26 percent in 1991 to 32 percent in 2000 (Martínez and Mesa-Lago 2003). The government strongly resisted World Bank proposals for neoliberal reforms and instead implemented a reform that improved the access of poorer sectors to health care via new primary care centers. As McGuire (2007) shows, Costa Rica has been enormously successful in lowering infant mortality, for instance, precisely because of consistent emphasis on public, basic, preventive care. Subsequent governments were able to do that because the PLN governments of the 1960s and 1970s unified the health care system under public sector predominance. By 1995, some 75 percent of all health spending came from the public sector, and 29 percent of that spending benefited the lowest quintile. Thus, the PLN government of Figueres Olson (1994–98) was able to make the establishment of Comprehensive Basic Health Care Teams (EBAIS) its flagship program and expand the program despite resistance from doctors' groups, business executives, and the political opposition (McGuire 2007). The EBAIS became very popular, and community groups organized to demand theirs and protect those established by putting pressure on the subsequent PUSC governments that were not particularly interested in promoting this new form of health care.

In Uruguay, some 90 percent of people over 65 receive some kind of pension (OIT 2004: 66), contributory or not, whereas there was very little support for working age parents who are poor and their children when the new Frente Amplio (FA) government took power. Accordingly, poverty was concentrated among children (OIT 2004: 40). The program of family allowances was reformed in 1995 and 2004, to improve its real value, target it to low income earners, and detach it from social security contributions and thus from formal sector employment. In 1995, the value of family allowances for private sector employees, the unemployed, pensioners, and small producers, was set at 16 percent of the national minimum wage for those with household incomes of less than six times the national minimum wage. Whereas the monetary value is low, it amounted to between 17 percent and 25 percent of the value of the basic nutrition basket for the poverty line in Montevideo between 2000 and 2004, and for 20–30 percent of that value in the interior (Vigorito 2007). Still, coverage remained restricted; only about 30 percent of families with children in the lowest income quintile received the allowances in 2003. Coverage expanded as a result of the 2004 reforms and has made a difference in lowering extreme poverty

(Vigorito 2007). Since total social expenditures in Uruguay are the highest in Latin America already, and the pension system weighs heavily and had a deficit of 4.5 percent of GDP in 2000 (before the crisis), the challenge for Uruguay is to redirect more resources from the elderly to working age unemployed or underemployed poor adults and their children. This, of course, is very difficult to do politically.

The FA government unleashed a flurry of initiatives in social policy. In May of 2005 they lauched the Plan de Atención a la Emergencia Social (PANES), targeting 40,000 households with 200,000 members in extreme poverty. In July of the same year they created a Social Cabinet which included the Ministry of Economy and Finance in addition to the sectoral ministries. By late 2005, they announced a tax reform and health sector reform. PANES established a citizenship income for each household below a certain income level, conditional on school attendance of minors in the household and on regular medical check-ups and participation in community activities. As of August 2005, 19,737 households were receiving a citizenship income. Families had to apply, and students were trained to find and assist them in their applications.

The citizenship income program was followed by an emergency employment program for community projects, linked to training for the labor market for unemployed heads of household. Selection for the program was by lottery and those selected stopped getting the citizenship income and instead got a salary of roughly twice that amount. As of November 2006 there were 7,500 people in that program, 71 percent of whom were women and most of whom had never had a formal sector job before. At the same time, efforts were stepped up to get all kids three to four years old into preschools and the older ones permanently in school, assisting kids from poor families to attend school regularly.

The health care reform aims at unifying the system and establishing control by the public sector, thus improving access to quality care for the lower income groups. By 2007 both the health care and tax reforms were well under way though negotiations continued about modifications. Given the complexity of the health care system in Uruguay, there is significant resistance from a variety of stake holders—resistance that had blocked far-reaching reforms under previous governments.

It is still too early for a comprehensive assessment of these policies in Uruguay, but the general trajectory of social indicators is encouraging. Poverty and inequality had increased between 2001 and 2004 because of the economic crisis, and they decreased between 2004 and 2006. Poverty in Montevideo increased from 12 percent to 23 percent from 2001 to 2004 and decreased to 18 percent by 2006; extreme poverty for these years was 1.9 percent, 6.6 percent, and 3.6 percent; and the ginis for those years were .46; .47; and .45. Clearly, the economic recovery contributed to the decline in overall poverty and indigence, but it is important to keep in mind that in most cases economic growth in the past decade in Latin America was NOT accompanied by a decrease in inequality, so social policy in Uruguay has to be credited with redistribution and therefore a significant contribution to poverty reduction. Income from total transfers (including pensions and public nutrition programs) amounted to 41.5 percent of household income for the bottom 10 percent of income earners, 33.6 percent for the next decile, and 21.6 percent for the top decile (19 percent accounted for by pensions and only 2.6 percent by other programs).

Brazil's *Bolsa Familia* is one of the two largest conditional cash transfer (CCT) programs in Latin America, along with Mexico's *Oportunidades*. It grew significantly in the second half of Brazilian President Lula's first term, to reach 11.1 million families by late 2006, about 100 percent of those eligible. The ministry in charge estimates 4.1 members per family, which would amount to about one-quarter of Brazil's population. Given the regional distribution of poverty, the share of families benefiting is much higher in the Northeast than in the large urban centers of the South. Still the program only absorbed roughly 7 percent of all social expenditures in 2006, or 2.3 percent of direct monetary transfers, compared with the 82 percent going to the much more regressive pensions. Hunter and Power (2007) make a very strong argument that this program greatly contributed to Lula's re-election, as he received the lion's share of the vote from lower income earners and the poorer geographical areas. A World Bank research paper (Rawlings and Rubio 2003) looking at Brazil along with Mexico and Nicaragua came to the conclusion that indeed these programs were an effective means for not only reducing poverty but also promoting human capital accumulation among poor households. The challenge for all left governments remains to raise new revenue to expand these programs and/or redirect social expenditures from upper to lower income groups.

A final area that needs mention is the minimum wage policy of left-of-center governments. The minimum wage in Chile under Pinochet had declined to total irrelevance, but it increased by 640 percent in nominal terms between 1990 and 2003, while the consumer price index increased by 280 percent in this period. The minimum wage as of 2002 was almost twice the poverty line, and 26 percent of wage earners received between 1 and 1.5 times the minimum wage, whereas 13 percent received less than that. In other words, about one-quarter of wage earners in Chile received a wage that was arguably influenced by minimum wage legislation and was sufficient to keep the worker and a spouse out of poverty. President Bachelet put a further increase in the minimum wage high on her agenda. Similarly, Lula greatly emphasized increases in the minimum wage. The real increase in the purchasing power of the minimum wage was approximately 23 percent in Lula's first term (Hunter and Power 2007). In Uruguay, the minimum wage had lost all relevance, but one of the early reforms of the FA government was to re-introduce the wage councils to deal with wage setting.

There are at least three intertwined obstacles on the path to effective poverty-reducing reforms faced by left governments. First, with the exception of Brazil, the tax revenue of these countries is still comparatively low, given their levels of development. This is heavily due to wide-spread tax avoidance and evasion. Second, in an effort to redirect at least some social expenditures from social insurance to social assistance, or from private to public health care, they all have to confront vocal and politically influential groups that are benefiting from the established social insurance and health care systems. This problem is particularly severe for social insurance in Brazil and Uruguay, and for health care in Chile. Third, the left parties by and large do not have solid majorities in the legislatures, so the left presidents have to negotiate with the opposition parties—and in Chile with the centrist coalition partners—that do not have the same social policy priorities. Still, their initiatives are going in a promising direction, and examples from OECD countries offer the hope that the policies will construct their own support bases.

REFERENCES

Bresser Pereira, L. C., J. M. Maravall, and A. Przeworski. 1993. *Economic Reforms in New Democracies: A Social-Democratic Approach*. Cambridge: Cambridge University Press.

Diamond, L., J. Hartlyn, J. J. Linz, and S. M. Lipset (eds.). 1999. *Democracy in Developing Countries: Latin America*. Boulder, CO: Lynne Rienner.

ECLAC. 2002. *Social Panorama of Latin America*. Santiago, Chile: United Nations Economic Commission for Latin America and the Caribbean.

———. 1998. *The Fiscal Covenant*. Santiago, Chile: United Nations Economic Commission for Latin America and the Caribbean.

Freedom House. 2002. *Freedom in the World: The Annual Survey of Political Rights and Civil Liberties, 2001–2002*. Lanham, MD: Rowman & Littlefield.

Hall, P. A., and D. Soskice (eds.). 2001. *Varieties of Capitalism: The Institutional Foundations of Comparative Advantage*. New York: Oxford University Press.

Huber, E., and J. D. Stephens. 2002. "Globalization, Competitiveness, and the Social Democratic Model." *Social Policy and Society* 1, No. 1: 47–57.

———. 2001. *Development and Crisis of the Welfare State: Parties and Policies in Global Markets.* Chicago: University of Chicago Press.

———. 2000. "The Political Economy of Pension Reform." Geneva: United Nations Research Institute for Social Development: Occasional Paper 7.

IADB. 1996. *Economic and Social Progress in Latin America, 1996 Report.* Washington, DC: Inter-American Development Bank, Johns Hopkins University Press.

———. 1995. *Economic and Social Progress in Latin America, 1995 Report: Overcoming Volatility.* Washington, DC: Inter-American Development Bank, Johns Hopkins University Press.

Kitschelt, H., P. Lange, G. Marks, and J. D. Stephens (eds.). 1999. *Continuity and Change in Contemporary Capitalism.* Cambridge: Cambridge University Press.

Larroulet V., C. 1993. "Introduction." C. Larroulet V. (ed.). *Private Solutions to Public Problems: The Chilean Experience.* Santiago, Chile: Instituto Libertad y Desarrollo

Londoño , J. Luisa., and M. Székely. 1997. "Persistent Poverty and Excess Inequality: Latin America, 1970–1995." Working Paper 357, Office of the Chief Economist, Inter-American Development Bank.

Mainwaring, S., D. Brinks, and A. Pérez-Liñán. 2001. "Classifying Political Regimes in Latin America, 1945–1999." *Studies in Comparative International Development* 36(1): 37–65.

Marshall, M. G., and K. Jaggers. 2002. *Polity IV: Political Regime Characteristics and Transitions, 1800–2001.* Dataset available for download at http://www.cidcm.umd.edu/inscr/polity/index.htm.

Morley, S. A., R. Machado, and S. Pettinato. 1999. "Indexes of Structural Reform in Latin America." Serie Reformas Económicas 12. Santiago, Chile: United Nations Economic Commission for Latin America and the Caribbean.

Müller, K. 2003. *Privatising Old Age Security: Latin America and Eastern Europe Compared.* Northampton, MA: Edward Elgar Publishers.

Munck, G. L., and J. Verkuilen. 2002. "Conceptualizing and Measuring Democracy: Evaluating Alternative Indices." *Comparative Political Studies* 35(1): 5–34.

OECD/ Statistics Canada. 2000. *Literacy in the Information Age: Final Report of the International Adult Literacy Survey.* Paris: Organization for Economic Co-operation and Development.

Portes, A., and K. Hoffman. 2003. "Latin American Class Structures: Their Composition and Change During the Neoliberal Era." *Latin American Research Review.* 38, no. 1: 41–82.

Scharpf, F. W., and V. A. Schmidt. 2000. *Welfare and Work in the Open Economy: From Vulnerability to Competitiveness.* New York: Oxford University Press.

Stallings, B., and W. Peres. 2000. *Growth, Employment, and Equity: The Impact of the Economic Reforms in Latin America and the Caribbean.* Washington, DC: Brookings Institution.

UNDP. 2002. *Human Development Report 2002: Deepening Democracy in a Fragmented World.* New York: Oxford University Press.

World Bank. 2000. *World Development Indicators 2000.* Washington, DC: World Bank.

II. THE CONTINUING INSTITUTIONAL CHALLENGE

MAKING CITIZENS FROM BELOW:
INDIA'S EMERGING LOCAL GOVERNMENT
Patrick G. Heller

In recent years the literature on participatory democracy has grown exponentially. Driven in part by important theoretical developments in normative democratic theory, the interest in participatory democracy has grown apace with the increasing recognition of the deficits of representative democracy, especially in the context of low-intensity citizenship (O'Donnell 1993).

The challenge of democratic deepening has both a vertical and a horizontal dimension. The vertical problem is essentially a Weberian problem: Many new democracies suffer from poor institutionalization and in particular weak forms of integration between states and citizens. The problem is two-fold. On the one hand, there is the problem of how citizens engage the state. State-society relations tend to be dominated by patronage and populism, with citizens having either no effective means of holding government accountable (other than periodic elections) or being reduced to dependent clients. In the absence of clear and rule-bound procedures of engagement, citizens can not engage the local state qua citizens, that is, as autonomous bearers of civic and political rights. On the other hand, there is the problem of where citizens engage the state, that is, the problem of the relatively narrow institutional surface area of the state. Given that local government is often absent or just extraordinarily weak in much of the developing world, there are in fact very few points of contact with the state for ordinary citizens.

The horizontal problem refers to the Tocquevillian view of democracy which focuses on the quality of associational life. Tocqueville argued that democracies function well when citizens make use of their associational capacities and recognize each other as rights-bearing citizens. If Indian democracy has endowed citizens with formal rights, pervasive inequalities within society limit the capacity of citizens to act on their rights effectively, in effect distorting the associational playing field and producing a wide range of exclusions (Mahajan 1999). Taken together, the vertical problem of state-society relations and the horizontal problem of perverse social inequalities undermine the associational autonomy of citizens, the *sine qua non* of any effective democracy (Fox 1993). Citizens can vote, but can they participate meaningfully?

But why should we accord so much importance to non-electoral participation? This question has received extensive attention in the literature, and I will only summarize it in bullet-point fashion. There are essentially five types of claims that have been made, none of which is mutually exclusive. First, meaningful forms of participation can serve as schools of democracy, allowing citizens to use and develop their civil and political rights. This is the Tocquevillian point, and it has informed much of the civic engagement and social capital literature. The general point is that the more often citizens engage each other and state institutions as rights-bearing citizens rather than as clients, supplicants, subjects, or dependents, the more likely they are to support and respect democratic rules and norms, including resolving conflicts through rule-bound mechanisms. Varshney's (2002) argument about civic life and ethnic conflict in India is a case in point. This thickening of civic ties can in turn have very positive spillover effects, such as increased trust and lower transaction costs in economic and social life.[1] Second, participation can help strengthen the accountability of democratic institutions by increasing the intensity and quality of ties between citizens and officials, and exposing state institutions to more continuous and noisier forms of scrutiny. In other words, it can help remedy the principle-agent problem. In turn, state actions that are seen as responsive to broad-based inputs will enjoy much higher legitimacy and stakeholder buy-in. Third, more direct forms of participation can have direct developmental benefits by providing decision-makers with better information about needs and problems (and hence better targeting) and better feedback on the effectiveness of interventions. Fourth, when participation has a pro-poor bias it not only gives the poor or historically marginalized a voice that is otherwise often lost through the aggregative logic of elections, but it can also give state reformers key allies with which they can then circumvent or otherwise neutralize traditional powerbrokers (Tendler 1997). The fifth argument has received much less attention in the literature on participation and decentralization, and yet in some respects may have the most profound implications for the quality of democracy. Theorists of deliberative democracy draw a direct link between the quality of participation and the validity of preferences in democratic societies. No one has made this case more eloquently than Amartya Sen:

Public debates and discussions, permitted by political freedoms and civil rights, can also play a major part in the formation of values. Indeed, even the identification of needs cannot but be influenced by the nature of public participation and dialogue. Not only is the force of public discussion one of the correlates of democracy…but its cultivation can also make democracy itself function better…Just as it is important to emphasize the need for democracy, it is also crucial to safeguard the conditions and circumstances that ensure the range of and reach of the democratic process. Valuable as democracy is as a major source of social opportunity … there is also the need to examine ways and means of making it function well, to realize its potentials. The achievement of social justice depends not only on institutional forms (including democratic rules and regulations), but also on effective practice….This a challenge that is faced both by well-established democracies such as the United States (especially with the differential participation of diverse racial groups) and by new democracies. (2000:158–159)

There are two key ideas here that need to be highlighted. The first is that Sen, in keeping with other theorists of participatory democracy, is arguing that we must not just have democracy, but that we must also *practice* democracy. Second, he moves beyond the traditional political science focus on how preferences are aggregated and represented to argue that democracy is first and foremost about how preferences are *formed*—and the key to how preferences are formed has to do with the quality and inclusiveness of public debate.

Local government looms large as the key terrain for developing these participatory dimensions of democracy. This is true at a general level, as well as for the specific circumstances of India. In a general sense, all these participatory dynamics of making citizens, both in terms of enhancing associational capabilities and improving the nature of citizen engagement with state, have their most immediate and palpable expression in local arenas. It is at the local level after all that citizens are most likely to first engage in public deliberation, to see and experience the state, to develop democratic norms, and to form associational ties. Political theorists and political sociologists have often lost sight of this simple fact in part because theories of citizenship have all too often simply been equated with histories of the nation-state. Yet, as Margaret Somers has shown in her critique of Marshall's stage theory of the evolution of civic, political, and social rights in England, social rights in some regions of England were effectively claimed and secured by workers well before the advent of the labor movement and the modern welfare state. Thus, as early as the 17th century, in those local communities where councils were not dominated by landed interests, subordinate groups were able use local public spheres to claim and secure a range of social rights. She concludes that "Recognizable popular citizenship rights have only emerged historically in the participatory spaces of [local] public spheres in tandem with "relationally-sturdy" civil societies" (1995:589).

The democratic and developmental significance of local government takes on added importance in the Indian context because it has been the weakest link in the chain of state-society relations. Three points need to be underscored. First, at the local level, development has been experienced as a largely top-down, bureaucratic affair, over which ordinary citizens enjoy little if any say. Second, the local incarnation of the state has, with notable exceptions, been dominated by elite interests, and linked to society largely through patronage. Third, the actual presence of local government has been so thin both institutionally and financially, that it has not provided a usable platform for public deliberation or action.[2] In sum, the form of the local state and the mode of its interface has been so circumscribed by social power and extra-legal authority as to vacate the actual practice of citizenship.

THE PROBLEM OF CIVIL SOCIETY IN INDIA

Much of the literature on civil society rests on classic liberal assumptions that view associational life as largely spontaneous, constrained only by an overbearing state authority. The recent emphasis on participation in policy and donor circles thus often slips into a form of boosterism that fails to acknowledge the extraordinary challenges that participation faces in any societal context, but particularly in societies marked by poorly formed civil societies and weak public authority. Any serious discussion of democratic deepening must begin with the sociology of actually existing civil society.

First, recent work in sociology has underscored just how resilient and durable inequality is. The term "durable inequality" comes from Tilly (1999), who has argued that most inequalities are organized around binary or hierarchical categories such as male/female, black, white, or in the case of hierarchical inequalities, class and caste. The point is that distributions of resources and opportunities are often organized around these categories, and the mechanisms of exclusion are mobilized or operationalized through the use of categories. The various forms of capital that groups mobilize to reproduce their positions in society—economic, social, and cultural capital—all flow within categorical boundaries. These boundaries are of course not airtight, but groups, and especially privileged groups, expend tremendous energy and capital in patrolling boundaries. Dominant groups have an interest in reproducing their privileges and do so through a whole range of cultural, social, and economic practices that enforce the boundaries of the privilege and ensure ongoing exclusion. This includes not only reproducing caste, class, and gender differences through daily practices, but also instrumentalizing institutions and governance in general to serve those interests. The weapons of the rich—to inverse Scot's famous line—represent a vast and powerful repertoire of techniques (material and discursive) to reproduce inequality.

The more general point is that inequality is relational—that is, it is constituted through struggles between groups, and inequality is produced. This point bears emphasis because in much of the literature and especially in the policy world, inequality is usually treated not in relational terms, but in residual terms. That is inequality is seen an unfortunate by-product of imperfect markets, bad policies, or historical legacies that can be removed through good policy, more complete markets, or changes in attitudes. The problem is that such views fail to recognize that because inequality is produced, better policy or more enlightened attitudes will do little to change inequality until the question of power is addressed.

The more careful analyses of civil society in India have provided very skeptical accounts. At a general theoretical level, Mahajan and Chaterjee have both questioned the viability of the very concept of civil society in India, and especially its democratizing character. Mahajan argues that because communities and group identities in India remain strong—and even have legal sanction—participation along group lines can often produce demands that are contrary to the principles of legal, individual equality. Chatterjee goes even further, arguing that civil society is a terrain of engagement with the state that has been dominated by elites, and goes on to assert that most Indians "are not proper members of civil society and are not regarded as such by the institutions of the state" (2001:8). And some recent empirical work by John Harriss and his collaborators has shown that the space of civil society is primarily populated with middle class groups that have crowded out lower class/caste groups (2006).

But one has to be very careful here. While we should be attentive to the kind of critical perspective Mahajan develops and note that there are indeed historically rooted forms of inequality in India that preclude any spontaneous associational life and make civic engagement a rather exclusive affair, we also have to recognize that there is a tremendous amount of variation in local civil societies. Let me provide two sets of examples: the first points to historically formed civil societies, the second points to a new churning of associational life.

First, Ashutosh Varshney has shown that there are places in India, specifically cities, where intercommunal associational ties have produced civic spaces where a wide range of actors can 1) participate in public life; 2) engage in more or less reasoned discussion about highly emotive issues such as communal conflict; and 3) resolve problems through cooperation. In addition, as is well known, the history of anti-Brahmin movements in the South has fundamentally transformed caste relations, opening up a range of political spaces and associational practices that simply do not exist in much of the North. Also, as I have argued elsewhere (Heller 2000), the extensive social rights that have been secured in Kerala can be tied directly to its historical pattern of civil society formation.

Second, there is enormous churning taking place among subordinate groups in India. The most remarkable expression of this has been in electoral patterns, and in particular in what Yadev has dubbed the "second democratic upsurge." But below the surface of electoral politics, many have also noted a new effervescence of associational life. As Corbridge, et al., write, "power is leaching steadily, and in some respects ineluctably, to the lower castes, and has been claimed by them in terms which often resist the presumptions of a benign and disinterested state" (83). From fieldwork in Bihar, Jharkhand, and West Bengal they conclude that it is "the indirect effects of a discourse of participation that have been most effective in carving out spaces of citizenship for poorer people, however small and disappointing these spaces might seem to be" (122). In his work on urban movements in Mumbai, Arjun Appadurai has pointed to a similar dynamic by showing that new forms of civic agency are fundamentally challenging dominant discourses and practices. One could point to many more examples, but I want to highlight two based on very recent, innovative fieldwork. The first comes from Paromita Sanyal's dissertation work (Harvard, Dept. of Sociology) on micro-credit schemes in West Bengal. Drawing on over 400 interviews with poor women, she finds that making small loans to women is having none of the desired economic effects, since men still, for the most part, end up controlling the capital. But she does find that for many of the women she interviewed, participation in women's groups has very significant effects in terms of expanding their associational capabilities. Women who had very limited if any associational life—that is contacts and social intercourse outside the extended family—found themselves attending village gatherings (and even extra-village meetings) and in the process developing a range of new capabilities, including critiques of patriarchal power, new solidarities, and expanding what Appadurai calls the "culture to aspire."

A second notable example of this churning is Rina Agarwala's dissertation work on informal sector women workers in the beedi and construction industries. Across three different states, she has documented new forms of organizing in what historically have been extremely difficult arenas for collective action. What is notable about the types of mobilization she documents is that they have taken place outside of traditional union or party-dominated structures, and despite not being linked to each other, have all developed forms of claim-making that revolve around their identities as citizens demanding rights and recognition (Agarwala 2006).

Yet what makes this churning all the more interesting and possibly transformative is that it is taking place in a rapidly changing political and institutional field.

PANCHAYATI RAJ: THE SILENT REVOLUTION?

The significance of Panchayati Raj is that it represents a potentially very significant expansion of the political opportunity structure. The 73rd Constitutional amendment mandates that states constitute panchayats as self-regulating governments, hold elections every five years and devolve power and resources to panchayats. As is always the case in Federal India, the actual powers and functions devolved are for states to decide. (Among other things this sets up a wonderful natural experiment. A single treatment—creation of democratic institutions where none existed before—but with actual take-up left to states.) However, even in its threadbare form, Panchayati Raj is a watershed.

Much as was the case with liberalization, decentralization was initiated by state elites at the center. Indeed, even as states elites were working ever more closely with an increasingly narrow dominant class base (Kohli 2007), state elites also led the process of reforming the local state. And the diagnosis that fed into the reforms is itself telling. On the one hand, there was a recognition that the Nehruvian developmental state had failed and that in particular the problem lay with command and control line department modes of delivery, which had proven to be heavy-handed (even authoritarian) and inefficient, a point of view famously expressed in Rajiv Gandhi's apparently improvised comment that only 15 paise of every rupee ever reached the intended beneficiary. On the other hand, there was a clear recognition that entrenched rural power structures had thwarted local development. Thus Panchayati Raj was specifically conceived as an instrument for leveling the playing field in favor of lower classes and lower caste actors.[3]

So what do we actually know about the impact of Panchayati Raj, 15 years after the legislation was introduced? First, it quite simply but dramatically expanded the surface area of the state. To borrow a phrase from Corbridge, et al., sightings of the state in rural India can be rather intermittent, and when the state is sighted, it is experienced more as top-down bureaucracy than as democratically accountable authority. With the exception of West Bengal, which has held local elections since 1978, most states have not held elections on a regular basis, and development has been the affair of silo-like departmental bureaucracies. With a firm constitutional mandate to hold elections,[4] the states now at least have a local democratic incarnation. In effect, the reforms have created 232,278 voter-accountable institutions (499 at the district level, 5,905 at the block level, and 232,278 at the village level) where none existed before.

Second, a whole new political class of 3 million elected representatives has been created, which in principle includes one-third of seats set aside for women and proportional representation for Scheduled Castes/Scheduled Tribes (SC/STs). Not surprisingly, many states have fallen short of the mandated representation of minorities, but a majority have achieved one-third representation for women, and a majority has close to or higher proportional representation of SC/STs (Chaudhuri 2007:174).

Third, while the actual amount of power devolved to local governments is hard to assess, and could only be done through very careful state-by-state analyses, there clearly has been some devolution of funds. Average annual funds available to local panchayats between 1990–1995 and 1995–1998 rose by an average of nearly 60 percent (Chaudhuri 2007:182).

But beyond these very broad observations, we actually know surprisingly little about the overall progress that has been made. What evidence we do have is at best fragmentary. Most studies focus on single states and only rarely look at a representative sample of panchayats. And those that have looked at multiple states (such as the series of papers by Rao and Beasely) do so at such a level of abstraction that it is hard to draw valid lessons. Chaudhuri (2007) has provided one of the few overviews.

Drawing on data from the eleventh finance commission, he constructs an admittedly crude index of performance that tracks political, financial, and functional devolution. Not surprisingly, Kerala and West Bengal are the highest performers. This underscores the Kohli thesis (1987) that complex reforms that are resisted by elites are most likely to be carried out by programmatic, disciplined, left-of-center parties such as the CPM. What is more surprising is the second tier of performers. This group includes Maharashtra and Karnataka, which already had solid track records of decentralization before the constitutional amendments. But is also includes Madhya Pradesh and Rajasthan, two states that are usually lumped with the low-performing BIMARU states. The achievements in West Bengal have been well documented by the careful work of Bardhan and Mookerjee. West Bengal however predates Panchayati Raj reforms, and is politically somewhat of an anomaly given the uninterupted rule of the CPM. To try and tease out some of the possibilities and limitations of Panchayati Raj, I want to focus on two very different cases, Kerala and Madhya Pradesh (MP).

THE PEOPLE'S CAMPAIGN FOR DECENTRALIZED PLANNING

The design and impact of Kerala's decentralization reform—officially the People's Campaign for Decentralized Planning—has been well documented. I present a brief overview here of two research projects that examined data from all 990 panchayats in Kerala and a survey of 862 key respondents conducted in 72 randomly selected panchayats.

In terms of its basic design, the campaign in Kerala represents the most ambitious decentralization initiative in India. The scale of financial devolution has been very significant (30 percent of plan expenditures) but just as importantly decentralization in Kerala has been marked by full functional devolution and the creation of a comprehensive, nested, participatory structure of local integrated planning and budgeting.

A number of studies have already established that in institutional terms the campaign has resulted in a significant reorganization of the state and governance, and that the level and scope of decentralization surpasses what has been achieved in Indian states since the 1993 constitutional amendments (Thomas Isaac and Franke 2002; Véron 2001; World Bank 2000). The increase in the discretionary portion of village panchayat budgets has been dramatic, jumping from Rs. 1,000 million in 1996–97 (the year before the campaign) to 4,204 million in 1997-98, and over 5,000 million in each of the three years following (Government of Kerala 2001). A World Bank report found that Kerala has the greatest degree of local expenditure autonomy and is the most fiscally decentralized state in India, and second only to Columbia in the developing world (2000: vol. I, 28–29).

The second decisive impact of the campaign has been on the level and composition of participation. Data collected by the State Planning Board from all 990 panchayats for the first two years of the campaign shows that 10.3 percent of the electorate participated in the first annual Gram Sabhas in 1996 and 10.6 percent in 1997. The social composition of the campaign improved drastically in the second year. If in the first year of the campaign, SC/ST participation was well below the average rate (relative participation was 0.53 with 1.0 = participation rate of the general population) by the second year it was 1.44, meaning that SC/STs were participating in greater proportions that non-SCs. Similarly, women's relative participation increased from 0.57 to 0.82, with women constituting 40 percent of all participants in 1997–98. The data from a sample of 72 panchayats shows that while overall participation has declined (falling to 4.7 percent of total population in 1999 from 7.8 percent in 1997), its social composition has stabilized (Heller, Harilal, and Chaudhuri 2007). In 1999–2000, women accounted for 41 percent of participants, and SCs accounted for 14 percent of participants, well above their proportion of the general population and their 11.5 percent representation in the sample. It is also important to note that the task forces—which were given the responsibility of actually designing and budgeting projects for different sectors—were also relatively inclusive. Women represented 30 percent of task force members, and SCs were proportionally represented. Moreover, 75 percent of all task force members were from civil society.

The high levels of participation appear to have ensured that the inputs of the Gram Sabhas and the Task Forces were incorporated into final budgets. Our survey respondents overwhelmingly reported that the "felt needs" expressed in Gram Sabhas and the projects designed by Task Forces were integrated into the final panchayat budget. Respondents also reported increased accountability of officials. The developmental impact of the campaign was also marked. Over 80 percent of respondents reported that across 13 different areas of development, the performance of the panchayat was an improvement over the past. The performance of panchayats was, however, uneven across areas. The campaign's most marked successes were in building roads, housing for the poor and anganawadis (child services) where almost two-thirds felt the difference was "significant." In contrast, less than a fourth of respondents felt that panchayats had made a "significant" difference in economic development (employment, agricultural support, and irrigation). What makes these survey findings especially robust is that the response rate did not vary significantly across respondent categories (politicians, civil society, and government officials).

There have been significant problems with the campaign. The "big bang" approach that was adopted in Kerala and that consisted of devolving resources and functions before building the necessary local institutional capacity was politically effective, but has left significant problems of system stabilization. Panchayats have found it difficult to manage and spend funds, panchayat plans are more often lists of demands rather than carefully integrated proposals for promoting development, and local plans were never effectively coordinated with block and district plans. Having said this, the campaign has irreversibly transformed the political geography of the state by creating substantial, well resourced, and democratically accountable local governments where none existed before. It is notable that this new institutional architecture and distribution of resources has survived two changes of government and now enjoys support from all political formations. Thus, even critics have concluded that the campaign has not only created a "public platform for a vigilant civil society" but has also ensured an "enabling environment for development" (Kannan and Pillai 2004: 39).

Of course, many will simply argue that these outcomes are just another example of Kerala's unique history and social structure. It is certainly the case that with its high levels of literacy and comparatively lower levels of inequality, Kerala presents a more inviting environment for democratic decentralization than most states. But such a deterministic view—that all these outcomes can be explained by Kerala's fixed attributes—misses two critical points.

First, the campaign represents a very decisive rupture with the past. Indeed, looking at Kerala in the 1980s one would not have thought in presented a favorable environment for decentralization. In the post-independence period, Kerala has enjoyed some of the most effective top-down governmental institutions in India. Thus traditional line departments have successfully provided universal education and heath care and an effective public food distribution system. The public employee unions in Kerala moreover are extremely strong and have long resisted decentralization. Neither party in Kerala has historically supported decentralization: the Congress because it has a weak local organizational infrastructure compared to the CPM, and the CPM because it has long been wedded to democratic centralism and to exerting direct party control over local units. Indeed, if anything, the strength and partisanship of the political party system has come at the expense of the growth of an autonomous civil society. As such, the campaign must be explained not assumed.

Second, the explanation for the adoption and success of democratic decentralization lies in politics, and in particular the relationship of the political field to civil society and changing social and economic circumstances. What made decentralization in Kerala possible was a complex set of political interventions, and what made implementation successful were key strategic choices and careful institutional design. To begin with, it was not the CPM as a whole that championed decentralization, but rather a reformist faction within the party that had the support of EMS Namboodirpad, the party's most respected figure. That faction itself had very close ties to the KSSP (Kerala Sastra Sahitya Parishad), a powerful and autonomous mass-based organization that had a long history of promoting development through grassroots initiatives. In other words, it was the colonization of the party by a civil society organization that pushed a key faction in the party to embrace a new vision of development and to support decentralization. Second, there was a widespread recognition that something had to be done to preserve Kerala's advanced social-welfare state in the face of liberalizing reforms and an endemic fiscal crisis. The traditional line department command and control state that has produced Kerala's universal services was poorly equipped to improve upon those services. Decentralization emerged as an attractive strategy of pushing forward a second generation of public sector interventions to promote economic and social development. Third, decentralization held the possibility of reaching out to new constituencies— women and younger people—to extend support for the party beyond its traditional constituencies of organized labor. Finally, these factors coincided with the passage of the 73rd amendment, giving the CPM both opportunity and political cover to push through reforms.

MADHYA PRADESH

That political contingencies can open up significant spaces for reform is underscored by the case of Madhya Pradesh. MP could not be more different than Kerala. In addition to being poor and having among the highest levels of poverty in India, the state is marked by entrenched structures of dominant caste power at the state and local level, and with the exception of the Narmada dam movements, has not enjoyed a very active civil society.

Despite this, MP is widely viewed as having made significant progress in promoting decentralization and greater participation by traditionally marginalized groups, most notably Dalits and Adivasis. James Manor has provided the most nuanced and detailed account of how Chief Minister Digvijay Singh, who served two terms (1993–2003), was able to push through a number of decentralization reforms. He significantly shifted power and resources downward by empowering local panchayats to spend money; introducing numerous single-sector user-committees in education, forestry, and water management; encouraging the formation of over 250,000 self-help groups encompassing millions, mostly women; formed para-professionals to provide help to councils; and launched mass mobilization campaigns, most notably a literacy campaign (Manor, forthcoming: 29).

The data on MP are not as rich as those we have for Kerala or West Bengal, so we must be careful in drawing conclusions. In comparative terms, MP's performance has been solid, if not spectacular. Average per capital expenditures for all local bodies increased 227 percent between 1990–95 and 1995–1998, second among Indian states only to Kerala (Chaudhuri 2007: 186).

Decentralization has by all accounts had its greatest impact in the area of primary education. The Education Guarantee Scheme (EGS) was the first dedicated program to be carried through the new decentralized structures. The goal of EGS was "to provide community-centered and rights-based primary education to all children in a quick and time-bound-manner" (Anderson 2006). The scheme specifically empowered any panchayat that does not have a school within 1 kilometer to request a school from the government. The government was mandated to respond within 90 days by providing the necessary funding. The panchayat was tasked with identifying a teacher from the community and forming a PTA.

Manor describes the EGS as an example of the government stimulating demand. The response, in Manor's evaluation, was "patently massive." By 1998, the scheme had achieved its target of almost complete access to primary education by drawing in 2 million children with over 31,000 villages getting new schools in a two-year period (McCarten and Vyasulu 2004). Drawing on a repeat household survey, McCarten and Vyasulu report that for the poorest 40 percent the probability rate for completing the 5th grade increased by 21 percent between 1992–93 and 1998–99, compared to 5 percent at the national level (2004: 736). By 2001, the primary education system in MP was entirely decentralized, with Gram Panchayats charged with recruiting and monitoring teachers. A nationwide study of teacher absence in India found that MP had the third lowest rate at 17 percent, well below the national level of 24.8 (Kremer et al. 2004). By one assessment, EGS has led to the "actualization of [individuals'] rights to elementary education from the State government" (Anderson 2006). The literacy rate in MP jumped 20 percent overall (including 22 percent for women) between 1991 and 2001, the second largest decadal growth record in India ever.

What was the political equation that made all this possible? As Manor argues (2007), at the most basic level it was a pragmatic effort to build a new electoral base for the Congress party. Because of increased electoral pressure from the BJP, Digvijay Singh had to break with the party's old reliance on the rural dominance of the Rajput caste and political bosses and to reach out to Dalits and Adivasis. And in response to the rising tide of Hindu chauvinism and caste-based politics, Singh opted to make a drive for development. But he knew he could not work through the traditional bureaucracy since it was corrupt and dominated by dominant caste interests. So instead he opted to stimulate demand from below by devolving resources and authority to the local level, by-passing the traditional patronage channels of local bosses and directing resources to elected councils and user committees. In doing so he worked with a close, hand-picked cadre of young bureaucrats and insulated the new development bureaucracy from patronage politics by creating special purpose delivery vehicles—Rajiv Gandhi Missions—in areas ranging from tackling illiteracy to watershed development and iodine disorders. Thus, even during a period when state-downsizing was the order of the day, Manor points out that during Singh's tenure "major progress [was] made in extending the downward reach of the state" (forthcoming, 26).

There are three dimensions of the MP story that need to be highlighted. First, the political configuration that made change in MP possible was not as idiosyncratic as a focus on Singh's leadership might suggest. What transpired in MP was a classic instance of the pincer strategy in which a determined executive bypasses traditional intermediaries to link directly with grassroots actors. This is for example what is described in Tendler's (1997) influential analysis of successful poverty reduction in the Northeastern Brazilian state of Cerea. Second, Digvijay Singh took advantage of a shifting electoral scene to reach out to historically marginalized groups. Without the loosening effect of the Second Democratic Upsurge, it is unlikely that any Congress leader would have staked her electoral fortunes on the direct mobilization of Dalits and Adivasis. Third, Singh strategically took advantage of opportunities that the center had created. Much as in the case of Kerala, opposition to decentralization was somewhat tempered by the fact that the center had provided the legal setting, some resources, and a lot of symbolic capital for reform.

The limits of a top-down process of reform should be emphasized. Many critics, including Digvijay Singh, have complained that panchayats in MP have been dominated by Sarpanchs. Gram Sabhas moreover have been found to be ineffective in holding elected officials accountable. This then underscores the limits of institutional intervention. In the absence of a well developed civil society, the danger of elite capture remains acute.

TAKING STOCK

The jury is still out on Panchayati Raj. From our limited knowledge we can say that most states have done little, some have done a bit, and a few either already had strong track records that they have extended (West Bengal, Karnataka) or broke new ground and made important headway (MP and Kerala). The reforms have however been significant on three counts. First, the initiative itself points to the existence and activism of a faction of state reformers. Even as the Indian state is being increasingly restructured in a pro-market direction (Kohli 2007), there are also significant pockets of reformers within the state dedicated to improving the accountability and effectiveness of the state in promoting development.[5] Those officials at the national level who support decentralization have significant and often very enterprising allies in the states. Second, new spaces and new rules of engagement have been created. Ordinary citizens have been afforded opportunities to engage public authority in ways that simply did not exist before. Whether such opportunities for engagement translate into the effective making of citizens depends on a host of factors, not least of which are local power configurations and local histories of civil society formation. Third, the participatory thrust of the reforms has lent new legitimacy and credibility to calls for mobilizing citizens. As Corbridge, et al., point out, even if the mandated structures of participation never quite function on the ground as prescribed, the very language of participation resonates with popular aspirations and can readily be turned against a non-performing state. Whether or not these patterns will converge into more robust and sustainable arrangements remains to be seen, but there is certainly an urgent need for more detailed and careful tracking of how decentralization is actually being implemented across different states and how it is impacting participation on the ground.

From the review of the two cases of Kerala and Madhya Pradesh it is possible to draw out some analytic observations. First, participation is more plastic than we generally assume. The conventional wisdom in political science is that participation is stratified and that stratification is driven by stock variables (literacy, race, income, etc.). Much of this literature is based on the U.S., but maybe the U.S. is the outlier. We already know that in the electoral arena in India this simply does not hold true. The social composition of participation— as Yogendra Yadev has shown—has changed dramatically. Just how plastic participation can be is underscored by the Kerala case. In the first year of the campaign, participation mirrored social structure. But by the second year of the campaign, women and Dalits were well represented. And Kerala is not unique in this respect. Alsop, et al., (2000) found that in Rajasthan and MP participation in Gram Sabhas was not stratified by caste, and Krishna (2002) has carefully documented how in the past two decades a new stratum of middle-caste, educated activists have come to play a new role in local politics, displacing the traditional upper-caste powerbrokers. If the extension of the franchise has provided subordinate groups with new avenues of political engagement, albeit with a significant lag, the creation of local participatory spaces is also certain to provide new opportunities for ratcheting up agency.

Second, if the plasticity of participation is in part a function of changing social structures—including various kinds of political empowerment from below—it can also be a result of state intervention. Associational life is artifactual—that is, an artifact of how the state structures political and civic life. In Kerala, the increase of women and Dalit participation was a direct result of new incentives and new fora created by the state. In Karnataka, Singh's EGS triggered a tremendous response from the rural poor.

Third, institutional design matters. In its rush to celebrate associational life, the literature on participation often fails to recognize the complex ways in which institutions structure incentives for participation and can favor or block pro-reform alliances. Much of MP's success can be attributed to the creation of parallel delivery structures and of the careful manner in which Singh built linkages to new constituencies while isolating or at least neutralizing traditional intermediaries. This has by definition not resolved the problem of entrenched powers, but it did allow for new and more effective forms of state intervention. In Kerala, the challenge was different. The patronage system had less to do with traditional social power than highly competitive electoral politics. The campaign was designed specifically with the intent of incorporating politicians and officials while at the same time reducing the opportunities for patronage. Delivery was structured through existing institutions, but the complex set of nested participatory structures increased transparency and reduced opportunities for elite deal-making (Heller, Harilal, and Chaudhuri 2006).

CONCLUSION

Because inequality is produced, it is durable. Because inequality is produced, it is plastic. Institutional reforms can change the transaction costs that the poor and the marginalized face in engaging the state. In this respect, Panchayati Raj represents an important step in the direction of deepening democracy. But those reforms will only be as effective as the type of politics through which they are constructed. What even the very fragmentary evidence I have reviewed here points to is that the politics of reform come in many shapes and configurations. Developing better typologies of these configurations and understanding how and why such favorable opportunity structures emerge calls for much more research. Having said this, there are clear signs of a Great Transformation. Even as rural power structures remain intact and a new urban dominant class secures its power, what has undeniably changed in post-independence India has been the slow, but increasing capacity of subordinate groups to voice their grievances, or to borrow a phrase from Habermas, to redeem the unredeemed citizenship claims of a democratic society. This is tangibly and unmistakably evident in the second democratic upsurge. The intriguing possibility that I would like to close with is that when the power shifts associated with the second democratic upsurge are combined with Panchayati Raj and the many stirrings of civil society, this may yet produce an upsurge of even far greater significance for strengthening citizenship.

REFERENCES

Agarwala, R. 2006. "From Work to Welfare." *Critical Asian Studies* 38 (4):419–444.

Alsop, R., A. Krishna, and D. Sjoblom. 2000. "Are Gram Panchayats Inclusive? Report of a Study Conducted in Rajasthan and Madhya Pradesh." *Background Paper no* 3.

Appadurai, A. 2002. "Deep Democracy: Urban Governmentality and the Horizon of Politics." *Public Culture* 14 (1):21–47.

Bardhan, P., and D. Mookherjee. November 12, 2004. "Decentralization in West Bengal: Origins, Functioning and Impact."

Beasely, T., R. Pande, and V. Rao. 2004. "Panchayats and Resource Allocation in South India."

Berman, S. 1997. "Civil Society and the Collapse of the Weimar Republic." *World Politics* 49: 401–29.

Chatterjee, P. 2001. "Democracy and the Violence of the State: APolitical Negotiation of Death." *Inter-Asian Cultural Studies* 2 (1):7–21.

Chaudhuri, S., and P. Heller. 2003. "The Plasticity of Participation: Evidence from a Participatory Governance Experiment." New York: Columbia University ISERP Working Paper.

Chaudhuri, S. forthcoming. "The 1994 Panchayati Raj Act and the Attempt to Revitalize Rural Local Government in India: What Difference Does a Constitutional Amendment Make?" in *Decentralization to Local Governments in Developing Countries: A Comparative Perspective,* ed. P. Bardhan, and D. Mookherje. Cambridge: MIT Press.

Corbridge, S. 2005. *Seeing the State: Governance and Governmentality in India.* Cambridge: New York: Cambridge University Press.

Crook, R. C., and J. Manor. 1995. "Democratic Decentralisation and Institutional Performance: Four Asian and African Experiences Compared." *Journal of Commonwealth and Comparative Politics* 33 (3):309–334.

Fox, J. 1994. "The Difficult Transition from Clientalism to Citizenship." *World Politics* 46 (2):151–184.

Harriss, J. 2006. "Middle-Class Activism and the Politics of the Informal Working Class." *Critical Asian Studies* 38 (4):445–465.

Heller, P. 2000. "Degrees of Democracy: Some Comparative Lessons from India." *World Politics* 52 (4):484–519.

———. 2001. "Moving the State: The Politics of Democratic Decentralization in Kerala, South Africa, and Porto Alegre." *Politics & Society* 29 (1):131–163.

———. 2005. "Reinventing Public Power in the Age of Globalization: The Transformation of Movement Politics in Kerala." *Social Movements in India: Poverty, Power and Politics,* ed. R. Ray and M. Katzenstein. New York: Rowman and Littlefield.

Heller, P., K. N. Harilal, and S. Chaudhuri. 2007. "Building Local Democracy: Evaluating the Impact of Decentralization in Kerala, India." *World Development* 35 (4):626–648.

Kannan, K. P., and V. N. Pillai. 2004. "Development as Freedom: An Interpretation of the 'Kerala Model'." Working Paper 361.

Kohli, A. 2007. "State and Redistributive Development in India." *Paper Prepared for Project on "Poverty Reduction and Policy Regimes."* Sponsored by UN Research Institute for Social Development.

Krishna, A. 2002. *Active Social Capital: Tracing the Roots of Development and Democracy.* New York: Columbia University Press.

Mahajan, G. 1999. "Civil Society and Its Avtars: What Happened to Freedom and Democracy." *Economic and Political Weekly* 34: 1188–1196.

Manor, J. forthcoming. "Digvijay Singh in Madhya Pradesh: Supplementing Political Institutions to Promote Inclusion." *Against the Odds: Politicians and Institutions in the Struggle Against Poverty.* ed. M. Melo, Ng'ethe N., and J. Manor.

Marshall, T. H. 1964. *Class, Citizenship, and Social Development; Essays.* Garden City, NY: Doubleday.

McCarten, W., and V. Vyasulu. 2004. "Democratic Decentralisation and Poverty Reduction in Madhya Pradesh: Searching for an Institutional Equilibrium." *Development and Practice* 14 (6):733–740.

O'Donnell, G. 1993. "On the State, Democratization and Some Conceptual Problems: A Latin American View with Glances at Some Postcommunist Countries." *World Development* 21 (8):1355–1359.

Riley, D. 2005. "Civic Associations and Authoritarian Regimes in Interwar Europe." *Amercian Sociological Review* 70 (2): 288–310.

Sen, A. K. 1999. *Development as Freedom.* New York: Knopf.

Somers, M. R. 1994. "Rights, Relationality, and Membership: Rethinking the Making and Meaning of Citizenship." *Law and Social Inquiry* 19 (1): 63–112.

Tendler, J. 1997. *Good Government in the Tropics.* Baltimore: Johns Hopkins University Press.

Thomas Isaac, T. M., and R. W. Franke. 2002. *Local Democracy and Development: The Kerala People's Campaign for Decentralized Planning.* Lanham, MD: Rowman & Littlefield.

Tilly, C. 1998. *Durable Inequality.* Berkeley, Calif.: University of California Press.

Varshney, A. 2002. *Ethnic Conflict and Civic Life: Hindus and Muslims in India.* New Haven [Conn.]: Yale University Press.

Veron, R. 2001. "The 'New" Kerala Model: Lessons for Sustainable Development." *World Development* 29 (4):601–617.

World Bank. 2000. "Overview of Rural Decentralization in India: Approaches to Rural Decentralization in Seven States." Vol. I.

Yadev, Y. "Understanding the Second Democratic Upsurge." *Transforming India,* ed. F. Frankel, R. Bhargava, and B. Arora. New Delhi: Oxford.

ENDNOTES

1. Not all forms of associational life have such positive effects. As Bourdieu (1984) always emphasized, social capital can be the basis of exclusionary practices and Armony, Riley (2006) and Berman (1997) have all shown how under certain political-historical circumstances, associational life can become the basis for very illiberal politics. The RSS in India also comes to mind.

2. At Rps. 45 per capita in 1990–95, Chaudhuri describes the resource base of local government before Panchayati Raj as "laughable."

3. D'Souza quotes K.C. Sivaramakrishnan—one of the drafters of the bill and secretary of Ministry of Urban Development—to this effect.

4. As of 2002, all states had held two local elections, except Bihar and Punjab, which had held only one election (Chaudhuri 2006: 171).

5. Mani Shankar Aiyar, the Minister of Panchayati Raj, has been a very vocal and articulate advocate of decentralization and a prominent critic of the distributional consequences of liberalization.

CIVIL SOCIETY AND SUCCESSFUL ACCOUNTABILITY IN PERU

Luis A. Chirinos

Six years alter the downfall of Alberto Fujimori, Peru is still suffering the consequences of twelve years of dictatorship, corruption, and political violence. The suffering is clear when we look at the polls about prestige and approval of the main institutions of the political system, and the mechanisms that social groups, especially the worse off, relate to the state. The polls also show that trust and approval of public institutions are at their lowest levels in history, as shown in Chart 1.

Chart 1: Confidence in Peru's Public Institutions

Institution	Great confidence	Some confidence	Low confidence	None
National government	5	18	51	25
Congress	3	15	45	36
Judicial power	2	12	39	45
Political parties	2	17	38	41

Source: PUC, 2007.

It is also worrying that the number of social conflicts outside of the institutional channels of the political and legal systems is increasing (see Chart 2). In August 2007, the *Defensoría del Pueblo* (Ombudsman) registered 76 conflicts: 29 of them active and 49 latent.[1] The annualized record indicates that between September 2006, and August 2007, there were 265 active conflicts, and the rate is increasing.

To add to the burden, 95 percent of Peruvians believe that corruption is still a serious problem (PUC 2007; Proética 2007), and 50 percent believe that it is a serious obstacle to development (Proética 2007). Furthermore, 73 percent believe that politicians get corrupted as soon as they enter into politics.

As a consequence, 60 percent of Peruvians are unsatisfied with the way democracy is functioning. These figures are not surprising, if we consider that almost 51 percent of Peruvians are considered poor, and that approximately 20 percent are in extreme poverty. Neither democracy nor the recent economic improvement has allowed them to overcome the dramatic obstacles of poverty and exclusion. This disaffection with democracy arises when citizens feel that their authorities and institutions are distant, do not hear their voice, and are not accountable and thus more prone to corruption. This reaction is common in many Third World countries, as shown in *Voices of the Poor: Crying Out for Change* (World Bank 2000).

Chart 2: Active Social Conflicts, September 2006–August 2007

Period	Number of active conflicts
August–November 2006	38
December 2006–February 2007	53
March–May 2007	84
June–August 2007	90
TOTAL	265

Source: Defensoría del Pueblo. Reportes de Conflictos Sociales.

Although Peru initiated a transition to democracy after Fujimori and the terrorist violence, it has not been able to find the virtuous path. It is not that Peruvians prefer an authoritarian regime, as 56 percent believe that democracy is the best political regime possible. What seems to be the case is that democracy has not been able to achieve the results Peruvians were expecting, such as, particularly, an improvement in their living conditions.

Peruvians' frustration with democracy is not so much indicative of a deficit in democracy as a political regime, but rather a result of the poor performance of extremely weakened political and social actors (state institutions, political parties, and civil society organizations [CSOs]). Such institutions have neither been able to design and approve the needed democratic reforms, nor to guarantee their adequate implementation. In order to understand this situation it is necessary to revisit the political crisis of the 1990s.

The roots of Peru's political crisis can be traced to the late 1980s, even before Fujimori. Adrianzen says that in 1994 Peru was facing a crisis of political representation that involved political parties and social organizations. "The parties do not organize the political arena through a new and universal system of norms and the creation of new arenas of political legitimacy for the democratic regime (…) capable of grasping the new consensus and channeling the conflicts." A key indicator of the crisis is that in 1989, *Izquierda Unida* (United Left), a coalition of democratic left wing parties, dissolved, leaving at least one-third of the constituency without a referent of political representation; in 2001, *FREDEMO*, a coalition of right wing parties also dissolved and saw many of its leaders and the entrepreneurs they allegedly represented move closer to the Fujimori government.

This situation also hit the party system as a whole; political identities were disrupted, the parties became mere vote-catchers, and politics became a media and marketing show. Furthermore, incentives were created for independents to enter into politics as opportunistic outsiders, often with radical proposals, but lacking a programmatic vision of the future for the country.[2]

The political crisis strongly affected the CSOs, especially those of the excluded sectors. On the one hand, political parties had often been their strategic allies and a key resource in their conflicts. Parties provided them with orientation, facilitated demand aggregation and hierarchization, and allowed access to the political sphere. The crisis of political parties implied a rupture of such relationships.

The Fujimori government strongly attacked CSOs. Adrianzen (1992, p. 17) says that Fujimori "established a fragmented and clientelistic relationship with some social groups; and a sporadic and caudillo type of dialogue with the economically excluded masses." It seemed clear that state-independent CSOs were not compatible with his political project. The consequences were devastating: CSOs were pervaded by corruption, individualism, and egotism in a ferocious struggle to obtain favors from the state. Even women's organizations (*comedores populares* and *comités del vaso de leche*) that were once strong and played an important role in the popular movement in the 1980s fell victim to the authoritarian seduction. It is important to point out that the private sector and its organizations were also seduced by Fujimori, to a great extent because they backed his neoliberal economic policy.

Shining Path (*Sendero Luminoso*) and the Tupac Amaru Revolutionary Movement (*Movimiento Revolucionario Túpac Amaru*) also attacked CSOs, since as autonomous social organizations they were incompatible with the movements' political project. These groups tried to dominate the CSOs and even assassinated democratic leaders. The overall consequence was a decay of CSOs and deterioration of their democratic values and communication and solidarity systems.

Finally, the impact of neoliberal economic policy was also crucial. The neoliberal reforms destroyed the old state, but were not able to produce an equivalent one in political terms. That is to say, they disrupted "the economic, social, political and discourse mediations through which the state established its relation with society.

The result is a profound fracture between the state and society that delegitimized the state, and generated an increasing political disorganization within society" (Adrianzen 2006, p. 41).

In general terms, the Peruvian state, traditionally inefficient, was incapable of responding to social demands and needs. Fujimori added authoritarianism, corruption, and systematic violation of human rights to this critical situation. In this context, the crisis was characterized by the increasing difficulty of the government to consciously manage the administration, to expand the legitimacy of the public sphere, and to aggregate social demands and satisfy them.

In this condition of astounding weakness of the main political and social actors, the return of democratic forms and procedures (elections, a competitive party system, etc.) was not enough. Democracy is not merely an issue of process, but also a system of interactions among actors. Thus, Peru became an incomplete and frustrated democracy. Peruvians could not see democracy as a political regime with the capacity to provide solutions to their problems, and a wave of disaffection swept civil society.

The transition to democracy initiated in 2001 brought the return of the democratic regime and a series of political reforms that were intended to increase the exercise of democratic rights in order to make the state more responsive, transparent, and accountable. Such rights included citizen participation, transparency and access to public information,[3] and the reform of political parties.[4]

In this chapter, I analyze the process of democratic reforms through three analytical perspectives in an attempt to explain role of political and social actors. The three perspectives are: a) the means of introducing democratic reforms; b) the structure of political opportunities they open; and c) their capacity to efficiently mobilize resources to take advantage of the political opportunities and guarantee the viability of reforms. I will argue that neither the state nor the political parties have had the necessary political will or capacity to provide crucial impetus to the process of democratic change. The most significant efforts in this sense have come from CSOs.

TRANSITION TO DEMOCRACY AND DEMOCRATIC REFORMS

The transition to democracy opened an historical opportunity to both the state and society, especially because its point of departure was a broad consensus between parties, social institutions and organizations, churches (Catholic and evangelic), and professional guilds to introduce key political reforms. That should not be surprising: transition to democracy always implies a realignment of political, social, and economic agents around consensual endeavors.

The most important issues covered by the political consensus were: a) restoration and consolidation of electoral democracy; b) economic reforms in order to ensure sustainable development, allow eradication of poverty and exclusion, and provide stability of the market economy; c) decentralization, establishing strong, democratic, development-oriented and participative subnational governments; d) transparency and access to public information; and e) establishment of rights of citizen participation in order to ensure a more active intervention in governmental processes.[5]

However, a transition to democracy could not be limited to restoration of minimal conditions of liberal democracy. The magnitude of the crisis demanded reforms oriented to the modification of the system of interaction among actors, that is, the structure, dynamics, and role of the state, as well as its relationship with society. For the great majority of Peruvians, democracy should include an ethical component that would allow reduction of the deep inequality and exclusion gap and increase the arenas of citizen participation (Macpherson 1991). This element triggered the potential for conflict because some of the most important reforms would seriously affect the participants in the democratic consensus.

Even though the democratic reforms were a result of a basic consensus between social and political actors, this did not necessarily mean full agreement on all of its terms and conditions. As mentioned by several authors, transition to democracy is characterized by a conflictive coexistence between the old and the new, between those who resist the loss of their traditionally owned power and those who want to occupy positions of power within the new scheme; in other words, between conservatives and reformers.[6] As a consequence, the process is bound to be underscored by a conflict during all phases: design, approval, and implementation.

It is not surprising then, that the transition in Peru generated some sort of a revolution of expectations. Dahl (1989, p. 196) had already foreseen this possibility when he pointed out that "when the barriers that block public debate and participation are destroyed, new interests and demands until then, unknown to the government tend to emerge." This was evident with the initiation of decentralization and citizen participation reforms because they substantially modify current power relations and generate competing expectations and fears within the various actors of the state and society.

Political parties (save for the democratic left-wing parties, which included it in their government plan) generally perceive citizen participation as a menace to the monopoly they hold on social and political representation. That is why their position towards it is often ambiguous, and they usually end up in overt opposition. This was clear from the beginning of the debate: The reformers were not only in the government party, but also in the opposition. Likewise, the conservatives were not only in the opposition, but also within the government party.

The executive branch was also riddled by conflict over the issue. While some sectors were enthusiastic backers of participation, others had serious doubts and even open discrepancies. The Congress presented similar issues. The most relevant supporters were a group of members of Congress, some of whom had been mayors as members of *Izquierda Unida* (United Left) and had established participatory mechanisms in their municipalities and the left wing parties. Members of Congress from other parties, such as *Partido Popular Cristiano* (Popular Christian Party, right-wing), *APRA* (American Popular Revolutionary Alliance, a center-right party) and others were firmly against participation, arguing it was intended to damage the political parties and to eliminate representative democracy.

The same occurred within the bureaucracy, which is often a loser in these kinds of reforms. As a general rule, it can be said that bureaucrats usually oppose citizen participation because it implies that they will lose their monopoly on providing the rationale for public decisions based on technical knowledge. It implies they will have to share the decision-making process with CSOs (Fung and Wright 2001, p. 20). Surprisingly enough, one bureaucratic sector, the *Dirección Nacional de Presupuesto Público* of the Ministry of Economy (*DNPP-MEF*), for diverse reasons, supported in 2001 (that is, prior to the decentralization law) the introduction of participatory budget pilot experiences in 11 regions. As early as 2003, the *DNPP-MEF* assumed a role in promoting the participatory budget, as established in the Law of Regional Governments. It was clear, though, that the state bureaucracy was not united on this issue.

For civil society, citizen participation is always a democratic advance, and that is why it is generally in favor, especially among CSOs of the excluded sectors. It must not be forgotten that CSOs' most important state demand is to participate in the decision-making process. However, CSOs from other sectors (such as the private sector) tend to see participation with distrust, since it implies that they will have to share their exclusive relationship with the state and their capacity to influence their decisions.

Thus there appears to be no unanimity over the value of citizen participation in public decisions. This is the primary reason the process of introducing participatory reforms is constantly conflictive, from its legislative approval through implementation.

The Legislative Process and Reform

A key issue in the transition to democracy is the way reforms are established, because it has different effects on the overall process. In fact, it is the first moment of conflict between reformers and conservatives. We identify three basic models (Chirinos 2004, p. 199–200): a) reforms "from above"; b) reforms "from below"; and, c) reforms through an "agreement among parties."

Reforms "from above" imply that the government approves the reform in the Congress as a universal and obligatory law that does not take into consideration particular and varied situations. Here, the key role is played by political party representatives in the Congress. CSOs do not have an active nor formal role, unless they develop advocacy actions. The consequence is that the reforms will tend to be the result of a negotiation process between reformers and conservatives that will be, as a general rule, limited, ambiguous, and will have weaknesses that generally include obstacles to implementation.

The second model is the reform introduced "from below," ordinarily generated by the pressure of a social or political movement at a particular juncture. Even though this situation implies a momentary triumph of social mobilization, it has extremely low possibilities of legal institutionalization and sustainability.

The third model is what we call an "agreement among parties" and connotes a situation in which the authorities, the political parties, and representatives of CSOs agree on a consensual initiative to introduce the reform. A key characteristic of this model is its high capacity to innovate, to be adapted to concrete situations, and to overcome problems that arise through new procedures or reforms. Experience shows that in these cases the reform has better chances of viability and sustainability since all (or most) of the stakeholders are part of the process. CSOs increase their organizational capacities and empowerment, and at the same time, the reform is more likely to be implemented and to overcome emerging problems. It is worth noting that the most successful experiences of citizen participation in local governments in Peru (Chirinos 2003)—as well as the famed participatory budget process in Porto Alegre, Brazil—were the result of an "agreement among parties."

This model has three important characteristics. On the one hand, it is a decision-making process that is unregulated by law; it is a public policy based on reformist political will and an openness to negotiate the rules of the game with CSOs.[7] Second, the authorities generally go "beyond the law," justified on the basis of their political autonomy,[8] and create new rights and institutions that have a wider coverage than the general law. Finally, this model is usually seen with regional and local governments[9]—not at the national level—because CSOs have more access to subnational governments. In his work on social movements, Hanspeter Kriesi identifies a similar pattern in centralized political systems where there are practically no relevant points of access to power at the subnational level. On the other hand, in federal political systems the points of access to power are distributed along the overall government structure (Kriesi 1995, p. 171).

In Peru, these reforms were introduced "from above," that is, they were the result of a negotiation between the parties in the Congress. As a consequence, the laws were limited, full of ambiguities and holes, and included rights with no sanction to transgressors. The Law of Regional Governments that established citizen participation in regional participatory budgets is perhaps the best example (Chirinos 2004).

The Structure of Political Opportunities

The creation of new democratic rights in a process of transition to democracy always opens political opportunities for civil society. This concept has been applied by Sydney Tarrow for the analysis of social movements and seems pertinent here, since it attempts to understand and explain collective action.[10]

The key components of the structure of political opportunities in Peru, at the beginning of the transition to democracy period, were:

- A new and democratically elected administration that generated deeply grounded expectations to overcome the authoritarianism, exclusion, and corruption that characterized Fujimori's government;
- Creation of new democratic rights for deliberation and participation. Among them, decentralization, citizen participation in the participatory budget, and access to public information and transparency;
- Realignment of political parties and elites with citizens looking for new reference points for political representation. This was blocked, however, "by the weakness of political parties and the inanity and ineffectiveness of civil society." Although it is true that Peru "was emerging from a deadlock, there were no institutional and political alternatives that may ensure a relatively trustable pathway" (Grompone, 2005: 43);
- Emergence of new social and political actors, new interests and new demands that under Fujimori could not be expressed: regionalists, environmentalists, opponents of privatization, and others. These movements "open an unforeseen political agenda (often) with non-negotiable demands, unless

dramatic changes are made at the institutional level and/or in key public policies. Furthermore, these demands usually are not considered by public institutions, because there are no pre-established procedures of negotiation in the existing legal framework, nor clarity on who is responsible in the state… its challenges to the authorities imply a great deal of uncertainty" (Remy 2005, p. 159);

- Emergence of important allies of CSOs, especially those from excluded social sectors. The most important allies were the Catholic and evangelic churches, NGOs, and the international aid agencies; and

- The presence of some groups within the state that were in favor of citizen participation. These included reformist congressmen who led the legal initiative on participatory budget; a group of bureaucrats at the *Consejo Nacional de Descentralización (CND),* and the *DNPP-MEF.* It is note worthy however, that the reformist bureaucrats at the CND had very little power and low capacity to develop actions.

As a consequence of the newly established rights, the emergent structure of political opportunities generated positive incentives to mobilization and also created arenas for conflict. It must be stressed though, that a favorable environment is not enough to guarantee viability to collective action, and it is clear that sectors negatively affected will try to oppose the approval and implementation of the new reforms, from within and outside the government.

Resource Mobilization

The key issue is whether civil society and its organizations, as beneficiaries of the democratic reforms, will be able to ensure approval and implementation of the changes. This question leads us to a concept used by the social movement's theory: resource mobilization (McCarthy and Zald 1977).

Resource mobilization implies that CSOs will successfully engage in collective action if they can take advantage of resources that put them in a better position of negotiation with their adversaries. Obviously, the most important resources are the CSO organization itself and its capacity to build strong alliances with external actors such as NGOs. In Peru, this CSO weakness posed a significant challenge. Among the main weaknesses of CSOs were the following:

- The crisis of political parties had a critical impact, because they had been frequent allies of CSO. Given their situation, it was impossible for them to provide their most important input, which was organizing, aggregating, and prioritizing social demands;

- The adversarial character of the relationship of CSOs with the state and other actors (especially the private sector), because of the latters' resistance to change. Such character often transforms interest conflicts into principle conflicts, making negotiation and agreement difficult. Institutionalized participation demands a change in both parties;

- CSOs often have low organizational capacities in crucial areas, such as streamlined procedures for decision making; degree of professionalism in their leaders; democratic representation; legal, economic, and technical information; and economic resources to finance activities and establish relationships with state officials and the media;

- The law established severe barriers to access. To participate in the *Consejo de Coordinacion Regional* (Regional Coordination Council, or CCR), CSOs had to have legal registration (*personería jurídica*). That posed a serious problem because the enormous majority of CSOs did not have it. It must be mentioned, however, that historically this has never been a requirement for establishing relations and negotiating with the state. The"costs of entering into legality" was a major concern; and

- In periods of transition to democracy, many CSOs present demands to the state that are not yet fully included in the public policy debate. This can cause problems of legitimacy of the demands and make it difficult to recruit allies.

On the other hand, among the main strengths of the CSO are the following:

- CSOs cover a great diversity of population and issues across all regions. Peru has a dense organizational network, especially among the excluded sectors;

- CSOs have a strong and vibrant participatory tradition that allows them a great mobility and versatility in their initiatives;

- CSOs possess strong identity based on bonds of diverse types: territorial or economic community, ethno-cultural, gender, generational, and the like;

- CSOs are prone to dialogue as a key component of their strategies. Most demands and conflicts begin with a formal request for dialogue that often does not receive a positive response from the government;

- CSOs have high capacity for direct action and other mechanisms typical of social movements; and

- CSOs have high capacity to recruit powerful strategic allies such as NGOs, churches (especially Catholic, but also evangelic and others), and international aid agencies. With the support of these allies, CSOs can override some weaknesses, such as technical knowledge and access to relevant information, logistics, training, and so on.

The efficacy of CSOs in struggling for new democratic rights depends greatly on their capacity to secure access to power centers in subnational governments—to take advantage of the incentives created by new political opportunities and the efficient mobilization of their resources. In addition, because of their organizational problems, the role of the allies became fundamental, as we shall see.

THE LEGAL MODEL OF THE PARTICIPATORY BUDGET

In this section we will explore the variety of actions that CSOs have performed to meet the challenge of securing approval and implementation of participatory rights in the participatory budget. These activities usually involve reformulation of strategies, innovation, and a role for allies—particularly NGOs—that are willing to intervene in the political process. The endeavor of CSOs was to address organizational problems and develop their capacity to represent their constituencies.

CSOs were facing a crucial challenge. The idea was to promote active citizens, as opposed to a passive and merely reactive citizenship. The creation of participatory rights was an extraordinary opportunity, the viability of which depended on the effective use of the incentives opened by the structure of political opportunities and the efficient use of their available resources.

The Base Law of Decentralization and the Law of Regional Governments established the right of all citizens to participate in the budgets of regional and local government, including the participatory budget and the regional development plan.[11] It must be stressed though, that the legislative process was very conflictive. The legal draft presented by the Decentralization Committee of the Congress (led by the reformers) encountered harsh opposition from the political parties, which argued that citizen participation was an attempt to replace representative democracy and to destroy the parties. As a consequence, after very tight voting, the first version of the law (Law 27867) did not include the institutional scheme for the participatory budget. Faced with this situation, CSOs and their allies launched a strong mobilization campaign to advocate for its inclusion. Negotiation between the government and some opposition parties was necessary and, as a result, Law 27867 was modified two months later (Law 27902).[12]

Some months later, the Congress passed the Law of Participatory Budget (Law 28056) that regulated the general procedure and established the mechanism of "participatory agents," apparently with the purpose of diminishing the role of the CCR and increasing the number of participants. This law was elaborated by the Economic Committee of the Congress, led by the conservative group, and not by the Decentralization Committee, which was comprised of a majority of reformers who favored participation.

The establishment of the participatory budget was a typical case of a right approved "from above," that is, through a general law, applicable to all situations. As mentioned, since the law resulted from a negotiation between conservatives and reformers, its contents were ambiguous; it had holes, and practically no sanctions for transgressors.

Thus, the legal scheme of the participatory budget had serious problems. The most important were:

- Restrictive access because of the requisite of legal registration of CSOs as a condition to participate in the CCR. As mentioned, this left the great majority of CSOs out of the game, since most CSOs from excluded sectors do not have it;
- CCR has an unequal membership: 60 percent should be provincial mayors and 40 percent representatives of CSOs. This criterion is more appropriate when decisions are made by vote, not by negotiation and consensus;[13]
- The participatory budget only includes capital expenditure (basically infrastructure investment), and leaves out expenditure in public and social services, human capital, and current expenditure;
- The participatory budget only includes income derived from central government transfers (the so called "budget ceiling"), which is decided by MEF every year. It does not include other sources such as mining royalties, *canon,* and *sobrecanon.* This is important because income from these sources has increased tremendously in the last five years due to the high price of minerals in the international market. Obviously, the income tax paid by mining (and other natural resource companies) has risen significantly. However, it must be mentioned that the distribution of these resources is extremely unequal: four regions receive 71 percent of the mining *canon;*[14]

- Institutional parallelism since, simultaneously with the CCR, a mechanism of "participatory agents" was established for which there are no access barriers and through which the participatory process actually takes place. This parallel mechanism, although it appears more democratic, in fact allows more control by the regional government;
- The consensus decisions of budget allocations require the approval of a technical team that has authority to modify the agreements, based on viability standards established by MEF. The risk is that the technical team implies bureaucratic control based on technical knowledge that Grompone (2005) and Fung and Wright (2001) point out is a key problem in this type of process;
- There are no sanctions for the authorities and bureaucrats that violate the law; and
- There are no incentives for authorities to conduct a truly democratic participative process. The law does not include measurement standards or benchmarking that might allow monitoring of the process.

Some authors have criticized the legal model. They argue that the participatory budget becomes the most important arena of citizen participation, forcing CSOs to focus their initiatives on it and leave aside other crucial problems in an attempt to "depoliticize" the society (Remy 2005, p. 172–173). This characterization has been labeled as "economicist reductionism" and is considered a menace to authentically democratic participation (Kliksberg 2000, p. 186). Although it is evident that four years of participatory budgeting is not enough to prove this hypothesis, the experience suggests that CSO participation in the participatory budget has not had a negative impact on their other roles.

The experience of participatory budgeting in Peru shows that several problems of implementation have arisen. Among them are:

- The CCR has lost importance because the "participatory agents" and the technical team have become the true protagonists of the process;
- Provincial mayors do not seem to be truly interested in participating in the CCR or in the overall process; they would rather go forum shopping to obtain economic resources from the national and regional government;
- Participating CSOs are mainly territorial, and much less sectoral organizations, because the legal model favors the participation of urban groups and local elites. Rural organizations are largely underrepresented. However, in the last few years this tendency is changing;

- The private sector does not participate because it does not perceive the CCR and the participatory budget as attractive to its interests, mainly because they can negotiate their demands and needs directly with the national or regional governments;

- Regional authorities tend to take the CCR into consideration only at the end of the process when the agreements have to be signed, because it is established in the law. Although the *Instructivo Anual del Presupuesto Participativo*[15] has introduced changes in order to improve its role, these have been notoriously insufficient;

- There is no effective coordination between the participatory budget and the development plan. Often, the budget allocations have no relation to the plan. This inconsistency is aggravated by the fact that the budget is made on an annual basis, whereas the plan is multi-annual. The phase of participatory debate and approval of the development plan in many cases has become a symbolic ritual;

- The resistance of regional authorities to complying with the participatory character of the process persists. This is mostly shown in their tendency to deny adequate and timely information to the participant CSOs and to ignore the changes introduced by the *Instructivo Anual del Presupuesto Participativo*;

- In some cases, the Regional Council in charge of approving the definitive budget does not respect the agreements of the participatory process. As a consequence, the distribution of resources is made allocating equal amounts to each province. This tendency however, is changing, as regional counselors have become more involved in the participative process;

- CSOs have little capacity to present technically proficient project profiles. That makes their initiatives highly vulnerable to the technical bureaucratic decisions of the technical team;

- Since social demands are not aggregated, they appear as disordered and strongly based on localism, making deliberation extremely difficult; and

- The oversight committees of the participatory budget established by the law operate precariously due to the opposition of the authorities, the lack of resources, and the low power they hold.

The introduction of the participatory budget opened, as mentioned, a crucial opportunity for civil society to increase participation in key state decisions, but as we have seen the legal model has had several problems that have hindered its efficacy. Thus, it becomes important to take a look at what the main social and political actors have done in this conflictive process.

The Role of the State

In spite of the problems, the central government did nothing to improve the situation. Neither the *CND*, the public agency in charge of conducting the decentralization process, nor the *Secretaria de Descentralización* (Secretariat of Decentralization), which replaced *CND* in 2007, have demonstrated political will to improve the process. Citizen participation and the participatory budget do not seem to be among their priorities.

In view of the problems generated, reformers in the Congress—with the active support of CSOs and NGOs—presented drafts proposing changes in the law, but lacked the necessary strength to succeed. The only public institution that paid some interest was the *DNPP-MEF,* which sponsored the formation of the so-called *Colectivo Interinstitucional del Presupuesto Participativo* (henceforth *Colectivo Interinstitucional*), an ad hoc working group with the participation of NGOs and some CSOs. This process is extremely interesting because it shows that even within the state there can be sectors subject to the impulse of democratic reforms. As early as 2002, MEF and the *Mesa de Concertación de Lucha Contra la Pobreza* (*MCLCP*) conducted a pilot program of participatory budgeting in 11 regions.

According to law, the main responsibility of *DNPP-MEF* in the process was to issue every year the *Instructivo Anual del Presupuesto Participativo*, a regulation for the participatory process. Apparently with a bureaucratic perspective (and without coordinating with *CND*, which was certainly unusual), *DNPP-MEF* convened NGOs and some CSOs to a workshop with the purpose of evaluating the 2003 participatory process; the workshops were repeated in 2004 and 2005. As a result, participants started to coordinate some activities such as dissemination (a poster) and standardization of training contents. Some time after, at the initiative of the *MCLCP*, participants agreed to formally establish the *Colectivo Interinstitucional* as a *sui generis* public-private forum dedicated to the analysis and evaluation of the participatory processes, and to introduce changes in the *Instructivo Anual del Presupuesto Participativo* (Shack 1995). Its activities went even further: In 2006, it called regional and local governments to a best-practices contest.

The importance of the *Colectivo Interinstitucional* is that it opened a dialogue platform between *DNPP-MEF* and civil society, which made an important difference in the previous situation of tension and conflict. Moreover, it became the arena where NGOs and CSOs were able to present the criticisms and initiatives. MEF was receptive to some initiatives, and as a consequence, some changes were introduced, such as: a) the obligation of the regional government to approve an ordinance at the beginning of the process; b) the technical team was to include civil society agents—universities, NGOs, CSOs, and *MCLCP*—as a means to control the power of bureaucrats in the technical evaluation of the investment projects; c) improvement in the role of the CCR; d) resource allocation to the overall process and to the oversight committees; and e) from 2008, the possibility to include multi-annual allocations in the budget, in order to improve its concordance with the development plan.

The case of the *Colectivo Interinstitucional* illustrates two important issues. On the one hand, within the state there exist some bureaucratic sectors with political will to dialogue with civil society, and eventually, open to changes in the regulations. It is clear that for *DNPP-MEF*, the purpose was only to ensure compliance with the law and the viability and efficiency of the legal scheme through the mechanism of the participatory agents, even if it diminished the role of the CCR. In other words, *DNPP*-MEF was not interested in the political aspects of the issue, but only in the technical ones. In the eyes of CSOs and NGOs, this did not exclude *DNPP-MEF* as an ally for specific objectives. It also indicates that some sectors within *MEF* have understood the seriousness of NGO and CSO criticisms and had become sensitive to the issue. It is interesting to note that currently the *Colectivo Interinstitucional* includes other state institutions such as the *Secretaria de Descentralización*, the Ministry of Woman and Social Development, and the Social Development Fund (FONCODES). On the other hand, it also shows that CSOs and NGOs have the capacity to force the state to establish this type of relationship as part of the strategy to improve the participatory process.

Even though it is not a typical state institution, the *Defensoría del Pueblo*, in charge of overseeing the citizen's rights, has performed an important role in promotion and oversight of the participatory rights. Its main activities covered: a) dissemination of the contents of participatory rights; b) periodical reports on the implementation of the law and its accomplishment, based on first hand information gathered through its regional offices; and c) recommendations to the Congress and the executive on possible legislative reforms to make the participatory process more democratic and accessible. The *Defensoría del Pueblo* has been a true ally to CSOs.[16]

The *Asociación de Municipalidades Rurales del Perú (REMURPE)* is the association of mayors of rural municipalities, especially the poorer ones with less relative development and populations on the poverty line or below. Thus it is not really a public institution, but because it is formed by mayors (who are political authorities), it should be considered here. One of the basic objectives of *REMURPE* is to advocate for legal changes to improve the situation of rural municipalities, as well as the democratic character of the participatory budget. This is mainly because the many mayors, members of *REMURPE,* had introduced successful mechanisms of citizen participation in their municipalities even before the decentralization and the participatory budget were approved by law. *REMURPE* has a good reputation in the decentralization political community and is perceived as a representative of its constituents. That is why *REMURPE* is often invited to participate in debates on decentralization and participation and is currently a member of the *Colectivo Interinstitucional,* where it has advocated improvements of the participatory process.

The Allies of Civil Society

From the beginning of the process, CSOs had important allies: NGOs, international aid projects—among them, *Participa Perú*[17] y *PRODES*[18]—the churches, and the *MCLCP*, institutions that have a long history of support for development and democratic reforms. Since 2003, these allies have intervened on different fronts: dissemination of the law and the rights of participation; training of CSO leaders in order to increase their capacity and technical assistance to present initiatives to the participatory budget and in the oversight committees; negotiation and decision-making processes; organizational strengthening of CSOs; generation of legal initiatives to modify the negative aspects of the legal model; public campaigns on key decentralization and participation issues; and legal aid in the acquisition of legal registration of CSOs.

It is important to stress the key role played by public international aid agencies, including the U.S. Agency for International Development, GTZ (Germany), COSUDE (Switzerland), the Swedish Agency for International Aid, DFID (United Kingdom), and others. From the beginning of the decentralization process they launched projects and activities to support the state efforts as well as civil society advocacy activities. Likewise, private international aid agencies from Germany, the Netherlands, United Kingdom, Spain, and other countries also supported programs implemented by NGOs.

Peruvian political parties, due to their current crisis, did not have the capacity to be effective allies as we have seen in other Latin American cases, such as Brazil, Uruguay, and Venezuela (Goldfrank 2006, p. 8–10).[19] It is noteworthy that the reformist members of Congress, the regional presidents and mayors that supported the participatory budget from the start in 2003 were former members of *Izquierda Unida*, the coalition of left-wing democratic parties that had an important role in the Peruvian political scene during the 1980s.

The CSO allies had a crucial role in the legislative process of the Law of Regional Governments and the Law of Municipalities. In both cases, they strongly advocated in the Congress, especially before the Decentralization Committee, presenting initiatives and providing relevant information about the importance and implications of the participatory budget. That the public campaign they launched for the modification of the first Law of Regional Governments did not include the CCR is especially relevant, because it turned out to be successful: one month later, the Congress passed a law amending the most negative aspects of the original law.[20] NGOs and other allies also advocated for other legislation on decentralization and participation, and they strongly supported the advocacy activities of CSOs in regional governments.

Unlike state institutions, allies developed multiple activities for dissemination of the new participatory rights and provided training and technical assistance to CSO leaders in order to improve their performance in the participatory process. A key component of these activities was the educational strategy that combined formal training in workshops and the practical exercise of the new rights, taking advantage of the capacity of CSOs to "learn by doing." CSOs produced a huge amount of high-quality materials such as posters, brochures, pamphlets, and studies that make part of the intellectual capital of CSOs.[21]

Citizen participation was perceived by CSOs and their allies as an opportunity to promote their organizational strengthening. That is why a significant component of the educational strategy included sustained efforts to increase the level of representation and organizational development of CSOs.

The allies also had an important role in launching programs of citizen oversight on the decentralization process and particularly on the participatory budget. *Vigila Perú*, a program implemented by *Participa Perú*, was probably the most successful, not only because of its positive results, but most of all because it was sustainable after the project ended.[22]

As for NGOs and other allies, there has been another collateral effect, namely, the consolidation of their role and public recognition of their contribution to development and democracy. However, this achievement has increased the distrust of many state segments and the private sector, which criticize their performance in issues such as human rights and environmental issues, especially in the mining sector.

According to most studies, the role of CSO allies in the process of transition to democracy is usually of the utmost importance. The Peruvian case is no exception. However, it did not include the political parties, which shows the significant gap created by the crisis. According to Tanaka (2007), this situation poses a poignant issue concerning the future of parties in Peru, because he perceives that most societal efforts are dedicated to the strengthening of CSOs and the participatory process as opposed to the reform of political parties. The most important allies to civil society had been NGOs, *MCLCP*, and the Catholic Church.

Political Advocacy

CSOs and their allies have presented since 2003 many legislative initiatives through advocacy activities, helped along in this by three factors: a) CSOs with strong leadership and a long-term political perspective; b) strong allies with capabilities to generate reasonable and high-quality legal proposals and persuasive arguments; and c) the openness of several regional presidents to build constructive relations with CSOs and their allies.

A crucial achievement was to persuade the regional governments to suspend the requisite legal registration of CSOs. This was important because CSOs and their allies thought that the Regional Council, the legislative body of regional government, should be the participatory forum *par excellence*. They thought that the Council could request an opinion on key governmental issues and that the CCR would develop a closer link between the participatory budget and development plan, which seemed to be extremely difficult.[23]

To strengthen the CCR, NGOs trained CSO leaders in advocacy and political bargaining, including methodologies that allowed them to build strong alliances with other sectors of civil society (Ballón and Chirinos 2007). The advocacy experiences carried out by *Participa Perú*, for example, were successful in four of the five regions in which they were implemented. Regulatory ordinances on the participatory budget, which adapted the law to each regional context, allowed greater access for CSOs, and simplified procedures were enacted in Cuzco, Ica, and Arequipa. In Huancavelica, an ordinance was passed approving the Regional Agenda, a document that organized the demands of civil society so as to incorporate them into the participatory budget and regional policies.[24] In other regions ordinances were passed to expand participation of women's organizations and peasant and native communities.

Within the participatory process itself, CSOs were able to prioritize budget allocation in human development issues (education and health) and to introduce gender criteria through the gender sensitive budgets (Flora Tristán and Escuela Mayor de Gestión Municipal 2007). A significant case was the approval of an ordinance recognizing the Women's Roundtable for Dialogue in nine provinces and another approving the Action Plan for Women's Development in the regional government of Junin.

Another important achievement was the inclusion of the resources of the Regional Compensation Fund, FONCOR, *canon* and *sobrecanon,* in the participatory budget, after a formal request by the CCR. The consequence was that the total amount of the budget was increased and allocation was more equitable.

The regional government's obligation to approve, in coordination with the CCR, an ordinance to regulate the process also became an opportunity for advocacy activities. Thus, these ordinances were enriched with key achievements such as:

- Members of CSOs and NGOs were included in the technical team, even before the *Instructivo Anual* required it. Cajamarca, Huancavelica, Cuzco, and Piura established it in 2005, and in the 2006 process, 90.5 percent of the regional governments did it. Government officials remain in the majority in these bodies, however (López Ricci and Pineda 2007, pp. 14–15).
- New criteria that combined territorial allocations with sectoral allocations were introduced to allow a more equitable distribution of resources. Cuzco and Huancavelica were cases in which these new criteria were particularly relevant (*Colectivo Interinstitucional de Presupuesto Participativo* 2007).[25]
- Strengthening of sectoral representation in order to ensure an increase in bargaining power over resource allocation through the establishment of thematic round tables.

It is also important to mention that regional governments created inter-institutional committees with CSO participation in key areas of the administration. Between 2003 and 2006, regional governments established approximately 125 committees of this sort. Even though there is no evaluation of their effectiveness, they represent the political will of regional presidents to build participatory mechanisms that go beyond the participatory budget. These sectoral committees are intended to work all year long, not just in the participatory budget period, and they are capable of generating initiatives and inputs by consensus, both for the participatory budget and for the overall administration. Consequently, they can present the hierarchy of social demands and orient budget allocation to long-term development policies and public and social services. Increased efficiencies in the sectoral committees will generate incentives for the private sector to participate more actively in the participatory budget.

The advocacy experiences of CSOs at the regional level allow us to identify their potential to introduce reforms and innovations to improve civic participation in the participatory budget. Given the negative response from the Congress regarding modifying some key provisions of the law, CSOs decided to advocate modification at the regional governments through political bargaining. The strategy consisted of generating conditions to change the legislative process, moving from a law "from above" toward a law produced as an "agreement among parties." When adequately implemented, this move was successful.

An analysis of the regional ordinances produced as "agreements between parties" shows that they exhibit four characteristics:

1) They go beyond the law, improving conditions for greater participation by different sectors of civil society;
2) They possess a greater legitimacy since they are a result of political bargaining that considers all stakeholders;
3) The "agreement among parties" is formalized through regional ordinances that give them full legal validity; and
4) The reforms produced under this model have a positive impact. Participatory budget decisions tend to be more deliberative (Fung and Wright 2001) and potentially can achieve a better articulation between the participatory budget and the development plan.

Fung and Wright believe this type of reform contributes to a decision-making model they label Empowered Deliberative Democracy (EDD). It is radically democratic because decisions depend on the participation and the capacities of citizens; it is deliberative, because they are a result of decision-making processes based on reasoning; and it is empowering (Fung and Wright 2001, p. 7).

Reorganizing Civil Society

For CSOs, the emergence of the right to participate in the participatory budget offered an opportunity to influence the decision-making process of public expenditure. Nevertheless, given their organizational weakness, CSOs had to address other crucial challenges, namely, strengthen their organizations, restore representation and internal democracy, and at the same time, actively exercise new rights.

The most important advantage in this endeavor was that Peruvian civil society has built a huge organizational network. Chart 3 presents the types of CSOs by economic or social sector and shows that civil society is organized in practically every dimension of social life. It must be stressed that the regional and local distribution seems to be unequal. Unfortunately, the lack of national, regional, and local CSO maps inhibits a more detailed view of the situation.

The survey of "Democratic Participation" (August 2001)[26] indicates that at least 56 percent of Peruvians belong to some type of organization, which shows a high citizen propensity to participate. As in the previous situation, these figures hide an unequal distribution at the regional and local level. The survey on "Citizen's Perception of the Decentralization Process,"[27] applied in seven regions, indicates that the number of people that say they belong to an organization is much lower: in 2003, it was 19.9 percent, and in 2005, it declined to 13.9 percent.

The greatest challenge of CSOs was to participate in the participatory budget process that started in 2003. Even though in the first year the number of participant CSO was very low, it increased in the following years. In 2006, the rate of growth was 25 percent nationwide (López Ricci and Pineda 2007). This was a result of increasing participation of women's organizations and peasant and native communities as well as universities and the private sector.

The most important improvement for women's organizations was carried out by the *Participa Perú* project, through which the *Centro de la Mujer Peruana Flora Tristán* implemented a program of legal registration in order to improve access to the CCR. The success was such that the majority of women's organizations not only received their legal registration, but also underwent organizational reform that included renewal of the governing bodies, restoration of internal democracy, and capacity building for investment projects in the participatory process (Durand 2005). Due to its success, this program has been replicated in others regions, such as Ayacucho and Huancavelica.

Little by little—though different among regions—the private sector has acquired a greater appreciation of the participatory budget, especially in Cuzco, Lambayeque, and Huancavelica. In 2006, global participation of the private sector reached 13.6 percent. Also relevant is the increased participation of state institutions. Between 2004 and 2006, average participation was about 50 percent (López Ricci and Pineda 2007).

Chart 3: Sample Types of CSO in Peru

Social sector	Type of organization	Level
Urban dwellers	Neighborhood organization (Organización vecinal)	Neighborhood
	Neighborhood committees (Juntas de Vecinos)	
	Housing cooperatives (Cooperativas de Vivienda)	
	Housing associations (Asociaciones de Vivienda)	
Peasants	Peasant communities (Comunidades campesinas)	Confederación Campesina del Perú-CCP at the national level
	Conveagro	
Amazon natives	Native communities (Comunidades Nativas)	Two national federations
Farmers	Juntas de regantes	National and regional federations
Workers	Labor unions in the private sector (Sindicatos de trabajadores del sector privado)	Two national federations: Confederación General de Trabajadores del Perú (CGTP) and Confederación de Trabajadores del Perú
	Labor unions of public workers (Sindicatos de trabajadores del sector publico)	
Women	Comedores populares	District and provincial level National federation
	"Glass of Milk" committees (Comités del vaso de leche)	
Youth	Cultural associations	Local level
	Popular libraries (Bibliotecas populares)	

Private sector	Associations by productive branch: Agrarian, industry, mining, fishery, and others	CONFIEP at the national level
	Local and regional chambers of commerce	Federación de Cámaras de Comercio del Perú
Provincial migrants	Asociaciones de provincianos	Local level
Professionals	Professional guilds and bars (Colegios profesionales)	Regional and national level

As mentioned above, CSOs developed diverse activities in order to enhance the legal role of CCR. With this objective, they created informal committees in several regions: the *Asamblea de Delegados* in Piura; the *Asamblea de la Sociedad Civil* in Cuzco, and the *Asamblea de Delegados de las Organizaciones de Sociedad civil* in Lambayeque. In spite of their potential significance, these committees have had severe problems and often are not recognized by regional governments. It appears clear, though, that they can play an important role in the propagation of legal reforms through the "agreement among parties" model discussed earlier.

In spite of its weakness, there are some ways in which the CCR has played an important role. The most representative case is that of Cuzco, in which the CCR requested that the Regional Council include the Regional Compensation Fund, the *canon,* and *sobrecanon* in the participatory budget. As mentioned before, this initiative was accepted.

From the beginning of the participatory process, CSOs have attempted—with the strong support of their allies—to strengthen their organizational structures. This allowed them to increase their participation and enhance the exercise of their new rights. As a consequence, some valuable experiences have been gained, though they remain isolated and incomplete. A long road lies ahead. In this sense, it seems that the appropriate strategy for moving forward is to promote reforms at the regional level through more-equitable "agreements between parties."

FINAL THOUGHTS

An important measure of Peruvian progress in the transition to democracy is the establishment of participatory budget rights. Granted after years of subpar governance and conflict, this right to budget participation caught Peruvian civil society in a moment of weakness, and Peruvian CSOs continue to search for the methods—and means—most likely to make a success of it. CSOs were able to mobilize their organizational resources, their long-standing participative tradition, and especially their large experience of learning by doing to find successful ground.

Yet it is also important to consider the cost of overcoming the legal hurdle. In Peru, issues of legal registration of organizations have not been the only barrier. Advocacy capacity, and, most importantly, leaders' ability to acquire new skills and the knowledge to be more effective with participatory budgeting is also critical.

In spite of some regional advances, problems remain, and challenges are still difficult and complex. Institutionalizing and exercising the right to the participatory budget is a long-term and conflictive process. However, it must be stressed that participation has become consolidated and is perceived by CSOs and citizens in general as a key component of the transition to democracy.

Finally, it is important to point out some key challenges for the near future. One is the need to "reinvent" the CCR, since it is no longer viable in its present form. Attempting to do this through the Congress is certainly not the most adequate strategy. Again, taking in consideration the experiences of the past years, the best possible strategy seems to be to advocate in the regional governments "agreements between parties."

Other crucial challenges must be faced in the near future, such as the need of CSOs to reconstruct their social demands in order to transition from the local to the regional agenda, the need to better articulate the participatory budget and the development plan, and the need to improve coordination between regional and municipal participatory budgets.

REFERENCES

Adrianzen, A. 1992. *Democracia y partidos en el Perú*. Pretextos, 3–4; Lima, DESCO.
———. 2006. *¿Crisis de gobernabilidad o inicio de un nuevo ciclo político en América Latina?* In: Grupo Propuesta Ciudadana. Democracia, descentralización y reforma fiscal en América Latina y Europa del Este. Lima; pp. 31–45.
Ballón, E., and L. Chirinos. 2007. *La incidencia política en la Descentralización peruana.* (Manuscript)
Bobbio, N. 2003. *Democracia Representativa y Democracia Directa*. In: El futuro de la Democracia; México, Fondo de Cultura Económica.
Centro de la Mujer Peruana Flora Tristan y Escuela Mayor de Gestion Municipal. 2007. *Manual de formación política y gestión local con enfoque de género*. Lima.

Colectivo Interinstitucional de Presupuesto Participativo. *Experiencias exitosas de Presupuesto Participativo en el Perú.* Lima, 2007.

Dahl, R. 1989. *Poliarquía. Participación y Oposición.* Madrid, Tecnos, 1989.

Defensoría del Pueblo. www.ombudsman.gob.pe.

Durand, A. 2005. *Participación Ciudadana y Empoderamento de la Mujer en Junín.* Lima. CRS/Flora Tristán.

Chirinos, L. 2004. *Participación ciudadana en los Gobiernos Regionales: el caso de los Consejos de Coordinación Regional.* In: La Participación ciudadana y la construcción de la democracia en América Latina; Lima, Participa Perú.

———. 2003. *La estructura de oportunidades políticas de la participación ciudadana en gobiernos locales.* Lima, Calandria-DFID.

Fung, A. and Awright, E. O. 2001. *Deepening Democracy: Innovations in Empowered Participatory Government.* Politics and Society 29, No. 1, March 2001.

Goldfrank, B. 2006. *Los procesos de "presupuesto participativo" en América Latina: Éxito, fracaso y cambio.* Revista de Ciencia Política, Vol. 20, No. 2; pp. 2006.

Grompone, R. 2005. *Argumentos a favor de la participación en contra de sus defensores.* In: Zarate, Patricia (ed.) Participación Ciudadana y Democracia. Perspectivas críticas y análisis de experiencias. Lima, Instituto de Estudios Peruanos.

Instituto de Estudio Peruanos (IEP). 2001. *Encuesta sobre "Participación Democrática".* Lima. Funded by USAID Perú.

———. 2007. *Encuesta sobre "Percepción ciudadana sobre el proceso de Descentralización."* Lima. Funded by PRODES.

Kliksberg, B. 2000. *Seis tesis no convencionales sobre la participación.* In: Kliksberg, B. and L. Tomassini eds. Capital social y cultura: claves estratégicas para el desarrollo. Buenos Aires, Banco Interamericano de Desarrollo.

Kriesi, H. 1995. *The Political Opportunity Structure in New Social Movements: Its impact on their mobilization.* Jenkins, C. and B. Kalndermans, eds. The politics of social protest. Minnesota, University of Minnesota Press.

Lopez Ricci, J. 2006. *Presupuesto Participativo 2005–2006. Seguimiento a cuatro casos regionales: Cusco, Piura, Huancavelica y Cajamarca.* (Unpublished working paper).

Lopez Ricci, J., and L. Pineda. 2007. *Seguimiento y evaluación nacional del presupuesto participativo 2006.* Informe preparado para La Mesa de Concertación de Lucha contra la Pobreza. (Unpublished working paper).

Macpherson, C.B. 1997. *La Democracia Liberal y su época.* Madrid, Alianza Editorial.

McCarthy, J. and M. Zald. 1977. *Resource mobilization and social movements: a partial theory.* American Journal of Sociology no. 82.

O'Donnell, G. 1998. *Accountablity Horizontal.* En: Ágora, Buenos Aires, no. 8, verano.

Offe, C. 1988. *Los nuevos movimientos sociales cuestionan los límites de la política institucional*; In: Partidos Políticos y nuevos movimientos sociales. Madrid, Editorial Sistema.

Pontifica Universidad Catolica del Peru. Instituto de Opinión Pública. www.pucp.edu.pe

Proética. www.proetica.org.pe

Remy, M. 2005. *Los múltiples campos de la participación ciudadana en el Perú.* Lima, Instituto de Estudios Peruanos.

Santos, B. de S. 2004. *Democratizar la democracia: los caminos de la democracia participativa.* México, Fondo de Cultura Económica.

———. 2005. *Reinventar la democracia. Reinventar el estado.* Buenos Aires, CLACSO.

Shack, N. 2005. *La programación participativa del presupuesto en el Perú: primeras lecciones de un proceso de concertación.* Caracas, CLAD.

Tanaka, M. 2007. *La participación ciudadana y el sistema representativo.* Lima, PRODES.

Tarrow, S. 1997. *El poder en movimiento.* Madrid, Alianza Editorial.

ENDNOTES

1. For the *Defensoría del Pueblo*, active conflicts are those that are overt during the period, whereas the latent conflicts are not, but remain unsolved and can burst at any moment.

2. At the end of the 1980s, as a consequence of the current political and economic crisis of the Garcia administration and its disastrous effects, the prestige of political parties fell abruptly. It is important to remember that one of Fujimori's arguments in the coup d' etat of 1992 was the need to put an end to politics and "traditional parties" and that it was largely supported by the population.

3. In August 2002, the Congress passed Law 27806 on Transparency and Access to public information. In February 2003, this law was modified to improve conditions to exercise the established rights.

4. In 2001 several draft laws on political party reform were presented to the Congress in order to make them more democratic, transparent, and representative. In November, 2003, after harsh debates, Congress passed Law 28094, which regulates political parties. However, it is a common opinion that its scope is limited and compliance is not a common practice.

5. These reforms are a consequence of new political and ideological currents that favor the widening of democratic rights through citizen participation and oversight mechanisms (Offe: 1988; Bobbio 2003). In Latin America, some Constitutions have explicitly included them, such as in Brazil, Colombia, and Peru.

6. The difference between conservatives and reformers is intended to identify general alignments. Within these blocks, there is a variety of subgroups, which coexist even within the political parties.

7. The most successful experiences of citizen participation in Peruvian local governments since 1980 were implemented by mayors belonging to *Izquierda Unida*. See Chirinos 2003.

8. Article 191 of the Peruvian Constitution says that regional governments have political, economic, and administrative autonomy. Article 194 says the same about local governments.

9. This type of situation arises when subnational governments acquire more power, resources, and functions as a result of decentralization policies, as occurred in local governments in Peru in 1980. At the regional level, this occurred in 2001 with the current decentralization process.

10. Tarrow defines the structure of political opportunities as "consistent signals— though not necessarily formal or permanent—provided by the political environment that stimulates or disincentivates collective action. The concept of political opportunities emphasizes external resources to the implied group … that can be used even by weak or disorganized groups. Social movements upsurge when citizens, sometimes mobilized by leaders, respond to changes in the opportunities that reduce the costs associated to collective action, when they discover potential allies, identify vulnerable points in the elites and the authorities."

11. The decentralization legislation also established other participatory rights that we will not discuss in this paper. They include among others: periodic public reports of the regional president of the state of the administration, referendum for regional integration, oversight of social relief programs, and citizen consultation for border interregional conflicts.

12. For a detailed analysis of the legislative process, see Chirinos 2004.

13. In this text, we only discuss the CCR. However, the same can be said about the CCL, the participatory organ in local governments.

14. The *canon* and *sobrecanon* is the regional and local government share in the income tax collected from companies that exploit natural resources (mining, fishery, timber, and others). The share of subnational governments is a percentage of the income tax collected by the state. The mining royalty is a percentage of the mining concentrate paid, as a compensation for the use of a nonrenewable resource.

15. The *Instructivo Anual del Presupuesto Participativo* is a regulation issued annually by the ministry of economy that establishes the procedure of the participatory process. It was established by the Law of Participatory Budget, and it is intended to provide a standard procedure to the process.

16. The activities of the *Defensoría del Pueblo* can be revised in: www.ombudsman.gob. pe. The international aid agencies that cooperated with the *Defensoría del Pueblo* were, among others, USAID and the Swedish agency for international aid.

17. *Participa Peru* was a project oriented toward civil society support to decentralization and was funded by USAID between 2002 and 2007. It was implemented by Catholic Relief Services, Grupo Propuesta Ciudadana, and Research Triangle Institute.

18. PRODES was a USAID-funded project to support decentralization. It was implemented between 2003 and 2007, by ARD.

19. Goldfrank says that the support of political parties as allies of CSO (*PT* in Porto Alegre, and *Frente Amplio* in Uruguay) were crucial for the initial implementation of the participatory budget.

20. The first law of regional governments did not include the participatory mechanisms. In view of that, an intense campaign and advocacy activities were launched. Members of the *Participa Peru* project participated in 29 radio interviews, 7 in TV, and 24 in newspapers.

21. These materials can be obtained in: www.participaperu.org.pe, www.prodes.org.pe, www.mesadeconcertacion.org.pe, www.redperu.org.pe, and www.care.org.pe, among others.

22. *Vigila Peru* is a system of citizen oversight on the performance of 13 regional governments that uses 65 indicators on 6 key issues: budget management, legislation, citizen participation, transparency and access to information, education, and health. It is currently managed by *Grupo Propuesta Ciudadana*. The website www.participaperu.org.pe includes all reports since 2003.

23. This option is notoriously different from the reasons that led MEF to support the participatory budget. For MEF, the strategy was to strengthen the mechanism of participatory agents.

24. These advocacy campaigns were carried by *Participa Peru*. Ballon and Chirinos analyze the experiences and describe the methodology.

25. In Huancavelica the decision was to distribute 50 percent to the territorial projects and 50 percent to the sectoral projects. In Cuzco, 50 percent was allocated to regional impact projects, 30 percent to other projects, 10 percent to road and highway maintenance, and 10 percent to finance prefeasibility studies. For more information, see *Colectivo Interinstitucional de presupuesto participativo* 2007.

26. The survey on "Democratic Participation" was made by IEP and financed by USAID. It had national coverage.

27. The survey on "Citizen's Perception of the Decentralization Process" was applied by IEP and financed by PRODES. The regions covered were those prioritized by USAID: Ayacucho, Cusco, Huanuco, Junin, Pasco, San Martin, and Ucayali.

DECENTRALIZATION AND DEMOCRATIC TRANSITION IN INDONESIA

Michael S. Malley

What a difference a decade makes. Ten years ago Indonesia was ruled by one of the least democratic and most centralized regimes in the world. It was also in the throes of its worst economic crisis in more than thirty years. The financial crisis that struck several Asian countries in 1997–98 affected Indonesia more severely than any other and touched off a process of political change that has made Indonesia the largest democracy in the Muslim world.

Indonesia's political transition was far from smooth. In addition to a national movement pressing for democratization, the country experienced separatist movements and communal conflicts on such a scale that observers inside and outside the country feared it would collapse. Despite these challenges, the interim government that ruled Indonesia between May 1998 and October 1999 managed to lay the foundation for a more democratic and decentralized political system, and the country emerged from that transitional period to join the ranks of the world's democracies, not its failed states. Today it is the only country in Southeast Asia that Freedom House considers entirely "free."

The twin processes of democratization and decentralization reflect a backlash against the authoritarian and centralized character of the previous regime. And their origins and impact are so deeply interwoven that they are, in many respects, inseparable. Indeed, that is one of the chief arguments of this chapter: it is, for the most part, impossible to draw a line between them in a way that allows us to ascribe various outcomes to one process rather than the other. Analyses that draw this line are common, especially in the donor community, but they succeed only by defining decentralization narrowly in terms of the laws and regulations designed specifically to shift power to the regions while neglecting others that contribute equally to shaping center-region relations.

Such an approach is no longer tenable. As recent studies have shown, the impact of decentralization depends heavily on the political context in which it is designed and implemented. And since these contexts vary so widely, Bardhan and Mookherjee find that "there cannot be any general presumption" about the impact of decentralization on either service delivery or the representation of local interests. Likewise, Treisman shows that across cases "one cannot generalize usefully about the consequences of decentralization."[1]

Quite obviously, these findings complicate the task of providing useful guidance to policy makers. Above all, they imply that we must devote as much attention to understanding the origins of decentralization as its effects. In particular, we need to consider more carefully the conditions under which political leaders are inclined to pursue decentralization, the reasons they offer for doing so, and the various ways they seek to distribute power across levels of government. Despite more than a decade of sustained research by political scientists, most literature on decentralization continues to reflect the longer and deeper research traditions rooted in public administration and economics, as well as the urgency that policy makers and advisers understandably place on gauging the impact of decentralization. Yet today even economists such as Bardhan and Mookherjee have concluded that understanding the origins of decentralization requires "rich historical description," and Treisman concludes that it is "important to understand the processes of politics in particular decentralized orders."[2]

In this spirit, I trace the origins of Indonesia's decentralization during the country's transition to democracy in 1998–99. My goal is to identify the key processes that reshaped the balance of power between national and subnational governments, and in that way to illustrate how broadening our notions of decentralization and its causes can reshape our view of its impact and of appropriate policy to address its less happy effects. Given this limited purpose, it is not necessary to trace the process of decentralization up to the present.

In the first section, I describe Indonesia's political transition and identify features of new democratic institutions that reshaped the balance of power between national and subnational governments before policies to promote decentralization were even drafted. In the second section, I describe how the legal basis of decentralization policy was created, and what its framers sought to achieve. In the third section, I return to the issues raised in this introduction. In particular, I show that "decentralization" preceded the adoption of policies intended to produce it, and that subnational political forces reshaped national decentralization policy even as that policy was being created. Consequently, it is difficult if not impossible to attribute subnational outcomes to "decentralization" rather than "democratization." And to the extent that problems commonly attributed to decentralization, such as corruption, actually result from shortcomings in democratization, efforts to ameliorate them are better addressed through democratic reforms rather than refinements of decentralization.

THE ORIGINS OF DEMOCRATIZATION IN INDONESIA

Indonesia's transition to democracy and decentralization occurred under conditions that impelled leaders of the authoritarian regime to enact reforms, but limited their opponents to indirect participation in the process of designing them. On the one hand, the regime had generally succeeded in disorganizing and intimidating its main opponents during the mid-1990s, so groups and individuals of national stature were unprepared to use the crisis as an opportunity to mobilize public opposition to the regime. On the other hand, President Soeharto resigned his position just two months after orchestrating his "reelection" to a seventh five-year term and only one month after a nascent student movement moved from university campuses onto public streets. In a short space of time, massive protests were mounted in cities and towns across the country, but these had not produced either a significant opposition organization or group of opposition leaders with whom the regime could negotiate the terms of a transition. Thus, the weakness of the opposition and Soeharto's sudden decision to resign created the conditions for an incumbent-led transition.[3]

Although the protest movement attracted support in nearly every region of the country, its demands were simple, straightforward, and essentially national rather than regional. Everywhere, students marched under the banner of opposition to corruption, collusion, and nepotism, and demanded Soeharto's resignation. Once he had left office, his successor, B. J. Habibie, was left to translate these demands into specific reforms. Seeking to head off further protests, he quickly committed his government to a three-stage timetable for reform: liberalization of laws on parties, elections, and legislatures within about six months, legislative elections at national provincial, and district levels within a year, and an indirect presidential election within about 18 months. He made no commitment to decentralization, and faced no significant criticism for failing to do so.

To draft the legal framework for democracy, Habibie's government turned to a small team of bureaucrat-scholars, mainly political scientists. In late 1998 the bills they drafted were presented to the House of Representatives, whose members had been elected in 1997 under conditions so illiberal that Freedom House assigned Indonesia its worst possible score for political rights. Fifteen percent of the members were military and police appointees, and the rest were either members of the regime's party or members of two other parties whose candidates the government had screened prior to the election. But like the executive branch drafters of the legislation, House members appreciated the need to present a "reformist" image to voters by supporting the proposed legislation. Despite the authoritarian conditions under which they had been chosen, they intensely debated several key provisions, particularly whether to permit civil servants to join political parties (yes, but with conditions), and how much to reduce appointed seats for the armed forces in the House (by half). And they rejected the drafters' recommendation to replace the traditional proportional representation system with single-member districts.

Even though the legal framework for democracy did not contain any reference to decentralization, it contained several provisions of tremendous importance to center-region relations. In the first place, it combined liberal rules on the formation of political parties with restrictions that effectively prevented regional parties from participating in elections, whether at the national or regional level. To take part in an election, a party needed to have a headquarters in Jakarta, and branches in half the provinces and half the districts in each of those provinces. Second, the closed-list proportional representation system strengthened national party leaders' influence over regional branches by allowing them to determine which members were nominated and where they were ranked on the party list. Third, the new framework called for legislative elections to be held simultaneously at the national, provincial, and district levels, which most election experts expect will further privilege national over regional concerns. Fourth, it distributed seats in the new legislature in a way that overrepresented sparsely populated regions outside Java, the demographic, political, and cultural center of the country. This was in keeping with the practice of the previous regime, and it meant that even though people on Java constituted nearly 60 percent of the country's population, they would receive only about 50 percent of the seats. And fifth, the new laws did not call for the early election of regional executives, so unlike either Soeharto, who was forced from office, or Habibie, who would face election in 1999, many regional heads would remain in office long after democratic elections had occurred.

THE ORIGINS OF DECENTRALIZATION IN INDONESIA

Laws explicitly aimed at decentralization were drafted and approved under much different circumstances. The same small team of drafters, on its own initiative, turned its attention to decentralization in late 1998 after completing work on the bills needed to prepare for elections in 1999. Its leader secured presidential approval for two parallel efforts under which his team would draft a new law on regional government and another team, based in the ministry of finance, would draft a law on intergovernmental fiscal relations. Both proceeded in highly technocratic fashion, with little public input, scrutiny, or even attention despite the team's high profile.

The members of the team that drafted the law governing political and administrative decentralization were almost entirely from regions outside Java, and they took for granted that the country was overly centralized. Moreover, they tended to believe that decentralization was needed to forestall a swelling cacophony of demands for autonomy. Most believed that decentralization was essential to maintain national unity. Their counterparts in the finance ministry had long debated the need for fiscal decentralization, and took largely for granted the common theoretical claims that some functions can more efficiently be performed by local governments, and that resources should follow function. The president, who had studied and worked in Germany for more than 20 years, seems to have been familiar with federalism and easily persuaded that decentralization would not be as dangerous as his predecessor had thought. And he may have viewed his support for decentralization as likely to enhance his own reform credentials ahead of the 1999 election.

The bills they drafted were radical, whether measured against previous Indonesian practice or the decentralization policies of other countries. They promised to democratize regional government, guarantee regional governments a large share of national government revenues, and turn over to regional governments millions of national government employees. Yet they generated few questions and no controversy when presented to the legislature for approval in early 1999. Indeed, in retrospect this is one of the most striking features of the process that produced one of the world's most ambitious decentralization policies. It merits little attention in either of the most comprehensive efforts to recount the transition, and only a few pages in the president's own account of that period.[4]

Unlike the bills that would underpin democratic elections, these laws promised no immediate impact on legislators' own career prospects. While elections were just a few months away, the new decentralization laws were not scheduled to take effect for nearly two years. And in the face of those elections and an electorate strongly inclined to oppose incumbents, they perceived their own support for decentralization as likely to enhance their image as proponents of reform. In other words, legislators had short time horizons, were very uncertain about their own prospects, and consequently heavily discounted the future costs of decentralization.

The 1999 regional government law granted the broadest range of rights to district-level, or second-tier governments (i.e., cities and kabupaten), rather than provinces. This was in line with Soeharto-era plans for decentralization, but drafters also readily acknowledge that they chose to grant less autonomy to provinces since they saw them as more likely than districts to demand independence. Only authority over defense, foreign affairs, justice, religion, and monetary policy remained solely with the central government. Most importantly, the law eliminated the district's status as an administrative unit of the national government. This had two practical implications. One was that regional chief executives (mayors and bupati) would no longer serve simultaneously as heads of regional government and chief representatives of the national bureaucracy in their regions, but only as heads of regional government. Accordingly, the national government surrendered to district legislatures the right to elect these officials. This marked a radical break with previous practice since these officials had, with the exception of a brief period in the late 1950s, always been appointed by the national government. As a result of this change, local governments were no longer accountable upward to national bureaucrats but, at least in law, downward to local legislatures and, indirectly, local electorates.

Secondly, the law provided that all district-level offices of national government ministries would be transferred to district governments or eliminated. As a result, the central government's administrative reach was limited to the provincial level, where the law preserved much of its authority. This marked a dramatic shift, since the New Order's dominance over regional affairs rested heavily on the central government's control of an administrative structure that paralleled regional government bureaucracies and through which it could monitor regional developments and funnel resources for development and patronage. Thus, these changes effectively severed the hierarchical administrative ties that had enabled national governments to subordinate local politics to central administration.

The second law revamped the fiscal relationship between the central and regional governments to give the latter greater autonomy in managing their own finances. It made two key changes. For the first time ever, the central government made legally binding commitments to share its income with subnational governments, a critical step considering Jakarta's tight control over major sources of tax revenue. The new law introduced a requirement that the central government distribute to the regions in the form of block grants at least 25 percent of its domestic revenues (i.e., all revenue excluding receipts from foreign aid and loans). Secondly, it committed itself to share revenues derived from natural resource production with the regions in which the resources are produced. Thus, regional governments became entitled to 15 percent of after-tax revenues from oil, 30 percent from natural gas, and 80 percent from forestry, fisheries, and general mining.

A few examples convey a sense of the massive changes the laws effected. During the first year, regional governments' share of government spending rose to 30 percent from just 15 percent prior to decentralization. Moreover, the bulk of fiscal transfers from the center to the regions was made as block grants, and no longer was tied to spending on specific programs, such as markets and schools. The elimination of central government offices at the district level also resulted in a massive shift of buildings and civil servants from national to regional control. According to a World Bank study, "Over 2 million civil servants, or almost two-thirds of the central government workforce, were transferred to the regions....239 provincial-level offices of the central government, 3,933 [district]-level offices, and more than 16,000 service facilities—schools, hospitals, health centers—were transferred lock, stock, and barrel to the regional governments throughout Indonesia."[5]

WHAT DID DECENTRALIZATION DO?

Since their passage in April 1999, it has become conventional among analysts of Indonesian decentralization to treat the laws on regional government and intergovernmental fiscal relations as though they alone define Indonesian decentralization policy. This seems especially common in donor-funded studies, perhaps exemplified best by a recent report in which major donors attempted to take stock of the progress made in implementing decentralization. Its opening sentence reads: "Indonesia has made significant strides in democratic decentralization over the last five years [i.e., since 2001], when reforms were first felt on the ground."[6] While it is true that Indonesia has made such progress, it is simply untrue that such reforms only began to be felt in 2001. This is the case even if we restrict our focus to the two official decentralization laws, but especially if we consider legal changes that fall outside those laws yet concern the transfer of authority from center to region.

The impact of reforms that strengthened local governments relative to the national government was felt as early as 1998. After Soeharto resigned, President Habibie released nearly all political prisoners and effectively removed all restrictions on freedom of expression and association. In this climate many regional protest movements turned their attention away from national debates and toward local issues. Chief among these were district heads and governors whom they frequently attempted to drive from office in the same way national protests had forced Soeharto to resign. In the province of Riau, which happens to produce half of Indonesia's oil, protesters compelled the resignation of their governor and brought about the election of a replacement who was a native of the province, unlike nearly all of his predecessors. By the end of the year, before legislation on decentralization had been submitted to the legislature, similar protest movements led to the removal of at least ten district heads. In other regions, the national government yielded to public pressure and agreed to replace district heads whose terms expired with people acceptable to the public rather than the home affairs ministry, as had been the practice since independence[7] and which, by law, remained its right.

Once the new law on regional government had been passed, but long before it legally took effect, regional legislatures put key provisions into effect with little opposition from the national government. In particular, legislatures in districts where local executives' terms were expiring asserted their "right" to elect a successor. And since the national government had not yet issued regulations on how the new law should be implemented, many of those legislatures devised their own rules on how candidates should be nominated and elected. By coincidence, the terms of nearly two-thirds of all district heads and mayors (second-tier governments) were set to expire in 1998 and 1999, thus creating a powerful incentive for legislatures—elected under the authoritarian rules that governed the 1997 elections—to assert their right to choose the next executive.

Similar movements emerged in late 1998 and early 1999 to demand two other changes. Leaders of wealthier regions traveled to Jakarta to demand that the national government return more resources to them, whether extracted from lucrative mining operations or manufacturing so, as one governor recently reappointed by Soeharto put it, "that we don't just collect the pollution." In many other places, groups emerged to demand that their region be split off to form a new province or district. And in 1999, before democratic elections were held and while the legislature was considering the decentralization bills, the government introduced a separate series of bills to create about three dozen new districts throughout the country. After the 1999 elections, local pressure groups enjoyed enormous success in persuading the national legislature to pass laws creating new provinces and, especially, districts. From fewer than 300 at the time Soeharto resigned, the number of second-tier regions has risen to about 450 today, and more than 100 new requests are said to be pending legislative consideration.

There are two important aspects to these developments. In the first place, they occurred prior to the implementation of official decentralization policies, and in some cases prior to the adoption of the laws intended to govern decentralization. This creates a serious challenge to any effort to account for the impact of decentralization, whether on democracy or any other variable of interest. How can we know that formal decentralization policies rather than democratization are the actual causes? Indeed, how can we know that decentralization itself is not mainly an effect of democratization?

Second, the process of creating new provinces and districts clearly has played a role in shifting political power from Jakarta to the regions, and in changing the distribution of power among regions. Nevertheless, it is almost always considered a phenomenon separate from decentralization. The USAID report mentioned above is characteristic of most donor-funded work in worrying that the creation of new regions "is leading to inefficient administration" (p. 5). What the report decries as "ulterior motives" that drive groups to seek their own jurisdictions differ little from other types of demands for political recognition, access to state resources, and local control. In a country that experienced widespread communal conflicts, separatist movements, and strident demands for autonomy, it seems realistic to consider whether the economically inefficient use of public resources to fund the construction of government offices in newly created districts might not have been a politically useful way of accommodating subnational demands and stemming centrifugal pressures.

CONCLUDING OBSERVATIONS

1. The timing and content of decentralization is much broader than the terms of the two laws that embody the government's official decentralization policy. Broadening our definition of decentralization has at least two benefits. First, it shows us that, in effect, political decentralization preceded fiscal and administrative decentralization. And second, it highlights the significance of subnational initiative and agency in bringing decentralization about; this is a useful corrective to the conventional view that a small group of people designed the policies on their own. Both benefits emphasize the role of democratization as a motivating force for decentralization, not a hindrance to administrative and fiscal efficiency.

2. Decentralization cannot be separated from the impact of democratization on parties, elections, and legislative behavior. Though more by accident than design, the crafters of Indonesia's democratizing and decentralizing policies seem to have struck an important balance between centrifugal and centripetal pressures by combining party and electoral institutions that privileged central authority with others that enhanced the authority of subnational governments.

3. Assessments of decentralization's impact must take into account the principal aims of the architects of decentralization, including politicians and the bureaucrat-scholars who drafted so much legislation. Their overwhelming concern was to maintain national unity, and on that point the record is in their favor. If they had not decentralized, in the ad hoc manner that has

yielded the shortcomings chronicled in so many donor-funded reports, would such sweeping decentralization have been possible at any point since then? And if not, would Indonesia be better off with centralized political parties, a centralized fiscal system, and a centralized administrative system? My guess, on both counts, is not.

4. Policies intended to "fix" decentralization's shortcomings must consider the broader set of policies that have redistributed power and authority to subnational governments. Local government problems such as the prevalence of corruption and an absence of transparency likely reflect shortcomings of democratization as much or more than decentralization. And some political institutions that seem to cause problems at the local level, such as centralized political party structures that undermine the accountability of local representatives to their constituents, may play an important role nationally by offsetting the centrifugal impact of decentralizing reforms in a way that promotes national unity.

REFERENCES

Bardhan, P., and D. Mookherjee. 2006. "The Rise of Local Governments: An Overview." Decentralization and Local Governance in Developing Countries. P. Bardhan and D. Mookherjee, eds. Cambridge, MA: MIT Press.

Habibie, B. J. 2006. Detik-Detik yang Menentukan: Jalan Panjang Indonesia Menuju Demokrasi. Jakarta: THC Mandiri.

Malley, M. S. 2007. "Inchoate Opposition, Divided Incumbents: Muddling toward Democracy in Indonesia, 1998–99." Interim Governments: Institutional Bridges to Peace and Democracy. K. Guttieri and J. Piombo, eds. Washington, DC: US Institute of Peace.

O'Rourke, K. 2002. Reformasi: The Struggle for Power in Post-Soeharto Indonesia. Crows Nest, NSW: Allen & Unwin.

Treisman, D. 2007. The Architecture of Government: Rethinking Decentralization. New York: Cambridge University Press.

USAID Democratic Reform Support Program for the Donor Working Group on Decentralization. 2006. "Decentralization 2006: Stock Taking on Indonesia's Recent Decentralization Reforms, Summary of Findings." August 2006.

van Dijk, K. 2001. A Country in Disrepair: Indonesia between 1997 and 2000. Leiden: KITLV.

World Bank. 2003. Decentralizing Indonesia: A Regional Public Expenditure Review Overview Report. June 2003.

ENDNOTES

1. Bardhan and Mookherjee 2006, p. 10; Treisman 2007, p. 293.
2. Bardhan and Mookherjee 2006, p. 14; Treisman, p. 293.
3. I develop this argument further in Malley 2007.
4. O'Rourke 2002; van Dijk 2001; Habibie 2006.
5. World Bank 2003, p. 1.
6. USAID 2006, p. 1.
7. Except for a brief period in the late 1950s.

LINKAGES BETWEEN CORRUPTION AND DEMOCRACY

Phyllis Dininio

This chapter examines the challenges of dealing with corruption in a democracy. It first looks at the corrosive impact of corruption on democratic governments and the more ambiguous impact of democracy on corruption. It then focuses on the underlying causes of corruption and corresponding interventions to fight it. It concludes with a discussion of efforts to promote democracy and combat corruption in Eastern Europe, which offer some encouragement and lessons to reformers elsewhere.

RELATIONSHIP BETWEEN CORRUPTION AND DEMOCRACY

Corruption undermines democratic government through many channels. Where money and influence trump rules, corruption makes hollow the core values of democracy such as equality, fairness, and justice. Citizens become cynical of the notion that the government is "of the people, by the people, and for the people"[1] and increasingly see the government as illegitimate.

Corruption also weakens the performance of government. Allocative inefficiencies caused by corruption lead to distorted markets, fewer investments, and lower growth. The weakened economy, in turn, lowers tax revenues and undermines the government's ability to provide services. At the same time, corruption can divert public spending to areas that profit the elite (like large defense contracts), and can result in the leakage of funds and supplies in health, education, water and other sectors, further corroding the delivery of public services.[2]

In addition, corruption hurts the poor disproportionately and further skews the distribution of wealth and power in a society. As highlighted by the work of Hernando de Soto, administrative barriers and weak property rights make it difficult for the poor to escape from poverty through small-scale entrepreneurial activity.[3] Bribes demanded by public officials can be considered a regressive tax because they constitute a greater share of poor households' and small firms' income than of wealthier households' and larger firms'. As the democratic literature explicates, inequality seriously diminishes democratic processes. Dahl notes, "That citizens ought to be political equals is...a crucial axiom in the moral perspective of democracy."[4] Higher levels of inequality undermine trust and confidence in fellow citizens and erode support for democracy.

Figure 1 shows the impact of corruption on democratic legitimacy. This graph comes from the Latin American Public Opinion Project of Vanderbilt University, which was funded by USAID. The research shows that corruption victimization was the largest reason for people to rate their government as less legitimate, ahead of crime victimization, personal income, and whether or not a person voted for the government in power.

Figure 1: Corruption Victimization Undermines Democratic Legitimacy

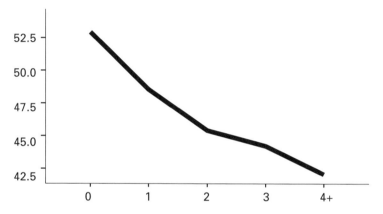

Source: AmericasBarometer 2006 by the Latin American Public Opinion Project of Vanderbilt University.

An analysis of similar data from Afrobarometer by Michael Bratton corroborates this finding for Africa. In that research, the perception that elected leaders are corrupt, and are monopolizing available resources, has a negative effect on people's perception of the extent of democracy in their country. Citizens question and condemn their leaders when corrupt benefits accrue narrowly to political elites.[5]

While the impact of corruption on democracy is clearly negative, the impact of democracy on corruption is less clear. On the one hand, democracy provides a framework for fighting corruption. Democracy allows citizens to throw corrupt leaders out of office and elect a new government. This threat of electoral defeat can act as a check on elected leaders' behavior. Indeed, the election of opposition candidates running on anticorruption platforms has become increasingly common and has spread to every continent. What is more, the dramatic color revolutions in recent years have shown the limits of corrupt regimes to manipulate election results in an effort to stay in power.

In addition to this form of vertical accountability, a democracy can also strengthen mechanisms of horizontal accountability, including independent judiciaries and legislatures. This separation of powers provides a check on abuses of power in democratic government. The executive branch carries out the law, the legislature makes the law, and the judiciary interprets the law. However, each branch is able to place limited restraints on the power exerted by the other branches. In the U.S. for example, the president appoints judges and departmental secretaries, but these appointments must be approved by the Senate. The Congress can pass a law, but the president can veto it. The Supreme Court can rule a law to be unconstitutional, but the Congress, with the States, can amend the Constitution. The framers of the U.S. Constitution separated powers in this way to check abuses that could arise in a more unified government.

On the other hand, democracy can provide new opportunities for corruption, especially in the electoral arena. The most notable forms of electoral corruption are vote buying, vote rigging, and campaign contributions that come with strings attached and function as bribes. Payoffs and the manipulation of election results are less common in advanced democracies, but campaign financing is a central challenge of political corruption in all democracies.[6]

On balance, data from Freedom House and Transparency International (TI) show that democracy and corruption are negatively correlated, although the relationship is not a strong one. Figure 2 shows TI's Corruption Perceptions Index (CPI) on the vertical axis and democracy scores compiled from adding Freedom House's political rights and civil liberties scores on the horizontal axis. A country is perceived as less corrupt if it has a higher CPI score and as more democratic if it has a lower Freedom House score. There is a lot of variation in corruption levels for countries at each level of democracy, but overall the corruption levels improve as countries become more democratic. In the middle category of countries with a democracy score between 1.5 and four, a lot of countries fall below the regression line. They are performing less well on fighting corruption than one would expect, given their level of democracy. By contrast, countries in the free category with a democracy score of one perform significantly better on fighting corruption.

Looking at different syndromes of corruption brings more clarity to the relationship between corruption and democracy. The four corruption syndromes delineated by Johnston[7] provide more nuance than the simple democracy scores of Figure 2 (See Table 1). Countries that would be characterized by Freedom House as free, having a score of one, for example, have different political and economic

Figure 2: Corruption and Democracy Are Negatively Correlated

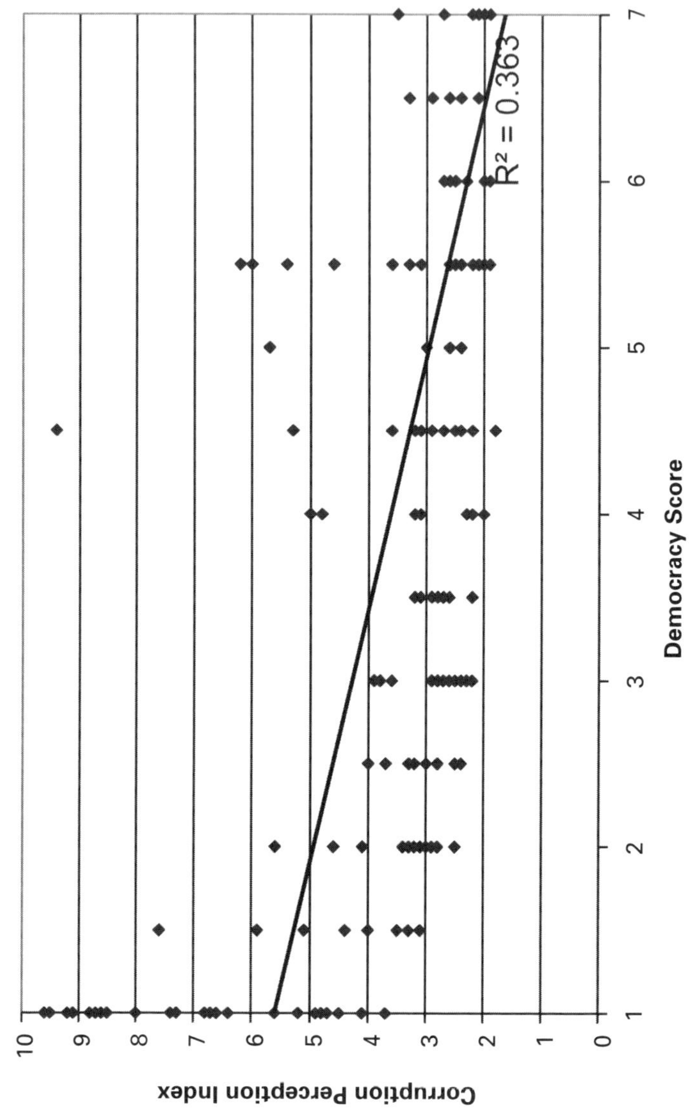

Source: Freedom House political rights and civil liberties scores, 2006, and Transparency International CPI, 2006.

profiles and fall into different categories. Some countries have mature democracies and markets and fall into the Influence Market syndrome with low levels of corruption, whereas others have reforming democracies and markets and fall into the Elite Cartel syndrome with higher levels of corruption.

In Influence Markets, the institutions are generally well established and have been developed over time, and the capacity of the state and civil society is extensive. There tends not to be much everyday, or administrative, corruption, but there is some political, or grand, corruption. The average CPI score (from 2003) is quite high at 8.1.

Table 1. Syndromes of Corruption

Syndrome	Political and Economic Profile	Average TI CPI (2003)
Influence Markets (most OECD countries)	Mature democracies and markets	8.1
Elite Cartels (Botswana, Central Europe, Chile, Italy, Korea)	Reforming democracies and markets	4.6
Oligarchs and Clans (Ghana, India, Mexico, Philippines, Russia, Thailand, Turkey)	Transitional democracies and new markets	3.1
Official Moguls (China, the Emirates, Indonesia, Jordan, Kenya)	Undemocratic regimes and new markets	3.0

Source: Johnston 2005.

In the second corruption syndrome, Elite Cartels, democracies and markets are reforming rather than mature. Interlocking groups of politicians, business figures, bureaucrats, military officials, and ethnic leaders share corrupt benefits and solidify their power. Corruption is more pervasive, with an average CPI score of 4.6.

Transitional democracies and new markets comprise countries in the third corruption syndrome, Oligarchs and Clans. Here, insecure elites build extended personal clans to exploit the state and the economy. The average CPI score is even lower, at 3.1.

Finally, undemocratic regimes and new markets characterize countries in the fourth corruption syndrome, Official Moguls. The officials exploit society and economy, and kleptocracy is likely. The CPI is again quite low, at 3.0.

CAUSES OF AND RESPONSES TO CORRUPTION

In general, the causes of corruption can be grouped into two categories: institutional and societal. Institutional causes of corruption include wide authority, little accountability, and perverse incentives. Wide authority is a cause of corruption because the more activities that public officials control, the more opportunities there are for corrupt behavior. Opportunities do not necessarily translate into corrupt acts, but if there are no opportunities, then there cannot be any corruption.

Little accountability is another institutional cause of corruption. If the probability of detecting and punishing corrupt behavior is low, then there is a greater probability that opportunists will engage in corruption. Measures like transparency and oversight allow corrupt acts to be detected, and the working of judicial system allows the corrupt to be sanctioned.

Perverse incentives also cause corruption. Low salaries, limited benefits and rewards for performance of duties, lack of professionalism, and no credible fear of job loss can contribute to an individual's decision to partake in corruption. Indeed, meritocracy has been shown to be a very big predictor of corruption levels across government institutions within a country.[8]

In addition to these institutional causes of corruption, there are a number of societal causes of corruption. Widespread poverty and conflict can fuel corruption because they create situations in which order and rules are challenged by the need to survive. Moreover, family or tribal, ethnic, religious, or political loyalties create systems of patronage in which advantage is given to members of a selected group and which subvert formal rules. An illegitimate government can also contribute to corruption: The extent to which people perceive their government as lacking legitimacy, whether it is due to repression or ineffectiveness or some other factor, can create an atmosphere of distrust and disregard for laws and rules. Finally, the dominance of a ruling elite can create an atmosphere in which the advantaged think they can operate outside the law because of their dominance, but the disadvantaged think that they can operate outside the rules because of the unfair playing field. These conditions often work in tandem, but they can be present to different extents.

Identifying the root causes of corruption facilitates a tailored intervention to fighting it. Where opportunities for corruption are seen as a problem, for example, reforms should aim to reduce those opportunities by simplifying and streamlining processes for permit or passport applications, reducing or eliminating import quotas and tariffs, and deregulating markets. Where little accountability is a problem, reforms should aim to increase transparency, oversight, and sanctions through passing freedom of information legislation; publishing rules and procedures so citizens have an understanding of what they're entitled to and how systems are supposed to work; criminalizing corrupt acts; and strengthening supreme audit institutions, attorney generals, and judiciaries. Where perverse incentives are a problem, reforms should aim to provide a living wage and improve meritocracy and professionalism in public administration.

In addition to these reforms to government institutions, anticorruption efforts need to mobilize civil society, the business sector, and media and enlist them as key stakeholders and partners in this effort. Coalitions of government and nongovernmental activists are the most effective way to make these changes and sustain them in the face of opposition.

Alongside these institutional reforms to fight corruption, a broader reform agenda can also seek to address the societal causes of corruption. Perhaps most notably, increasing economic development can contribute to this effort. In most cross-country studies, higher income levels are the best predictor of lower corruption levels.[9] Increasing economic development makes possible capacity building and other improvements in institutions and reduces the drive to cheat the system if the system is providing a means to meet one's needs. This is not a short-term undertaking for most developing countries, and suggests a focus on alternative livelihoods in post-conflict settings may be warranted.

Emphasizing government effectiveness can also address societal causes of corruption. Citizens are more likely to abide by rules when they are actually seeing the government deliver what they want, particularly security and essential services.

Decreasing the concentration of wealth and power can also address societal causes of corruption by reducing the privileges of the dominant elite and improving the fairness of economic and political systems.

RECENT EXPERIENCE IN EASTERN EUROPE

An analysis of TI corruption scores and Freedom House democracy scores between 1999 and 2006 in Eastern Europe affirms that improving democracy and fighting corruption are closely linked. Figure 3 shows the first ten countries that joined the EU—the eight that joined in 2004, and Romania and Bulgaria, which joined in 2007—in alphabetical order followed by the four Balkan countries. The paired columns point to a strong link between the changes in corruption and the changes in democracy: the R-squared in fact is .87. This shows that accession helps countries take on political and economic reforms that result in increased freedom and lower corruption. These countries have also experienced increasing per capita incomes.

The EU accession process requires the accession countries to adopt the acquis communautaire—the EU's legislation and policies and standards—which creates a more coherent, accountable, and democratic government. At the same time, the accession process substantially increases the amount of aid that's given to these countries and requires careful formulation of national development policies in order to help them catch up to EU standards of living.[10] Through both channels, theory suggests that the accession process helps to reduce corruption.

Figure 3. Changes in Corruption and Democracy in Eastern Europe

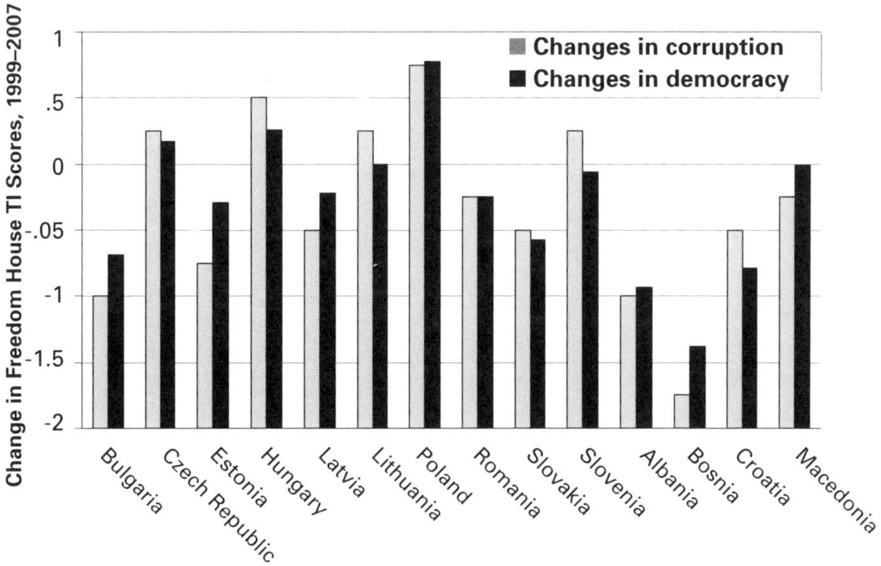

Source: Freedom House and Transparency International, various years.

The World Bank's analysis of these countries in their report from 2007, Anticorruption in Transition 3,[11] shows another way in which evidence supports theory. The accession countries have progressed further in reducing administrative day-to-day corruption than other countries in the region, but continue to have difficulty addressing grand corruption, such as public procurement. This corresponds with a move from Johnston's Elite Cartel syndrome to the Influence Market syndrome. With these EU accession countries, corruption levels in general are falling, day-to-day administrative corruption is falling, but political corruption continues to be a problem just like it is for the OECD countries.

The political and economic reforms carried out by the accession countries in Eastern Europe offer lessons and encouragement to reformers elsewhere. Above all, they show that encompassing political reforms and foreign aid can bring about notable improvements in governance and standards of living. In other words, the standard package of assistance offered by development agencies can lead to clear successes. What is missing in many countries where assistance is given, however, is the domestic political will to carry out the full array of reforms and to use the foreign aid for its intended purpose.

CONCLUSION

Corruption is a problem that all democracies have to face, although advanced democracies tend to have less corruption than newer democracies. The relationship between corruption control and democracy is not linear, however: A democratizing country may make quite significant gains in freedom before it experiences notable reductions in corruption levels. This corresponds, in part, to changes in the corruption syndromes that a country may experience. Regardless of the corruption syndrome or level, countries can make progress in the fight against corruption. As highlighted by the East European experience, incentives and politics are critical to sustaining the multi-faceted effort to improve governance and reduce corruption.

REFERENCES

Bratton, M. 2007. "Formal versus Informal Institutions in Africa." Journal of Democracy 18. no. 3 (July 2007): 96–110.

Dahl, R. A. 1989. Democracy and Its Critics. New Haven: Yale University Press.

de Soto, H. 2000. The Mystery of Capital: Why Capitalism Triumphs in the West and Fails Everywhere Else. New York: Basic Books.

Johnston, M. 2005. Syndromes of Corruption. New York: Cambridge University Press.

Kaufmann, D., and P. Dininio. 2006. "Corruption: A Key Challenge for Development." The Role of Parliament in Curbing Corruption. R. Stapenhurst, N. Johnston, and R. Pelizzo, eds. Washington, DC: World Bank Institute.

Knaus, G., and Cox, M. 2005. "The 'Helsinki' Moment in Southeastern Europe." Journal of Democracy 16, no. 1 (January 2005): 39–54.

Pinto-Duschinsky, M. 2002. "Financing Politics: A Global View." Journal of Democracy 13 (October 2002): 69–86.

Treisman, D. 2000. "Causes of Corruption: A Cross-National Study." Journal of Public Economics 76 (3): 399–457.

World Bank. 2006. Anticorruption in Transition 3. Washington, DC: World Bank.

———. 1997. World Development Report 1997. Washington, DC: World Bank.

ENDNOTES

1. Abraham Lincoln, Gettysburg Address, accessed at http://en.wikipedia.org/wiki/Gettysburg_Address on August 22, 2008.

2. Kaufmann and Dininio 2006.

3. de Soto 2000.

4. Dahl 1989, p. 325.

5. Bratton 2007.

6. Pinto-Duschinsky 2002.

7. Johnston 2005.

8. World Bank 1997.

9. Treisman 2000.

10. Knaus and Cox 2005.

11. World Bank 2006.

III. LIMITATIONS AND THREATS PRESENTED BY CONFLICT

CONSTRUCTING DEMOCRACY
IN KOSOVO AND THE BALKANS
Tim Judah

On September 6, 2007, Miroslav Lajcak, whom one might describe as the international community's governor general in Bosnia-Hercegovina, told parliament in Sarajevo that now was not the time for "business as usual" and that the country had slipped into the "dark valley of isolation and self-indulgent rhetoric."[1] Who is this man, a Slovak, to tell the Bosnians what to do and why was he doing it? Broadly speaking that is what this chapter will be about.

So, why should Kosovo or Bosnia or the rest of the region we now call the Western Balkans (that is, the former Yugoslavia minus Slovenia but plus Albania) be fundamentally and absolutely different from the rest of the world? Simple: It is in Europe, or more particularly surrounded by the European Union. So? So, the region has what is called a "European perspective." That means the EU has given a commitment that this region will, sooner or later, join the now 27-member body. And, as I will describe, everyone knows (up to a point) what has to be done. This is what Mr. Lajcak, who is also the EU's special representative in Bosnia, was talking about. "Integration or isolation," he thundered to parliament in Sarajevo; or as is often said, the choice is "Brussels or Belarus."

At its simplest the theory is this: There are 100,000 pages of laws, rules, and regulations which need to be harmonised with the EU, subdivided into 35 chapters of subjects which need to be gone through to make sure you are a fully functioning modern, European democracy. If you can fulfil, these targets you can join the EU. That is the target, that is what you have to aim for. And that is the difference between Peru and Afghanistan and Kosovo. What is the target in Peru? What is the right model for Afghanistan? How is it going to be done there, what is going to be done? "For countries such as Turkey, Serbia, or Bosnia," says Mark Leonard, the head of the European Council on Foreign Relations, "the only thing worse than having the bureaucracy of Brussels descend on your political system, insisting on changes, implementing regulations, instigating state privatizations, and generally seeping into every crack of everyday political life, is to have its doors closed to you."[2]

And this says Leonard, correctly in my view, is "the contrast between how Europe and America have dealt with their neighbours…the threats are similar— drug trafficking, large flows of migrants across leaky borders, networks of international crime—but the responses could not be more different. The United States has sent troops into its neighbours more than fifteen times over the last 50 years, but many of the countries have barely changed—limping from crisis to crisis and often sucking American troops back into their problems."[3] In other words, the EU says "do this, join us, be part of the big club, not a lonely little powerless country" while the US says, "do this" or "we are giving you cash to fight drug smugglers," or whatever, because it is in the interest of the US but there is no big, long-term motivating factor for change within the country otherwise. There is no major incentive. After all, what is it that the average Bosnian or Haitian might like, apart from freedom or prosperity in his own country? It is the right to live and work legally and travel freely, without restriction wherever he would like in the EU in the first case or the US in the second. The Bosnian knows what his leaders have to do to make this happen. The Haitian does not, because it is not on the agenda.

I have not talked yet about ethnic and other challenges. We need to examine the theory of the issue more closely before we get on to the practice. What we need to do now is look at the map. Today, Bosnia, Macedonia, Kosovo, Serbia, Croatia, Montenegro, and Albania, countries whose combined populations are a little over 20m are an enclave surrounded by the EU. Sometimes we call this the "Balkan ghetto." Let's forget so-called "enlargement fatigue" for the moment. The theory is that these small and often weak countries need to be tied down with the EU framework to make them functional, stable, and democratic. The system to do that has been evolving for decades. Firstly, it absorbed the formerly authoritarian states of Spain, Portugal, and Greece and then of course, the ten former communist countries of central and eastern Europe.

Let me describe here the path. Firstly the Copenhagen criteria. These are rules laid down in 1993 which describe, in outline, what a state needs to do:

> Membership requires that the candidate country has achieved stability of institutions guaranteeing democracy, the rule of law, human rights and respect for and protection of minorities, the existence of a functioning market economy, as well as the capacity to cope with competitive pressure and market forces within the Union. Membership presupposes the candidate's ability to take on the obligations of membership, including adherence to the aims of political, economic and monetary union.[4]

Ever since then these rules have been subject to interpretation and definition, but at its simplest, any country which does not fit the criteria, as say Switzerland or Iceland would (more or less) if they applied today, needs to be completely overhauled. And this is the great success of the recent enlargements, that is to say, taking ten former communist countries, and in effect rebuilding them as modern democracies.

The procedure for doing this has, of course, varied over the enlargements but let me describe here, very briefly, the pathway outlined for the Western Balkan states. This is the Stabilisation and Association Process (SAP). After a period of negotiation a country signs its first contractual agreement with the EU, a Stabilisation and Association Agreement (SAA). The modernisation process begins in earnest, leading after the European Commission has given a green light, to Candidate status. After gaining this, all sorts of intensive harmonization and so-called screening begins. This is done chapter by chapter. Now there are 35 chapters, and their subjects range from justice, freedom, and security to food safety to tax to the judiciary and fundamental rights. During all of these years EU money to assist in the transformation is disbursed via the Instrument for Pre-Accession Assistance. Twinning arrangements are another feature of assistance, in which for example, civil servants might be despatched from say Finland, specialists in maritime safety for example (this is a real example), to help their Estonian colleagues upgrade their maritime safety, rules, regulations, and procedures to meet EU standards. At the end of this procedure, the political decision is made, and then the candidate becomes a member.

Where are the states of the Western Balkans in this process? Croatia and Macedonia are candidates, but Croatia is much further advanced down the track than Macedonia and has the realistic chance of completing the so-called *acquis communautaire* and joining the EU within a few years. Albania and Montenegro have both signed SAAs and they should come into force soon. Serbia has finished negotiating an SAA, but whether it will be initialled will depend on, above all, cooperation with the UN Yugoslav war crimes tribunal, and a report to be submitted by Carla Del Ponte, its chief prosecutor. Kosovo is of course not a state, but it has what is called a tracking mechanism so as to keep it on course until its status is decided. Bosnia has negotiated an SAA but the political conditions laid down by Brussels before it can be signed have not been fulfilled. These are highly intrusive, and the main one concerns police reform and how the police forces of Bosnia should be run and organized. Let me quote here from that speech by Mr. Lajcak before the Bosnian parliament, talking on the question of police reform, and you will see what I mean:

The first EU principle requires that all legislative and budgetary competences for all police matters be vested at the State Level. [Bosnia is divided into two "entities"—one Serb dominated and other Croat and Bosniak.] This means, among other things, that only this body, the BiH [Bosnian] Parliamentary Assembly, can adopt legislation and budgets related to police matters. It means that all police bodies in the future will be legally defined as organizations of the BiH state. The second principle—that there should be no political interference in the operational work of the police—means exactly what it says: There will be oversight at the policy level, but operational independence must be guaranteed. Getting politics out of the daily work of the police is something that we know the overwhelming majority of BiH citizens agree on. The third principle—that functional local police areas must be determined by technical policing criteria, where operational command is exercized at the local level is the best way to bring policing to the community that it serves.[5]

One thing the EU is particularly bad at is singing its own praises. However, despite the grumbling you sometimes hear that the rules were softened for Romania and Bulgaria, no one doubts that enlargement has been a huge success in terms of modernizing the ten former communist countries. There is no time now to examine in great detail the effect of EU conditionality, but let's just take Bulgaria. A decade ago it was considered an economic and political basket case. Now the country is growing by leaps and bounds. Since 1998 the economy has been expanding at annual rates of more than 4 percent a year. Unemployment was 18 percent in 2001, but by last year had fallen to half that. From 1992 to 1996 annual average FDI was $153m, since 2003 it has been $2bn a year. "European member-state building," write Gerald Knaus and Kristof Bender of the European Stability Initiative (ESI), "does contribute directly to the building of more transparent public institutions through the adoption and enforcement of European standards in public procurement, state aid and financial auditing, the requirement of increased participation of non-governmental interest groups in government decision making and the provision of activity reports, policy plans and financial data to the public."[6]

So much for the theory then. Now for the practice. The question is whether what worked for eastern and central Europe will work for the Western Balkans, which, after all, are not just countries in transition but also recovering either from war or conflict directly, the trauma of the collapse of Yugoslavia and its legacies, or just collapse as in the case of Albania. Also, unlike eastern and central

Europe, many of the issues which produced the wars have not been settled, the most important of course, being Kosovo and to a lesser extent Bosnia. On top of this, notes Heather Grabbe of the European Commission:

> …when it comes to the most sensitive and difficult issues in the region, such as the status and treatment of minorities, human rights, corruption, organized crime and constitutional reform, the EU has no detailed policy guidance to offer from its own rule book. Although potential members have to meet the political conditions, the EU has no democratic *acquis* on which to draw to provide detailed guidance to the candidates. The member states themselves have diverse policies on the provision of bilingual education for ethnic minorities, or on tackling corruption in the public sector. Although the members form part of a community of nations and share norms on what is and what is not acceptable behaviour on the part of the state, the trickiest dilemmas of democracy cannot be solved by drawing on a codified guidance set down in EU law.[7]

So, now we come to the core of the issue. Let me describe briefly where we are in terms of Kosovo and the rest of the region. The war in Kosovo ended in 1999. The territory was then put under the jurisdiction of the UN. In the wake of the conflict, hundreds of thousands of ethnic Albanians who had fled or been ethnically cleansed flooded back and then tens of thousands of Kosovo Serbs fled or were ethnically cleansed in their turn. Today there are some two million people in Kosovo of whom about 90 percent are ethnic Albanians while about half of the rest are Bosniaks, Roma, and other minorities and the other half Serbs. In many places the Serbs live in enclaves. So, most of the north of Kosovo, which abuts Serbia proper, is Serb, plus a swathe of land around Pristina, the capital, and in certain other places. Serbia argues that because Kosovo was its province in the old Yugoslavia and not a republic, like Croatia or Macedonia, it has no right to independence. Albanians argue that they have the right to self-determination.

In March of this year, after 14 rounds of mostly fruitless talks between Serbs and Albanians, Martti Ahtisaari, the former Finnish president, presented the UN with a plan for so-called "supervised independence." This meant that Kosovo would become an independent state but that a large and powerful EU justice and security mission would replace the UN along with a so-called International Civilian Office (ICO), which would play a role similar to that played by Mr. Lajcak in Bosnia, i.e., a kind of international governor general.

This plan was torpedoed by a resurgent Russia. Mindful of several "frozen conflicts" in the former Soviet Union, Russia, whose diplomats were also keen to take revenge for their humiliation in 1999 in being unable to prevent the bombing of Serbia, simply said it would veto the Ahtisaari plan. A new mediation mission expected to report to the UN in late 2007 could head off the Kosovo's Albanians declaration of independence. The US has already said it would recognize the new state, and much of the EU looks set to follow. This may not happen, but as of now it looks like the most likely scenario. What then? The plan the diplomats had devised was that Kosovo would in effect be taken over by the EU and hence put on the path to membership. The justice and security mission would have come under the aegis of the EU's European Security and Defence Policy (ESDP) and the ICO head would also have been the EU Special Envoy. This may yet happen, but without a UN mandate his power will be weaker, and if Europe is divided, then there may be no ESDP mission. However, here we are talking in the realms of speculation. We simply do not know what is going to happen.

What does this mean for democracy in Kosovo, especially with elections due on November 17, 2007? Indeed, where are we in terms of democracy? The answer is that we have in effect two parallel societies that don't meet much. Given instructions from Belgrade, Serbs barely participate in Kosovo's institutions, and they have been instructed not to take part in Kosovo's elections. Anyone who does will, as has happened before, be branded a traitor. Albanians for their part will do the minimum necessary to make politically correct statements about inclusion but these are widely disbelieved. The division is best seen in Mitrovica, a town which has an Albanian south and a Serbian north, divided at the river Ibar. In the south they talk Albanian, use euros, have Kosovo papers and number plates and look forward to independence. Across the bridge everyone speaks Serbian, uses dinars (and euros), has Serbian papers and documents, and in almost every way is fully part of Serbia. To a lesser extent this situation prevails in the enclaves too. In the years after 1999 it was dangerous for Serbs to venture into Albanian areas, and in the main Serbs tend to avoid them today, even if the danger has subsided. On both sides politics is to a great extent a kind of party patronage system, and as in the rest of the Balkans, there is an overlap with big business, tycoons, and organized crime. This is one of the central problems of Kosovo, the wider region, and for outsiders who have to deal with it. That is to say that in a nontransparent system like this, it is hard for a democratic culture to flourish, especially if some of the mafia-bosses, for reasons of realpolitik, are coddled by western protectors. This is a major problem, and it is one that is not talked about. In Kosovo journalists cannot write about many sensitive issues because of the structure of media ownership and because they don't want to get killed. People like me cannot inform the rest of the world about such things—even in this context—because of the constant threat of litigation.

In Bosnia the legacy of the war, is as I have said, a country divided into two "entities" with a weak central government. The Serbian dominated Republika Srpska is run as one unit while the Croat-Bosniak federation is sub-divided into ten cantons. There is also an autonomous region called Brcko. This is not an efficient way to run a country of 3.5 million people (Bosnia has some 16 police forces). The country needs reform, but in a way the biggest failure of the country, post-war, is that it is a state without people. That is to say that its citizens are Bosniaks (Muslims), Serbs, and Croats. And, Serbs and Croats are there, not because they want to be, but because the war ended this way. Today Croats are a declining factor in Bosnia—but many would like their own federal unit, something resisted by Bosniaks who see that as a prelude to the eventual demise and formal partition of the country between Serbia and Croatia. Bosnia's main Bosniak leader, Haris Silajdzic, wants to abolish the entities, arguing that he wants a state of citizens—which Serbs see as code for domination by the more numerous Bosniaks, while the Republika Srpska's leaders are fighting to maintain their autonomy and constantly threatening a referendum on independence. And yet, there has been good news from Bosnia, too. The country is unrecognisable as the Bosnia of 1995 and, unlike Kosovo, levels of inter-ethnic alienation are much lower.

One reason Bosnia is now politically blocked though is Kosovo. In that sense, this is another major difference from central and eastern Europe. Yugoslavia may no longer exist, but the Yugoslav space does. Much remains connected. At the moment Kosovo dominates politics in Serbia. Bosnia to a great extent remains a hostage to Serbia via the cues given to the Republika Srpska leadership from Belgrade, which is happy to encourage the leadership of the Republika Srpska to be intransigent because it is a threat related to Kosovo; i.e., if Kosovo, not a former Yugoslav republic has the right to independence and even, maybe, union with Albania, then the Republika Srpska can have the same right. Macedonia is also umbilically linked to Kosovo since a quarter of its population is ethnic Albanian. If ever the borders of the Western Balkans were redrawn then Macedonia would be divided with its western part joining a greater Albania or perhaps a greater Kosovo. Over the last fifteen years a process of ethnic winnowing has been taking place with Albanians and Macedonians who lived in mixed areas separating out. Like Bosnia though, the news is not all bad. Indeed

Macedonia, given candidate status, is not doing so badly. A brief conflict in 1991 was rapidly snuffed out and indeed the prospect of EU membership is the glue that has kept the country together, just as it is, in part, in Bosnia. Power-sharing is not perfect and in Macedonia, as elsewhere, often means patronage or loot-sharing, but it is a system that has kept the state on the road for the last 15 years.

Are the Balkans different from elsewhere in Europe? Yes and no. Conflicts are fresher and deeper. But compare with Northern Ireland, with Spain, and with Belgium. Will Belgium exist in 15 years, let alone Bosnia? Belgium had elections in June, and if this were Bosnia or Serbia we would lament the fact that it still has no government. How many Spanish flags do you see in Catalonia or the Basque country? Not many. Is there panic in England that Scotland's election was won by a pro-independence party? No, of course not. Thus far, the democratic process has been capable of addressing or at least accommodating deep societal cleavages. But of course these are countries with a long experience now of the democratic tradition reinforced by the EU. But as Heather Grabbe pointed out, the EU is not the answer to everything. Cyprus is, of course, the case in point.

And yet, it is the only tool we have. The prospect of EU membership in 15 years cannot solve the Kosovo question or make Bosnians happy to be Bosnians. But what other tool is there? And this is where the question of "enlargement fatigue" comes in. Experience has shown that when EU membership is in serious prospect, serious amounts of foreign direct investment (FDI) begin to flow in, and that FDI, beyond privatization, is the oil that lubricates the process of modernization, the demand for the rule of law, and helps nurture a democratic culture. (Though this need not be so.) Even though it is arguable that enlargement had little to do with the defeat of the EU's constitutional project in the French and Dutch referenda of 2005, the loss of nerves when it comes to enlargement is potentially disastrous. Why take on the difficult questions, why make people endure pain if the end of the tunnel is not in sight? If joining is a receding prospect then modernization stretches out too. In that sense the argument should perhaps be to accelerate giving candidate status to those countries in the Western Balkans that do not have it so that, as Knaus and Bender argue, "it would be up to political elites in these countries to ensure that the Bulgarian miracle of the past decade [is] repeated in Serbia, Albania [and] Bosnia and Hercegovina."[8] There are important tools that can be used for this but none is more important than visa liberalization. If the people, and especially the young people of the region, are literally penned in and cannot travel freely to the EU, then how is it possible to maintain over a long period of time the necessary enthusiasm for joining, and hence the work that needs to be done by politicians and leaders for their countries to join?

Kosovo, which is now a football in the international arena, has the potential to derail the progress made in the Balkans in the last seven years. Indeed turbulence is definitely ahead. Serbia's leadership is already bitterly divided between those who, broadly speaking, say Kosovo is more important than the EU and those who argue the contrary. But, in the long run, after the formal loss of Kosovo, what has Russia to offer Serbia? Not much. Can Serbia stay out? Yes, of course, but it is not Switzerland or Norway to have such a luxurious choice. And besides, Serbs want to work and travel freely in the EU and sell their goods there, not Russia. In the long run, the EU and its 100,000 pages are the future, as they are for the rest of the region, but its leaders need a credible promise of accession to keep the momentum of reform going and Kosovo needs a solution. Given both of those (which of course is not a given), Bosnia will simply fall into the slipstream of a Brussels-bound Serbia and Croatia. None of this will be easy though, and I will not end with a cliché of there being no other future. There is, as Lajcak has indicated, "the dark valley of isolation," and if integration and all that it promises falls off the agenda, then as Ivan Krastev, the Bulgarian political scientist argues, empire, as in the maintenance of protectorates in Kosovo and Bosnia and much oversight or crisis—management elsewhere is in prospect:

> In the language of *realpolitik* blocking the accession of the Balkans to the European Union equals the destruction of pro-reform leaders and constituencies in the region and turning the Balkans into the land of "unknown unknowns"...The nature of the Balkan crisis could make the European public aware of the real danger of the decline of the EU's soft power and force them to make a different choice than the one that it is making now. If not, let's pray for the efficiency and benevolence of the new empire.[9]

In Europe we don't have the answer to everything. But we do have some answers. The Balkans are ripe for reform and EU enlargement is the way to do it, even if it cannot solve everything. Enlargement provides many of the pointers but it needs political will on the ground and in the EU member states; in other words, leadership. The process may not work, or may take much longer than it did in eastern and central Europe, but the price of failure and all that that entails in the Balkans—this island within the EU—would be much higher than the costs involved in making it work.

EPILOGUE

Much water has flowed under the bridge since this chapter was originally written one year ago. In fact the political landscape of the Western Balkans has changed radically —but still the thrust of my argument remains valid: "The prospect of EU membership in 15 years cannot solve the Kosovo question or make Bosnians happy to be Bosnians. But what other tool is there?" That remains the case.

The single most important development in the region over the past year is that Kosovo declared independence on February 17, 2008. Since then it has been recognized by the US, 21 out of 27 EU countries, and several more, coming to a total of 47. Russia, China, India, Brazil, Egypt, and almost all Muslim countries have refused to recognize the new state. This has been a major disappointment to Kosovo Albanians.

Serbian areas of Kosovo remain under de facto Serbian control, but despite a couple of violent incidents, the doomsday scenarios of conflict and a major Serbian exodus have all proven unfounded.

Kosovo's declaration of independence provoked the downfall of the Serbian government. Elections were subsequently held on May 11, 2008. Opinion polls all pointed to the victory of a nationalist coalition led by the Serbian Radical Party. However, in a demonstration of EU soft power, the Serbian electorate was in effect bribed to vote for pro-European forces.

Just before the poll the EU agreed to give Serbia a Stabilisation and Association Agreement (SAA) and open talks on visa liberalisation. This helped swing enough voters to President Boris Tadic's Democratic Party, which in July succeeded in forming a new government.

In fact the SAA was immediately frozen and now, despite the arrest and despatch to The Hague in July of Radovan Karadzic, the former Bosnian Serb leader, remains so.

Still, President Tadic and his government are utterly committed to EU integration and want all possible obstacles that remain in the way to be cleared. For this reason, although Serbia says it will never recognise Kosovo, since July its officials have been in almost daily, discreet contact with members of the Government of Kosovo in order to solve problems and prevent flare ups.

Bosnia, too, now has an SAA, which means that all countries of the Western Balkans are finally in some form of contractual arrangement with the EU. Progress in Bosnia has been slow and patchy, but Bosnia will inevitably follow Serbia and Croatia on their paths to European integration.

While intervening in the Serbian election was a good example of Brussels making use of its soft power, subsequent developments in Kosovo have not been. Because there was no new Security Council resolution on Kosovo, UNMIK, the UN mission there, remained as did that of the OSCE. This had not been foreseen.

At the same time the ICO (as discussed above) began to deploy, as did EULEX, the EU's showcase police and justice mission. This was hobbled by a slow deployment and legal and political problems. These included the fact that it was unwelcome in Serbian areas and that several EU states did not recognise Kosovo, although they had all supported the deployment of EULEX.

All this led to what one Kosovar minister called "organized institutional anarchy" with the US Embassy, UNMIK, EULEX, OSCE, and the ICO all vying for power and influence.

Finally the Russian-Georgian war of August 2008 helped change the international context of the Western Balkans. Russia's position as a principled defender of the territorial integrity of Serbia was undermined by its recognitions of South Ossetia and Abkhazia. But, by contrast, Kosovo Albanian observers pointed out that their leaders were slow to take on board the long-term strategic implications of this, i.e., the relative decline of US power and influence in which they continue to place almost blind faith.

Nevertheless, in terms of Europe, the Serbian example of pledging not to use force over Kosovo while pursuing the goal of European integration was not lost in hitherto similarly pro-American Georgia. Only Western Balkan countries have a promise of eventual accession, while countries like Georgia are linked to the EU through the European Neighbourhood Policy.

If the conflict had done nothing else, said Tamar Beruchashvili, deputy state minister for European Integration, it should at least show people in the rest of Europe that Georgia was not in the neighbourhood, but was in fact in Europe. Diplomats and strategists meanwhile discussed the idea of an "SAA minus" for Georgia, i.e., the idea of giving it an SAA without the promise of membership.

The EU is not a state, and with 27 members consensus is always hard to find. And yet, in Europe, we have no alternative. The fact that the European flag flies in front of every official building in Georgia shows that the idea that has taken root in the Western Balkans is strong elsewhere, too; i.e., the only thing worse than being in the EU is (unless one is rich enough to live without it like Switzerland, Iceland, or Norway) to be left out.

REFERENCES

Bender, K., and G. Knaus. 2007. "The Bulgarian Miracle and the Future of EU Balkan Policy." *The Balkan Prism: A Retrospective by Policy-Makers and Analysts.* J. Deimel and W. van Meurs eds.

Grabbe, H. 2007. "What the EU Can and Cannot Do for the Balkans." *The Balkan Prism: A Retrospective by Policy-Makers and Analysts.* J. Deimel and W. van Meurs eds.

Krastev, I. 2007. "European Union and the Balkans: Enlargement or Empire." *The Balkan Prism: A Retrospective by Policy-Makers and Analysts.* J. Deimel and W. van Meurs eds.

Leonard, M. 2005. *Why Europe Will Run the 21st Century*. UK: Fourth Estate.

ENDNOTES

1. http://www.ohr.int/ohr-dept/presso/presssp/default.asp?content_id=40431
2. Leonard 2005, p.51
3. *Ibid.*
4. http://ue.eu.int/ueDocs/cms_Data/docs/pressdata/en/ec/72921.pdf
5. http://www.ohr.int/ohr-dept/presso/presssp/default.asp?content_id=40431
6. Bender and Knaus 2007, p. 449.
7. Grabbe 2007, p. 436.
8. Bender and Knaus 2007, p. 450.
9. Krastev 2007, p. 100.

BUILDING A DEMOCRATIC REGIME AMID CONFLICT: THE CASE OF AFGHANISTAN

Larry P. Goodson

In 2002 I flew into Qala-i-Nau District of Badghis Province in northwestern Afghanistan on a UN helicopter to observe a Phase II election for the Emergency Loya Jirga (ELJ), a key step in the transition to democracy then underway in that country. I was serving as one of a handful of international monitors for this process, and this was one of the district elections I had drawn to observe. Not long after we had gotten there, and as we mingled with the electors, some of whom would also be candidates to go on to the ELJ in Kabul, it became quite apparent that one female teacher, fully veiled in the traditional burqa, possessed the education and maturity of thought to be an excellent representative for this district. Although there were a handful of seats set aside for female candidates, here was one woman who appeared worthy of winning an open seat in head-to-head competition with male candidates. Alas, it was also quite clear that no such outcome was going to occur if the majority male voters had anything to do about it. So, my colleague from the Loya Jirga Commission (LJC) began to joke, in typical Afghan fashion, with the voters. In this land of limited literacy, each candidate had been given a symbol to go along with their name and our female had drawn, by chance, a book. As I stood guard over the entrance to the room with the ballot box, one elector at a time would come forward to cast his/her vote, and my colleague would say something like, "Learning is good, and books are for learning." Everyone would chuckle and in the person would go to cast whatever vote he was going to vote anyway. Finally, the voters grew a bit tired of the joking, which had begun to take on an admonitory tone, and one of them paused on the threshold of going in to vote, looked me in the eye and said, "We are letting them vote this time. In the future maybe some can be elected."

I have never forgotten his earnest effort to educate me on the pace of change in a traditional society like Afghanistan. Thus, I begin with this anecdote to illustrate the complexities of Afghan society, which constrain its efforts to make a rapid, successful, and sustainable transition to democracy. Let me add to this beginning four persistent ground realities of Afghanistan.

First, the most important thing is the resilience of local identity structures in this country that have historically trumped efforts at state-building. The ethnolinguistic, sectarian, racial, and spatial divisions within Afghanistan are huge, and many cleavage lines have resurfaced or been rubbed more raw than is usual by Afghanistan's long and destructive war. I do not wish to insult anyone's intelligence here, and indeed, the average person knows a great deal more today about Afghanistan than was the norm a few years ago. What I would emphasize is that Afghanistan's deep and multifaceted cleavages tend to be reinforcing. People are divided basically along ethnic and linguistic lines, but sectarian, tribal, and racial divisions also exist, and all of these are reinforced by a spatial pattern of population distribution into different regions of the country. In a country where tribal social groupings still exist, the social system is based on communal loyalties and emphasizes the local over higher-order identity formations. The rugged topographical features and geographical position of Afghanistan, coupled with its lack of economic development, further isolate it internationally and magnify the distance of its people from the government. Often these factors combine to reinforce each other, other times they overlap each other, but collectively they create a complex foundation for modern Afghan politics.

Together, these factors provide the foundation for understanding the difficulty of Afghanistan's initial state-building, especially during the Abdur Rahman period a century ago (1880–1901); their resurgence today gives us insight into the difficulties inherent in Afghanistan's state-*re*building. Afghanistan's ethnic mélange, reinforced by varying Islamic practices and terrain so rugged that dialects can change from one valley to the next, has produced a country where Pashtuns, Tajiks, Hazaras, Uzbeks, and 20-odd other groups tend to live in differing areas and reinforce their differences in numerous ways (religious practice, dialect, facial features, dress, etc.). Most important, Afghanistan today is once again a country defined by localism, and every effort to understand it must peel away layers of identity to find the core. The recent Northern Alliance, for example, can be understood as a collection of several militias primarily constructed along ethnic lines; or understood *more completely* in terms of each militia having several or multiple factions; or understood *best* as made up of hundreds of small groups of armed men who share local *qawm* identity and who are affiliated with one or another of the larger factions (not always permanently). Afghanistan is also a place shaped profoundly by its history, and although elements of its earlier history are of great importance, such as the traditional national political dominance of the Durrani Pashtuns, its recent history of highly destructive, transformative war has altered the landscape there to the extent that we must be careful drawing too many conclusions about the lessons of Afghanistan's past.

I would suggest that it is here that the U.S. faces one of its greatest strategic weaknesses in regard to nation-building operations—that is, that we just do not possess the requisite knowledge of other cultures to be able to make our efforts to help them develop appear anything other than clumsy, and that is when we are well-intentioned. I don't wish to tease this out as another underlying factor, but the reality is that when local identity structures enjoy great autonomy then the national government tends to be weak or strong but brittle/limited. This has been the historical pattern since the creation of the modern Afghan state, so it is no surprise that it continues today.

A second underlying factor of great importance is that Afghanistan has no basis for a modern economy. To reduce Barnett Rubin's work on Afghanistan's political economy to an overly simplistic point, prior to the Communist era in Afghanistan the economy in this extremely poor country was overwhelmingly agrarian and that dominated by essentially subsistence farmers and herders. As for the urban economy, it was largely rentier, reliant on Soviet largesse. Afghanistan, then and now, did have a famously active trading culture, which some label a smuggling culture, but until the advent of the poppy economy, there was little of value smuggled through Afghanistan that was from Afghanistan. All of the higher end products—TVs, refrigerators, air conditioners, and the like—came through Afghanistan. So, as we try to rebuild Afghanistan's economy I always ask David Ricardo's simple question—"In what does Afghanistan have a comparative advantage?" Other than poppy, of course.

Third, and of course I defer to Asta Olesen and Olivier Roy here, but Afghanistan's religious framework is based on a syncretic blend of various interpretations of Islamic doctrine with local customs, making the country simultaneously unified by one faith and divided by hundreds of variations on its practice. Interestingly, Afghanistan is one of the most average of all Muslim countries in two important ways. Demographically, its 82–18% Sunni-Shi'a split closely mirrors the split among the Muslim umma worldwide. Doctrinally, Afghanistan has little that makes it a center point for Muslims. Unlike Saudi Arabia, with Mecca and the Grand Mosque; Egypt, with Al Azhar; Palestine, with the Al-Aqsa Mosque; Syria, with the Umayyad Mosque in Damascus; Iran, with its hawza at Qum, and Iraq, with its hawza at Najaf; and India, with the Darul-Uloom madrassa at Deoband; Afghanistan has nothing. There are no great mosques, mudaris, or anything in this country, which is decidedly part of the Islamic periphery. Consequently, it has long been a place where Islamic practice, as melded with local customs and tribal codes, has unified the people throughout their life cycle events. But, it is also a place particularly susceptible to outside Islamic influences, since pretty much all of the ulema and their philosophy/theology come from elsewhere. Of course, as Charles Allen has recently chronicled, this includes the mixture of Deobandism and Wahhabism whose most recent manifestation has been the Taliban.

The fourth and last underlying factor that I will take a moment to mention is Afghanistan's geopolitical position on the Asian and global stage. Everyone remembers Afghanistan as the playing field of the Great Game, midwifed into birth by British and Russian empires bent on having a buffer state to prevent their accidental blundering into a disastrous great power war. Prior to that, Afghanistan's territory served as the crossroads of Asia, where its Silk Road caravanserais served innumerable invaders and traders crossing the steppes of Inner Asia. Both of these geopolitical characteristics have manifested themselves following the Soviet defeat in Afghanistan and the collapse of the Soviet empire (1989/1992). All regional actors—that is, Pakistan, Iran, India, China, Russia, and Saudi Arabia—see Afghanistan today as both a playing field for a new Great Game and as a crossroads for trade and influence. Thus, all regional actors are attentive to what is happening in Afghanistan and all are appropriately active there in advancing their own interests and attempting to thwart those of their rivals.

Now, to add to these underlying factors of Afghanistan's past and present, I would add a theoretical framework. As in virtually all recent nation-building cases (or, if you prefer, post-conflict stability cases), for post-conflict Afghanistan to undergo successful nation-building several significant challenges would need to be met, and met in a way that reinforced success across these challenges. These were provision of security, relief of displaced populations, rehabilitation of the economy and accompanying reconstruction of infrastructure, governance (or state-building), and transitional justice. With that theoretical framework as an overview and keeping in mind the underlying characteristics just discussed, I consider key areas of American strategy for Afghanistan and assess how we are faring in each area. Most Americans (and probably most Afghans) would begin with "Destroy Taliban and Al-Qa'ida" and I would give us very low marks here. As I am a professional educator, I'll give us a grade of D in this area. This is not to denigrate U.S. efforts, replete with rules of engagement (ROE) authorizing cross-border hot pursuit and all sorts of lame arm-twisting of Pakistani generals to get them to perform better at anvil and hammer tactics, but we haven't nabbed or nailed the Big Three, nor closed down the operational capacity of either Al-Qa'ida (AQ) or the Taliban (TB), both of which have resurged quite publicly of late. Unless one and/or the other are/is achieved, I do not think we can score this area very high.

What about the areas of nation-building? I will divide nation-building into four areas, setting aside refugee repatriation, which in fact has gone quite well in Afghanistan to date, but which has not been that critical to the overall success of the effort there, and give a short assessment of each. First, as everyone always notes, there is Security. In general, security was fairly good in Afghanistan after 2002, at least as compared to Iraq, but there are some unsettling trends here, the main one of note being a downward trajectory, especially along the border with Pakistan. There has been an increase in quantity of attacks and a shift in their tactical quality, with more emphasis on suicide bombings and improvised explosive device (IED) attacks, more use of civilians as shields, and more mobilized efforts against forward operating bases (FOBs). A more generalized downward trend with regard to attacks on soft targets, especially Afghan civilians, has gone on even longer, but the greater focus by the international media on the dismal security situation in Iraq has allowed this slipping security situation in Afghanistan to simmer along in the shadows. The early breathing space in late 2001 and through much of 2002 afforded the Operation Enduring Freedom (OEF) Coalition by the TB/AQ in disarray and the then-focused international community—that is, all of this was pre-Operation Iraqi Freedom (OIF)—allowed for much progress in security sector reform (SSR), especially in the American-led pillar of Afghan National Army (ANA) and Ministry of Defense (MOD) development. Thus, and again relative to Iraq, Afghanistan has seen much progress over the post-9/11 years in the development of its army and MOD, and the training cycles of its soldiers, with less success on the other pillars of SSR (disarmament, demobilization, and reintegration (DDR) of militias; Afghan national police (ANP); Ministry of Justice (MOJ); and counter-narcotics (CN), probably in that order). Though I give Security a B pointing the fall of 2007, that grade is slipping downward.

On Economic Development and Infrastructure Reconstruction the grade is worse, perhaps a C-, which is sad given the amount of effort made in this area. As with all grades, this one is a bit perceptual, which is to say that the cup could be perceived as half-full here rather than half-empty. After all, Afghanistan was enormously destroyed going in to OEF and needed everything reconstructed, and there have been substantial positives on the macroeconomic side, especially with gross domestic product (GDP) growth rates over the past five years. But, the half-empty reality is that the drug economy has boomed, providing much of the impetus to the overall GDP growth rate, and much infrastructure rebuilding in the south has stalled or been forestalled by declining security. Moreover, the project-driven construct of our infrastructure program makes its rebuilding very problematic, while the broader issue of economic development for Afghanistan is almost impossible, since this is a country with a rural underclass that has been off the farm for over a generation and cannot return successfully. Afghanistan never had a robust development picture prior to its quarter-century of war, and it cannot easily construct such a picture now.

As someone who was intimately involved in the State-Building/Governance component of Afghanistan's nation-building project, I feel a sharp desire to report that here, at least, there is something good to say. I managed the electoral processes at the ELJ in 2002, or, to put it more bluntly, I elected Hamid Karzai. This is not to say that I made Karzai president—Zal Khalilzad, Lakhdar Brahimi, and Barney Rubin all had a hand in that—I merely supervised his final, formal election to the post. And so I would love to give this area of Governance a high grade, but even at that first LJ it was clear to the international observers that justice was being sacrificed to expediency, that too many war criminals, warlords, drug lords, and just generally unsavory characters were being allowed into power because the U.S. had decided on a light military footprint that would leverage local guys who controlled guns, some aspect of the illicit economy, or both. As the drug economy took hold and regional actors began (correctly) to conclude that U.S. focus on and staying power in Afghanistan were indeed running out, the Governance part of this project started to decline from its early grade of B to something far lower. Again, low starting conditions mitigate against the assignment of an even lower grade, but it is a bit like testing someone on reading comprehension of "War and Peace" who scores a bit poorly and then you discover they've just learned how to read. You feel like a bit of grade inflation is in order. On the other hand, however, some political maturation just takes time to occur, and patience and a strong stomach are all that is really needed.

The last important pillar for a nation-building country like Afghanistan is Transitional Justice, and in this area we have all failed miserably—the grade is F. What's more, this is not an area where we are losing ground on initial progress; rather, we made no provision in our initial strategy for this area. I have spoken and written before of how we tried hard in the ELJ process to keep war criminals out of the big tent, only to see everyone who had been anyone in Afghanistan get credentialed and put into the ELJ anyway. The biggest of these folks ended up in the seats of honor down front (which I called "Murderer's Row"), and it has been downhill ever since, from the point of view of average Ahmed on the streets of Kabul. DDR, for all its statistical successes, and the new Constitution, for all of its provisions that ministers possess some technical competence, have not brought about one simple change for Afghanistan—namely, that people who committed wrongs during the long period of past violence admit to some culpability, or at least a truth and reconciliation process. In such a deeply scarred and troubled society, healing may not be possible without some sort of transitional justice.

Now, I have given U.S. efforts to date fairly low marks, which probably help to suggest how successful the consolidation of democracy in Afghanistan has been, but let me conclude by looking at three specific questions the organizers asked me to consider. First, "to what extent are core democratic values, such as compromise, influential in addressing the societal cleavages that need to be overcome?" Frequently, when we are asked anthropological questions about Afghan culture, such as this one, the answers are provided according to the Pashtunwali, or code of the Pashtuns, which at most applies to some 40 percent of the population. The principle of compromise, or rogha in Pashto, does exist among the Pashtuns, and indeed more broadly among Afghans, although it has more relevance in the context of reconciliation between groups that have been in conflict with one another. Male Pashtuns, and again, most Afghans, are also notoriously egalitarian, although females, as my opening anecdote made very clear, do not enjoy equal political or social status. Realistically, though, Afghan society has been transformed utterly by the long war there and is now a narco-state. The khan-malik class of local elites were dispersed by the long conflict, or detached from their sources of patronage and influence, and the new class of local elites are increasingly relying on money generated from the narcotics industry. The era of warlordism and militias also did great damage to the underlying social constructs that might support democracy, especially by pushing people toward local identity formations, as outlined at length above. Moreover, other traditional factors that have been correlated strongly with successful democratic transitions, such as earlier democratic experience, an independent and educated middle class, and a robust civil society, are all essentially absent from present-day Afghanistan. The democratic experiment of the 1960s is too far in the past to be relevant for most Afghans, the most educated and wealthy of whom fled abroad and have made their lives in diaspora. In the capacity gap that resulted from this refugee exodus, civil society organizations came largely from abroad and operated on the fringes of government. There has been only limited success at reestablishing such organizations in Afghanistan. Overall then, the indicators for democratic transition in Afghanistan are bad. This is not a place that will embrace democracy enthusiastically, and the difficulties will be exacerbated by resistance from increasingly enriched and entrenched elites.

Second, what are some guiding lessons for building democracy in the midst of religious, ethnic, or other divisions? In light of the foregoing, it may seem that Afghanistan offers us little in the way of useful guiding lessons, but there is one important thing that it can teach us—democratic transitions in divided societies where conflict continues are unlikely to take root for a considerable period of time. If we commit to fostering such a transition, we must make certain that we can and will stay the course, or we will likely make it more difficult down the road. It is entirely likely that over time the kind of societal change that can produce a supportive environment for democracy in states that are now pre-democratic in orientation will occur, but it is almost certainly the case that democracy is not the first priority to people in those circumstances. Usually, higher-order goods like security and economic well-being must be satisfied first, especially when traditional forms of governance that may have been authoritarian but effective have been disrupted by conflict and/or societal transition.

A lesser but not unimportant lesson occurs to me in response to the question, "Are we asking too much of democratic process (i.e., elections)?" The broad answer here is, "yes, we are," because democratic processes in a place like Afghanistan tend to reinforce preexisting local identity orientation rather than produce the kind of mature democracy found in developed Western societies. Having said that, though, I have maintained consistently that for Afghanistan the beauty of democratic processes, if we can stay the course, is that over time they transform ethnically-based warlords and drug traffickers into sleazy ward bosses and petty politicians—not, perhaps, unlike some U.S. Congressmen or national representatives in other governments—and that is progress for a faction-riven and conflict-ridden society like Afghanistan. Of course, some psephological tricks and other basics of political science can hasten a democratic transition, although they must be appropriate to the cultural circumstances of the case in question. In Afghanistan, the use of the single non-transferable vote (SNTV) system with candidates having to stand as individuals rather than as members of competing parties for the 2005 Wolesi Jirga (lower house) election is an example of how not to use basic political science advantageously. This system appears to be undergoing reform prior to the 2009 elections, and such changes are in keeping with the maturation of democratic processes in fledgling democracies, but a more proportional system and an orientation toward greater consociational processes might have gone further from the start to help move Afghanistan along in its democratic transition.

Can an effective transition to stable democracy, of any sort, occur in Afghanistan today? Unfortunately, there are quite significant negatives that are making this very difficult. Most significant is the ongoing conflict by primarily indigenous Afghan forces against the Karzai regime. These forces are the resurgent Taliban, or neo-Taliban as some call them, who again have Pakistani support despite ongoing U.S. pressures to push Pakistan into a more ally-friendly position. The pressure on Pakistani President Pervez Musharraf to form a more moderate government with less of a role for the Muttahida Majlies-e-Amal (MMA) did not lead to a decline of the Talibanization that has deepened along the frontier over these past few years; Pakistan will continue to play both sides against the middle, in part at least to keep the lid on militant Islamism at home and in part to maintain an ethnically Pashtun proxy in Afghanistan. Why the Taliban have resurged strikes me as one of the most frustrating questions for any of us to have to deal with, because of course they were going to resurge! They were not really crushed, most of them just went home in late 2001 or early 2002 when they saw which way the wind was blowing. Or they went to Pakistan, where they could have sanctuary and the Pakistani Inter-Services Intelligence Directorate (ISI) could prep them for another round, which following the handover of the Eastern Zone combat space to the International Security Assistance Force (ISAF), now from the North Atlantic Treaty Organization (NATO), many in Pakistan believed had come. Moreover, as Tom Johnson and Chris Mason have ably documented, the decision to construct a Kabul government that systematically excluded the non-Durrani Pashtuns (especially the Ghilzai and Ghurghust) has done a great deal to alienate those Pashtuns and drive them into the anti-regime ranks. More generally, the U.S. never figured out how to have a proper reconciliation with the Taliban, whose early alienation was a clear by-product of the strategic approach the U.S. adopted from the outset.

The booming narcotics sub-sector of the rural and trading economies is a second persistent negative. The data here seem to worsen every year, such that now Afghanistan is a narco-state, as Ashraf Ghani once presciently warned us it would be. According to Wordnet Dictionary, a narco-state is "an area that has been taken over and is controlled and corrupted by drug cartels and where law enforcement is effectively nonexistent," which, of course, sounds exactly like Afghanistan.

A narco-state always has a very high rate of corruption, which Transparency International does not reveal for Afghanistan because it is one of a relatively few countries for which data are inadequate. But our anecdotal knowledge of the corruption in Afghanistan tells us that it is very high, and extremely debilitating to the recovery of this war-torn society. The problem, as with Iraq, is exacerbated by the local-identity orientation of Afghan society, and the low levels of personal security, and the uncertain economic conditions, all of which combine for people to try to get whatever they can as early as they can. With regular reports of the heroin trade having infected the highest levels of the government with its corrupting influence, to include Wali Karzai, younger brother of Hamid Karzai, and many others, as well, it is hard to imagine that this narco-state can stabilize itself in the time that remains for international community engagement.

Which leads me to my last point on the negative side of the ledger, the growing problem of alliance management. As someone who advocated (and worked to realize) NATO involvement in Afghanistan, I regret to say that I did not see the downside of this policy. I saw, and still see, substantial upside to all the international community involvement in Afghanistan, the absence of which continue to make the looming disaster in Iraq all the more problematic for the U.S.. Having said that, though, there is no question that alliance management has been a challenge in Afghanistan, from the flawed SSR pillars of various other lead donor nations to the national caveats of various European security partners to the rather underwhelming support for the Afghan mission in key alliance country publics. The reality is that, sooner or later, this alliance will crack in Afghanistan, as one or another (or more) of the countries chooses to go home. And then what? Bringing NATO into the fight has not substantially increased combat power there—rather it has increased the political commitment to the mission when no one wanted to do Iraq—but failure for NATO in Afghanistan would likely be disastrous for that organization, in ways that failure for the U.S. in Iraq likely will not be. So, the potential downside is very great.

I have painted a fairly dismal picture of the situation in Afghanistan, but I do not mean for it to be unremittingly gloomy, for indeed, there is much to celebrate in Afghanistan. The sad reality is that there could and should be much more to celebrate there, were our initial policies not so hamstrung by a senior policy-making aversion to nation-building, neo-conservative commitment to abandoning the Afghan project for the more lucrative target of Iraq, the growing anti-Americanism of Islamists due in large measure to both of the foregoing mistakes, and the willingness of other actors—especially, but not solely, American rivals—to make moves of their own. Especially interesting in regard to this last point are the activities of three regional actors, one of which is a rising great power rival to the U.S.. Pakistan, as has already been mentioned, has a long investment in Afghanistan, whose societal collapse spilled over into Pakistan, causing the Talibanization, Kalashnikovization, and heroinchi ills faced by that country. Pakistan believes with great reason that its investment in Afghanistan must pay off and sees Indian Research and Analysis Wing (RAW is India's foreign intelligence agency) agents behind every rock in eastern Afghanistan, while it sees Iranian Ministry of Intelligence and Security (MOIS) agents behind every dust mound in western Afghanistan. Hence, Pakistan's willingness to allow the Taliban and other associated groups to engage in cross-border activities in Afghanistan. Iran is the second regional player whose involvement in Afghanistan has been quiet of note. It has no natural rival for influence in western Afghanistan, where its commercial activities have provided both a point of ingress into Afghan society and a beginning point for intelligence operations. Lastly, Afghanistan has become fertile ground for China's re-entry to the Great Game in Central Asia as well as a wider corridor for Chinese overland influence in Pakistan, especially the strategically significant, resource-rich, and under-populated barren wasteland of Balochistan.

All of these regional actors illustrate a reality of Afghanistan's future, which is that it will be as it always has been—an Asian future. Although many Afghans are especially fond of the U.S. and most things American, as they have been for many decades, it does not take strategic genius for them to see that America will not be in Afghanistan's neighborhood for much longer, at least to a level that can shape decisively its future. As America has left or ignored Afghanistan in the past, so it will in the future, since the strategic imperatives that shape U.S. involvement so far from the homeland remain for now essentially unchanged. Afghanistan is not that significant to the U.S., so long as its state failure does not dip to the crisis level of allowing the Taliban and Al-Qa'ida or similar such organizations to threaten American security. The U.S. can lead from afar, or stay and lead there, but in the same way that we engage in Nepal, or Bangladesh, or other lesser Asian states. The U.S. is too far away, too self-centered, and too focused on higher profile strategic interests to remain the biggest player in Afghanistan for much longer.

So Afghanistan's future is most likely one that will be shaped more by actors other than the U.S.. Yet continued U.S. engagement is crucial both to Afghanistan having a stable future and the U.S. having a secure one. Given that the U.S. is headed to failure in Iraq, the U.S. must not fail in Afghanistan. To avoid failure there the U.S. must commit to staying, by exercising the kind of strategic engagement and patience that runs so counter to American foreign policy. Thus, I wonder what U.S. exit strategy for Afghanistan should be. It began and has largely stayed a "Vietnamization" strategy, as has U.S. strategy for Iraq—namely, that America build indigenous Afghan institutions, especially its government and security forces, so that the U.S. can hand off control of the country to them, allowing the U.S. to take its highly professional (and highly expensive) military home, or elsewhere. This strategy, however, has shown little sign of working, and the impending failure in Iraq will imperil U.S. efforts in Afghanistan in manifest ways. To really rebuild a country's institutions you have to understand that country and the regional milieu it sits within. The U.S. does not have, and never really has had, the aptitude for it, and now that it has become essential to U.S. national security the U.S. has been mighty slow to embrace this challenge.

A second factor is that most Americans could care less about nation-building, certainly not for humanitarian reasons. If the U.S. has to engage in such silly nonsense, there had better be a pretty damn good strategic reason and it had better not be very costly. To America's xenophobes, though, there are virtually no good reasons to do nation-building, which leaves America with this vexing problem—what happens when Usama bin Laden and Ayman Al-Zawahairi are finally caught, killed, or exfiltrate from the region? Why, then, will America be in Afghanistan? Perhaps the Afghan diaspora in Northern Virginia and California can exert a similar influence on American foreign policy to the influence brought by Zionist Jews in the late 1940s, but most likely Afghanistan will slip back to its accustomed back burner spot on the American foreign policy stove. At that point, "Afghanization" or not, America will go home.

Or, perhaps not. Perhaps in the new U.S. foreign policy, Afghanistan is too important to abandon. Perhaps here we will see, correctly, a confluence of grand strategic imperatives to stay with the most important test case for an effective anti-militant Islamist foreign policy anywhere—that is, a robust and successful nation-building effort. We need Afghanistan—indeed, we always have—and perhaps now we can begin to see that. And Afghanistan needs the U.S.. So, can the U.S. really afford to leave?

DEMOCRATIC PROGRESS OR PERIL? INDIGENOUS AND POPULAR MOBILIZATION IN BOLIVIA

Brooke Larson

THE MOUSE THAT ROARED: BOLIVIA'S OUTSIZED SIGNIFICANCE TO EUROPE AND THE US

Historically, Bolivia has occupied a critical place in the shifting geopolitical politics of Latin America. The manifold reasons for its strategic importance are familiar to most of us: Bolivia's licit and illicit export commodities (from silver through to industrial tin and, most recently, to hydrocarbons and coca) have periodically swept this landlocked nation into the swift currents of transnational trade. Further, Bolivia's geopolitical location in the interior of the continent, together with its volatile political history, have long captured the political and military attention of the US, as well as Cuba, in their expansionary phases (recall the sudden US interest in Bolivian tin during WWII and its strategic "soft" intervention in Bolivia after 1952; or Che Guevara's 1967 mission to create two, three, many Vietnams, starting in Bolivia's jungles). More recently, Bolivia has emerged as a fascinating, and troubling, case for scholars, policymakers, and hands-on practitioners interested in the structural challenges of democracy and development: its endemic poverty, radical inequalities of class and race, deep regional divisions, and cyclical dependence on mono-exports.

The overarching question that vexes us is this: how can an internally fractured, desperately poor nation like Bolivia build a sustainable democratic order capable of addressing those endemic social problems? The question is complicated by the fact that Bolivia is Latin America's most indigenous nation (64 percent of Bolivians self-identified as being members of an ethnic group in the most recent census). Since the 1980s, many popular movements have traded on that fact. Indeed, as I will argue, Bolivia's return to democratic rule in the 1980s unleashed an array of popular and indigenous movements, which have since reconfigured around the Movimiento al Socialismo (MAS). Today, it is the most powerful indigenous movement in Latin America, and since 2006 the MAS has become the new driver of democratic politics and social policy in Bolivia. Thus, Evo Morales' recent rise to power on the wings of grassroots movements represents a fundamental turning point in the broadening of participatory democracy in that difficult social and institutional environment.

I want to cast historical light on the democratizing process that brought indigenous and labor movements into power. In so doing, I will highlight what I believe to be some of the most compelling challenges confronting this fragile democracy today. As a historian, I am uncomfortable with predictive and prescriptive forms of analysis, but I do think Bolivia's recent experiences with neoliberalism and democratic reform provide a rich context for understanding the daunting challenges facing Evo Morales and his ethnopopulist party today.

BOLIVIA IN THE 1980S AND 1990S: LATIN AMERICA'S POSTER CHILD OF NEOLIBERALISM

If we are to understand the radical rupture that neoliberalism represented for Bolivia after the return to democracy in 1982, we need to recall how it redefined the mission of the Bolivian state vis-à-vis the economy and civil society. Bolivia's 1952 nationalist-populist revolution had transformed the government from being an instrument of the tiny mining and agricultural elite to a populist-corporatist state beholden to a broader citizenry. Although the '52 state eventually reneged on many of its social goals, it did create the institutional basis for coalitional politics, broader political representation (universal rights to suffrage and literacy were legalized), and delivery of "social rights" to militant constituencies of mineworkers and peasants (through the nationalization of mines, land redistribution, the extension of public schooling, and cultural reforms celebrating Bolivia's mixed "mestizo" heritage, etc.). That historic moment of populist-corporatist rule came to an abrupt halt in 1964, when the military overthrew the MNR government and ruled for the next 18 years. As with her Southern Cone neighbors, Bolivia's struggle for re-democratization was a contestatory and uneven process.

The restoration of civilian rule in 1982 reinstated parties and allowed civil society to flourish, but it quashed the social goals of the 1952 state and redefined the Bolivian state. The return to civilian rule marked a dramatic turning point in state-society relations: the 1952 corporatist, developmental model of statism now, in 1982, morphed into a neoliberal regulatory model of statehood. The state's primary goals were to control Bolivia's hyperinflation, encourage the creation of efficient enterprises, reduce corruption, induce foreign investment, and increase economic growth. The results of Bolivia's first round of privatization were decidedly mixed. Monetary stabilization brought hyperinflation under control after 1985, and many urban middle class Bolivians quickly jumped on neoliberal-gobalization bandwagon. But the closure of large state mines proved catastrophic to the most militant sector of Bolivia's working class, as 23,000 out of 30,000 miners were sacked. Thousands of ex-miners ended up as coca farmers in the eastern semi-tropical regions of El Chapare and Santa Cruz. Meanwhile, massive unemployment followed in the public sector, with 10,000 government employees and nearly 25,000 rural teachers losing their jobs. In short, neoliberalism's first cycle of structural adjustment plunged the lower income sectors into deeper poverty. The scenario was alarming in the late 1980s: real wages throughout the country fell sharply; unemployment soared; severe drought spread across the arid western highlands, dislocating tens of thousands of indigenous peasants; rural migration was transforming the center of Bolivian cities, as destitute Indian day laborers and beggars converged on downtown La Paz and other cities. Such profound social dislocations (what many Bolivian intellectuals called "savage neoliberalism") forced the Bolivian government to renege on many of its market-driven goals and reach out to the multitude of political parties now beginning to appear on the scene. Problems of governability forced the Paz Zamora government (1989–1993) to deploy traditional political tools (multiparty alliances, patronage, and pact making) to secure middle-class support and shore up the state. Weak social institutions and political imperatives therefore undercut a basic neoliberal goal to shrink the government bureaucracy, eliminate corruption, and end patronage. Systemic corruption continued to undermine government legitimacy in the eyes of ordinary Bolivians.

In the 1990s, Bolivia's version of neoliberal restructuring took an innovative turn under President Sánchez de Losada (aka "Goni"). Under his 1994 Law of Capitalization, the government sold off the largest state-owned firms (Bolivian oil company, YPFB; national railroad and airlines; telephone and electric companies, etc.), while retaining minority public ownership of those firms. The idea behind capitalization was to channel the proceeds into pensions and social security for the nation's most vulnerable sectors of the population. Backed by the IMF and World Bank, the capitalization plan was part of Goni's larger political program to turn savage capitalism into "neoliberalism with a human face," as he sought to secure the hegemony of market capitalism in this polarizing political climate. Concretely, Goni's government auctioned off half of the five largest state-owned firms to multinational corporations, keeping 50 percent of the shares for the "shareholding citizens" of Bolivia (i.e., pensioners and social security recipients). The so-called *Plan de Todos* put forth utopian projects: a flood of foreign and domestic capital investment, a spurt in GDP growth rates up to 11 percent by 1997, the rapid growth of jobs.

Again, as scholars look back on Bolivia's second cycle of neoliberalism, they argue about its mixed and ultimately disappointing results. There is no time to delve into details here, but suffice it to say that the policy of Capitalization did effect a massive infusion of foreign investment in Bolivia's petrochemical export industry—namely, oil and gas exploration and pipeline construction. Dramatically, the full scope of Bolivia's vast hydrocarbon ("gas") reserves was discovered. But the new export boom in oil and gas (a capital-intensive enclave economy) provided little stimulus to the broader economy. Predicted growth rates fell far short of the mark: between 1989 and 1996, average annual growth was about 4 percent, but fell to 2 percent in the late 1990s. Moreover, partial privatization triggered massive firings on a scale not seen since the 1980s. Finally, but not least, the government revenues were not sufficient to sustain the new welfare system. Indeed, government revenues declined precipitously in the late 1990s, leaving the Banzer government (1997–2001) with huge budget deficits. By the late 1990s, Bolivia was in for another devastating round of privatization, tax hikes, budget cuts, and overall belt-tightening. Neoliberalism's "human face" had turned ugly, once again.

Taking stock of neoliberalism's boom-bust cycle in the 1990s, Bolivian critics and policy makers repudiated what they saw as "pervasive market failures, new forms of social polarization, and a dramatic intensification of uneven development at all spatial scales" (Brenner and Theodore 2002, p. 122). Certainly, popular perceptions held that neoliberalism's "trickle down" agenda had gone into reverse by the end of the decade, redistributing income upwards towards the top of Bolivia's rigid class hierarchy and within the international entrepreneurial elite. What was also starkly apparent by 1999, however, was that the correlation of political forces had drastically changed over the 1980s and 1990s, with the resurgence of grassroots participatory politics and revitalized civil society. In short, state-society relations had shifted rather silently but dramatically during the whole neoliberal experiment of the late 1980s and 1990s. It is to this political reconfiguration of civil society under neoliberalism that I now turn.

RETURN OF BOLIVIA'S CIVIL SOCIETY, GRASSROOTS STYLE

One of deeper ironies of Bolivian neoliberalism is that it opened up political spaces for new social groups to press their claims on the government and search for progressive and radical alternatives to the neoliberal order. The rising tide of popular mobilization was, of course, built into the very process of redemocratization taking place across the Southern Cone region in the 1980s and 1990s. But in Bolivia, there was a paradoxical shift away from militant trade unionism in the mining sector (due to the massive sacking of mineworkers under the privatization policies of the 1980s) towards a broad indigenous movement based on the Aymara *altiplano,* where peasants, laborers, and a few indigenous intellectuals forged the militant *katarista* movement with links to trade unions, political parties, and the university. The recomposition of the *katarista* Indian movement had a crucial impact in the cultural sphere, by bringing issues and identities of *indigeneity* back into the public sphere after a long hiatus in which nationalist-populist narratives and class ideologies had dominated political discourse. After the 1952 revolution, Bolivia was refashioned as a unifying "mestizo" nation, while the ethnic question was relegated to the margins of national consciousness. All that changed in the 1980s with *"el retorno del indio."* Aymara-led movements in and around the capital of La Paz had a crucial impact on shaping popular consciousness and identity policies through Aymara-language radio programs, street-theater, bilingual books, oral history workshops, and the spread of literacy and adult education. The roots of Bolivia's resurgent indigenous movement, today the most powerful one in South America, grew in the subsoil of the Aymara movement during the transition to liberal democracy and market-driven reforms.

But if we are to understand the reinsertion of indigenous and popular sectors into the political process, we need to take another look at neoliberalism's "structural adjustments"—this time in the sphere of political reform and social institutions. During the 1990s, Bolivia's increasingly bankrupt party system gave way to new forms of popular representation, new political subjects, and new conflicts. Bolivia and other democratizing regions in Latin America witnessed the explosive growth of grassroots organization and strategies of mediation that articulated new political constituencies. Indigenous groups, peasant producer associations, *barrio* organizations, subsets of workers and women, environmental and human rights activists, evangelical groups, and the plethora of NGOs that began to inhabit much of rural Bolivia in the 1990s all populated the interstices between civil society and the state, as they fashioned new forms of sociability, identity, and political agenda. Here, I borrow the idea of "associative network" from Doug Chalmers, et al., (1997) to argue that those forms and forums of popular representation originated in the base, percolating upwards towards the institutional spheres of power and political influence. This resurgence of popular politics and networks did not, however, mark the return to Bolivia's old-style populist-corporatist model under a centralized interventionist state (although political patronage still served as a vital instrument of cooptation and control).

Rather, the emergence of new forms of popular representation grew out of the need to solve social problems and to press their specific, issue-oriented agendas into the political sphere. They rushed in to fill the vacuum left by the bankruptcy of the traditional party system and by the destruction of militant trade unionism and class-based politics.

But the mushrooming of grassroots politics and networks in Bolivia during the 1990s also reflected the growing pressure on the central government to shift revenues (and slough off the intractable problems of development and governance) to Bolivia's regional and municipal governments. Goni's 1994 Law of Popular Participation (LPP) had a measurable impact on political decentralization: for example, the LPP committed 20 percent of national tax revenues to municipal governments to cover the cost of roads, schools, health clinics, irrigation systems, etc. The LPP recognized grassroots organizations, and by 1997 some 15,000 rural peasant communities, unions, and *ayllus* were pursing territorial agendas to recover their rights to land. The LPP also created a host of new municipalities in remote rural areas that now could compete for federal funds to jump-start local development projects. Finally, the LPP introduced electoral reform at the municipal level, opening up Bolivia's 311 municipalities to indigenous and *campesino* representatives for the first time. Another key player to benefit from administrative decentralization was the ubiquitous NGO, which often served to leverage (or control) the agenda of rural grassroots associations. Indeed, many scholars have argued that the overall impact of NGOs in Bolivia during the 1990s was to steer grassroots organizations away from mobilizing activities in order to promote specific market-friendly projects in harmony with the IMF's globalization agenda, and that Goni's highly-touted agenda of multiculturalism (including his promotion of bilingual educational) was but part of his effort to put a human face on neoliberalism's painful economic policies.

Perhaps, but it is equally clear that neoliberalism's *political reforms* opened the way for a deeper, more participatory form of civil society and democracy. Bolivia's popular and indigenous sector exploded on the national stage in 1999-2000, in the famous Water War of Cochabamba. In the view of many social analysts, this massive grassroots movement protesting the sale of Cochabamba's municipal water system to an international consortium (including the US company, Bechtel) marked the end of Bolivia as the IMF's poster child of neoliberalism. For it triggered a series of popular mobilizations that peaked in October 2003, with nation-wide *bloqueos,* marches, hunger strikes, and military counterattacks. It sent Goni into exile and later forced his successor, Carlos Mesa, to resign. These events presaged the transformation of the MAS from social movement into a broad, inclusionary "ethnopopulist" party, which catapulted Evo Morales into power in the landslide election of December 2005.

Thus, paradoxically, the social and institutional transformations that neoliberalism engendered, or inspired, in the *political sphere* opened the way for the direct political participation by people who now challenge the basic precepts of neoliberal capitalism. The election of Bolivia's first Indian to the presidency is not purely symbolic, although indigeneity has proven to be a powerful mobilizing and legitimizing tool that the MAS has skillfully deployed. The electoral victory of MAS represents, I would argue, a fundamental shift in state-society relations, the composition of the state, and its political orientation. Consequently, it has raised sharp dilemmas in the sphere of public policy—such fundamental issues as: how to promote economic development with equity; dismantle the century-old structures of racial discrimination; carry out an agrarian reform program; rewrite the political "rules of the game" in the shape of a new, more inclusive political constitution; and not least, strengthen and reform the state apparatus in the face of growing political and regional polarization. The MAS agenda is, by any measure, an ambitious (perhaps utopian) one, and the jury is still out. But already there have been significant successes (notably, Morales' renegotiation of the terms under which Bolivia is exporting gas to Brazil, Argentina, and Spain), as well as some serious setbacks (dramatically, the implosion of the Constitutional Assembly). In light of Bolivia's ongoing social tensions and the constitutional meltdown, the cohesion and viability of the nation now seem to be more at risk.

Rather than focus on unfolding political events and prospects for policy reform, however, I want to briefly highlight the unresolved ethnic and regional tensions that have historically burdened the Bolivian nation and that now threaten to create acute problems of governability.

CONFRONTING ETHNIC AND REGIONAL TENSIONS

The persistence of ethnicity in Bolivian society and politics has permeated the development of the nation state and class politics for most of the 20th century. That ethnic politics are not disappearing (in spite of state policies and rhetoric designed to marginalize ethnicity in favor of "mestizo nationalism") was dramatically demonstrated by the 2001 census, in which 62 percent of the population self-identified as belonging to an ethnic group (the largest groups being the Quechua (31 percent) and Aymara (25 percent), or one of 31 other named indigenous groups distributed mainly through the eastern lowlands). Historically, ethnicity (namely "Indianness") was created and utilized by Spanish colonial society, and caste divisions were reproduced under republican laws, policies, and practices until the mid-20th century. The 1952 state went a long way towards incorporating illiterate Indians who still constituted the great majority of the population. Universal suffrage, rural schools, agrarian reform, and new forms of *campesino* unionization brought Indians into the nation, as they extended the reach of the state into the countryside. But, as historians have pointed out, the state-directed process of incorporation came at the price of obliterating the cultural identities and communal rights of Bolivia's massive indigenous population. The legitimate pretext to suppress Indian identities in favor of *campesinización* was part of the effort of the corporatist state to bring the rural masses into government-controlled unions, while also dismantling the discursive apparatus of racial discrimination. But the imposition of a unifying national "mestizo" identity in the 1950s did not obliterate local indigenous identities, as became all too clear when, in the 1980s under Bolivia's restored democracy, militant indigenous parties merged with labor unions to create the powerful *katarista* movement in the Aymara region in and around La Paz.

The fusion of ethnic and class politics is the mantle that Evo Morales and MAS inherited and redefined, as they moved into power. However, unlike the militant separatist movement of *katarismo*, MAS has harnessed the idea of "indigenous rights" (that is, customary law, or *"usos y costumbres"*) to a broad coalitional agenda that has tried to make common cause with diverse urban popular sectors and the middle class. So while Morales rode into power calling for the "recuperation of national patrimony" and "economic self-determination," he has located those issues in the resurgent indigenous movement. "The MAS is born and draws its strength from the struggles of the indigenous peoples, for the defense of our identity, which is the coca leaf, for the defense of our land, who is our mother, for the defense of our natural resources, which are our hope and our patrimony." (Morales 2004, quoted in Albró 2005: 447) The indigenous struggle has become the basis for broader concepts of *social rights* (to economic livelihood, education, health care, cultural inclusion, etc.) and *national sovereignty* (the repatriation of the nation's natural resources). MAS' strategic brilliance in the political campaign was to use indigenous rights as a rallying point to build a broad cross-class coalition of workers, peasants, and progressive sectors of the middle class against the moral bankruptcy of neoliberalism. No surprise, then, that Morales' presidential inauguration was suffused by rich ethnic symbolism that capitalized on the idea that Bolivia's first Indian president marked the culmination of 500 years of resistance to colonialism and oppression.

Looking back over 2006, MAS' crucial first year, we can trace the outlines of a public policy agenda driven, in large part, by an effort to redress historical injustices and social marginalization of the rural indigenous population. In brief: 1) Bolivia's increased hydrocarbon revenues will help finance social programs (social security, education, health care) for the 65 percent of Bolivia's population that lives below the poverty line; 2) the government's new hybrid coca/cocaine strategy celebrates the coca leaf as an indigenous cultural symbol and as a licit commodity with great industrial potential, while maintaining a firm line on drug trafficking (utilizing cooperative, instead of forced, policies of eradication); 3) the government has promoted an Agrarian Reform process, promised more than a decade ago, that would redistribute privately-owned, but uncultivated lands, thus threatening the huge *latifundia* in the eastern frontier regions of Bolivia; and 4) as 2007 opened, the government announced plans to promote job creation, micro-enterprise development, and improved services in health, education, and welfare –all skewed towards the rural poor. Undergirding these domestic reforms are Bolivia's international realignments in trade and diplomacy: its crucial trade relations with Brazil and Argentina, the economic and technical aid and trade packages Bolivia has negotiated with Venezuela (and, to a much lesser extent, Cuba), its growing trade relationship with China and India, and the cancellation of debt to the international credit cartel. These realignments, along with the US's relative disengagement from Latin America, have made the US much less salient to Bolivian domestic politics and policy making.

In spite of these policy outcomes (or potential benefits), MAS increasingly confronts a restive base that expects the rapid delivery of lands, jobs, and social services. Bolivia's highly mobilized popular sector both inside and outside the MAS is positioned, as perhaps never before, to stir up opposition in the case that MAS reneges on its promises to attack poverty, social exclusion, and inequality. Militant labor leaders, like Oscar Olivera, who led the 2000 Water War, are deeply critical of the compromises the Morales regime has made to the imperatives of functioning within the parameters of global capitalism, for example. And Morales confronted an acute crisis in October 2006, when the confrontation between Huanuni's unionized mineworkers and self-employed *cooperativistas* left many people dead. Such violence and disillusionment inevitably feed militant class politics and ethnic fundamentalism, which threaten to boomerang. Indeed, it can be argued that MAS itself has fanned the flames of ethnic fundamentalism with its own fiery rhetoric and symbolism. Nativism rallied the masses and helped define MAS' political identity, but ethnic separatism fundamentally perverts MAS' broad ethnopopulist agenda of coalitional policies and multiethnic inclusion.

Far more dangerous to the democratic order, I would argue, is the longstanding problem of regionalism, newly articulated to a racialist anti-Indian agenda. As historians have shown, the history of regional fragmentation goes back to the 19th century and is exacerbated by the country's three-tiered ecology (western backbone of mountains, intermontane valleys, and vast eastern lowlands) and historically weak infrastructure of roads and rails. In recent times, regional cleavages have acquired a new bipolar dynamic that bifurcates Bolivia into two warring racialized and regionalized identities, the highland indigenous *colla* and the lowland white/mestizo *camba*. This normative bipolarity of region, race, and national identity has assumed a new, more threatening dimension since the resurgence of indigenous social movements in the highlands. The *cambas* of Santa Cruz (and the whole arc of eastern provinces known colloquially as *la Media Luna*) cast themselves as the nation's forward-looking entrepreneurial elites leading Bolivia into the future, as against the primitive backward-looking *collas* of the western highlands. The discovery of gas in the Tarija region (part of the *Media Luna)*, together with Santa Cruz's buoyant agro-export economy, has exacerbated debates over how the nation should be governed and in whose interests. Key disputes include such vital issues as how the rents from hydrocarbons should be allocated, how much political "autonomy" each department should be granted, and what sort of model of development should be promoted. Reduced to its starkest polarity, this regional conflict is about what sort of nation Bolivia is, or hopes to become. Santa Cruz elites look towards Brazil and capitalist modernity, wishing themselves to be white, modern, and cosmopolitan. Indigenous leaders of the western highlands find inspiration in their own communal past and in popular forms of representation, and they want to impose popular sovereignty over the nation's natural resources.

However much Evo Morales would like to unify the nation under his vision of economic development with equity (with a rural, pro-indigenous twist), the counterforce of regional politics is proving to be one of the most difficult challenges facing the government. The imploding Constitutional Assembly is perhaps the most visible venue in which these polarizing regional, racial, and class tendencies are playing themselves out. For the elites of the eastern zones have created a political bloc within the Constitutional Assembly to sabotage MAS and promote the cause of "regional autonomy," which would give them greater control over the region's vast territorial and natural resources (everything from lumber and land to hydrocarbons). Most recently, the country's legitimate capital (Sucre, in the south versus La Paz, in the north) has become another flashpoint in the larger theater of regional power struggles. As many scholars have warned, this dynamic of regional/racial dualism has become a powerful new force that could break asunder the viability of Bolivia as unified territorial nation.

CONCLUDING REMARKS

I want to end this chapter with a few observations about the promises and perils of democracy in Bolivia today. In my view, the rise of MAS, the most powerful indigenous social movement/party in Latin America, has had a largely positive impact on Bolivian democracy because it has leveraged the political influence of traditionally marginalized groups and articulated an economic project of development with equity. Certainly, Bolivia's electoral democracy has been strengthened by the significant increase in voter turnout in indigenous areas over the past five years. It has made mistakes and indulged in excesses, but overall MAS has navigated the transition from social movement to political party with relative success. On the other hand, MAS continues to have a dual character: this mass party grew out of the vigorous social movements and popular citizenship organizations of the 1990s, and it is still articulated to a heterogeneous (and increasingly factious) social movement.

How the MAS manages to sustain good governance in this highly mobilized, extremely polarized society is a challenge of a higher order of magnitude. On balance, the Morales government has accomplished notable domestic reforms, reintegrated itself on favorable terms into South American diplomatic and trading networks, and demonstrated an unusual degree of political transparency. On the other hand, the new regime has not shied away from militant pro-Indian symbolism, which has frightened or alienated much of the urban elite. Politically, the most intense struggle has taken place in the constitutional convention to "refound the nation." Precious months were lost in the battle over voting procedures, thus squandering the opportunity to bring the country together under the powerful electoral mandate that put Morales into office in the first place. Meanwhile, longstanding tensions between regionalism and centralism have flared up, feeding fuel to the "Regional Autonomy" movement of the *Media Luna* and to right-wing opposition parties like Podemos.

Thus, Bolivia seems to be at a historic impasse over how to rewrite the political rules of the game and, more fundamentally, how to consolidate a centralized state committed to solving Bolivia's desperate social problems—poverty, inequality, marginality, and discrimination. Symptomatic of this breakdown of unity and dialogue is the resurgence of street politics—marches, *bloqueos,* demonstrations, hunger strikes, and even brawls—being deployed by both MAS and the opposition forces. As a result, racial-ethnic polarization is, once again, on the rise in both the "Indian highlands" and "white lowlands." Today, it is the convergence of the regional-ethnic schism that constitutes what is, perhaps, the most sinister threat to Bolivia's fragile democratic order.

REFERENCES

Albó, X. "The 'Long Memory' of Ethnicity in Bolivia, and Some Temporary Oscillations." Forthcoming. In J. Crabtree and L. Whitehead, eds., *Unresolved Tensions: Bolivia Past and Present.* Pittsburgh: University of Pittsburgh Press.

Albró, R. 2005. "The Indigenous in the Plural in Bolivia Oppositional Politics." *Bulletin of Latin American Research* 24 no. 4: 433–453.

Chalmers, D., et. al. 1997. "Associative Networks: New Structures of Representation for the Popular Sectors?" *The New Politics of Inequality in Latin America. Rethinking Participation and Representation.* D. Chalmers et al.

Kohl, B., and L.Farthing. 2006. *Impasse in Bolivia. Neoliberal Hegemony and Popular Resistance.* London: Zed Press.

Kreuger, C. "A Bold and Difficult First Year." *Bolivia Ground. Independent Information and Analysis on Bolivia* (kregerchris@hotmail.com). Distributed by the Andean Information Network.

Lazar, S., and J. A. McNeish. 2006. "The Millions Return? Democracy in Bolivia at the Start of the Twenty-first Century." Special Section, *Bulletin of Latin American Research Review* 25 no. 2: 157–162.

Ledebur, K. 2007. "Bolivian Conflict: September Stalemate in Sucre." *Andean Information Network* (www.ain-bolivia.org).

Madrid, R. 2007. "The Indigenous Movement and Democracy in Bolivia." Paper presented at the symposium, "Prospects for Democracy in Latin America," April 5–7, University of North Texas.

Martinez, N. 2007. "Bolivia's Nationalization of Oil and Gas. Understanding the Process and Creating Opportunities." *Institute for Policy Studies (www.ips-dc.org).*

Postero, N. 2007. *Now We Are Citizens. Indigenous Politics in Postmulticultural Bolivia.* Stanford: Stanford University Press.

Yashar, D. 2005. *Contesting Citizenship in Latin America. The Rise of Indigenous Movements and the Postliberal Challenge.* Cambridge: Cambridge University Press.

LEBANON'S PARALLEL GOVERNANCE
Rami G. Khouri

This chapter is about not just Lebanon but most of the Middle East, because I think Lebanon is quite representative of what's happening all around the Middle East. It's easy to get stuck in some of the details of local politics and political contestation inside Lebanon. But I think we need to accurately see it as a symbol of really wider trends that I think are going on all over the region, at least all over the Arab world, while Turkey, Israel, and Iran are slightly different.

In Lebanon today, the public sector has failed quite badly. I mean, the public sector is effectively dysfunctional today at the level of political governance. At the level of day-to-day routine bureaucratic activities, it's functioning fine. We just bought an apartment in Beirut, went through the whole process of registering it with many little bureaucratic steps, and everything was done normally. Sometimes you have to wait a month or two because the minister had resigned or was refusing to go to the office. And then you just wait a while, and it gets done, or you find ways to speed up the process. So the system functions without an effective government. And this is another Lebanese contribution to world history, along with the alphabet, which is that you can run a country without an effective government.

Somalia gave us that same lesson a few years ago. Palestine is giving it to us. It's one of the new Arab contributions to global civilization and the work of political scientists, which is how societies govern themselves without official governments in place. Or, the most fascinating new development, which we see in Lebanon, Palestine, Sudan, and Iraq and other places, is that you actually have several governments. And they're all legitimate. If they're not official governments, they're at least legitimate governing authorities or power authorities that actually deliver services and exercise power, including significant military power. They are seen to be legitimate by their own people, and you have several of them at the same time within the same country.

So a single sovereignty with multiple government authorities is one of the latest Arab contributions to global civilization. We're very proud of it. We haven't quite figured out how long it's going to last, what it really means, if it's going to continue, or if this is just a transitional stage. But I think these are some of the kinds of issues that raise themselves for us to consider when you look at Lebanon, and at the region.

The public sector governance challenges and the stresses in Lebanon reflect a whole series of different things that are happening simultaneously. There is a local power struggle between the Siniora government and the Hezbollah-led opposition. They're vying for a different share or a different combination of power within the cabinet, a different electoral system so that they have different shares of power in parliament. So there's a very local power struggle going on.

At the same time, you have a bilateral struggle going on between Syria and Lebanon, which is still a consequence of the modern history of Lebanon. Many Syrians still have not accepted the fact that Lebanon became an independent country and part of it was taken out of Syria by the French. This is an old problem between the Syrians and the Lebanese. And recently, Syria dominated Lebanon for many years; some people say it occupied it. But there's a terribly stressful situation between Lebanon and Syria that is still working itself out.

You have regional tensions and power struggles going on between Israel, Syria, Saudi Arabia, which manifests in Lebanon, as well. You have a wider contest between Iran and the U.S. more or less leading to constellations of forces within the Middle East and further afield that are confronting each other. And Lebanon is one of the arenas where this struggle is taking place.

You have the historical weakness of a pluralistic consensus based on power sharing, consociational democracy, as the Lebanese call it. This is a process that has been going on since the 1930s and 1940s. And it really has not worked very well in recent years. It worked okay up till around the 1950s or 1960s. But then it started showing its weaknesses.

Finally, you have a problem emerging—at a much higher level—which is about the very viability of statehood and the legitimacy of nationhood. These are bigger-ticket items. But they really need to be worked into the issues that we have to consider as we are looking at Lebanon or most of the other countries in the Arab world.

At the moment, the main government institutions, the public sector institutions of government, have failed and are totally immobilized. The cabinet—it's still working, but it doesn't represent all the Lebanese. Many of its decisions are being challenged. So the cabinet is not working very well. The parliament hasn't met for months and months. And the national dialogue committee that was established last year, and that met a few times to try to overcome the immobility of these other institutions, the informal national dialogue, is no longer meeting, either. So the three mechanisms of the cabinet, the parliament, and the national dialogue that were very vibrant at one point and were inclusive, because everybody was there, have all stopped functioning in any significant way.

But at the same time, the good news is that the political contestation process has been largely peaceful within Lebanon. There were some explosions and assassinations. But those were presumed to be done by external powers; many Lebanese blame the Syrians or the Israelis or others. And who knows who is responsible. Or, some were done, as is now clear, by Fateh al-Islam, some of these small Al-Qaeda-like terror groups that are springing up partly as a consequence of the Anglo-American adventure in Iraq. But that's a separate point for a different book.

But the proliferation of neoterrorist groups, small terrorist groups all over the Middle East, is something that's now just becoming clear in Lebanon as probably the most dramatic arena for this in the short run, because it's the arena where you've actually had a little war recently, a three-month war between Fateh al-Islam and the Lebanese Army in the north of Lebanon. So this is the, again, new phenomenon that we're seeing in Lebanon, which we're probably going to see in other places, which is very localized wars between Arab armies, heavily funded and supported and armed by the U.S., fighting against small spontaneously emerging terror groups that ally themselves to al-Qaeda. But that kind of violence has very specific causes, and it's separate from the political contestation within Lebanon, which has been and continues to be largely peaceful.

The other good news is that there are intense mediation efforts. And I would suggest to add an item to your list of how do you grade democracies. If your former colonial masters have to keep coming back as mediators to mediate among your people, you should probably lose a couple of points, too. The French foreign minister is now coming regularly to Beirut to mediate among the Lebanese—it's extraordinary—as are Saudi envoys, Arab League envoys. There's more per capita mediation in Lebanon, I think, than any other country in the world. But this is probably a constructive sign because it means that the Lebanese are looking to solve their political problems.

I think the situation causes us to look at the issue in a wider context and say, "Well, what are the problems? What is this—is it a question of the quality of democracy as we are talking about, or is it a wider question?" And I would say that there are several simultaneous issues that we have to look at. One is that the system is structured around confessional proportionality, which is what we have in Lebanon. There are 18 different religious and ethnic groups that formally have a place in the system, in parliament or in the government bureaucracy, or in the cabinet, or in the senior army officers.

A system structured around confessional proportionality has reached the limits of its efficacy due to several factors. One is that so many of these

Lebanese groups have formal and enduring links with outside powers, military links, financial links, whatever, whether it's the Shiites with Iran or the Sunnis with Saudis or the Christians with the French or others with the Americans. This structural reliance on foreign support, funding, and protection makes democracy a mockery. And we're seeing this in Lebanon.

Also, the changing demographic balance in Lebanon has really brought this system more or less to the end of its useful life. The Shiites are emerging as the largest group in the country. The combination of Sunni and Shiite Muslims is now more than the Christians. The Christians themselves have become relatively a minority in the country. And the Christians have also split politically, so Michel Aoun is aligned with Hezbollah. The other Christians, most of them are allied with the government. So there's a really serious demographic shakeup taking place, which is, again, making this traditional system no longer functional.

The second point is that the dominance of group rights over individual rights degrades the quality of public life and any attempt to have a functioning democracy or an efficient government system. I think this is pretty clear. If the tribe dominates the citizen, you can't have a real serious democratic system. You can have a governing system based on a tribal confederacy, which is essentially what most of the Arab countries are, but you can't have a real functioning democracy.

One of the problems here is that when you have groups that define political life and identity and interests, and these groups have access to external resources, as all of them do in Lebanon, whether it's money from Iran or guns from Syria or money from the U.S., or whatever, from France or Saudis, these external resources mean that most of the key players inside Lebanon don't need a functioning political system in the country. They don't need either power or validation from their own political system because they get it from outside. Therefore, they can let the state stagnate. They can let the public's governing system deteriorate and stagnate and freeze up, as it's doing now.

The third element is that the weak central government, which Lebanon has always had, means either you're going to be dominated by foreigners from outside, which Lebanon has experienced (Syria, Israel, or others have dominated it, and that wasn't satisfactory), or the weak central government has to be offset by strong sectarian, ethnic, and tribal groups. So we have a situation where real power is now shared, partly by the state, which still functions. It's not as if the government isn't there. It's there. There's a police. There's an army. But it doesn't rule the whole country.

Real power is shared by the state and non-state actors whom—though I don't think we should call them non-state actors any more. When you have a group like Hezbollah, which is very powerful, I would call them a parallel state. So you have states and parallel state actors. Hezbollah's military capabilities are far greater than the Lebanese government's. Its service delivery capacity is far greater than the Lebanese government's. But at the same time, Hezbollah doesn't want to take over the government. So it's a parallel state actor to the official state.

That raises issues of why people like Hezbollah, why groups like Hezbollah have become so strong. I think we need to look at them dispassionately, which I know in this town is very difficult to do. I look at Hezbollah rather dispassionately. I respect and admire some of the things they do. I criticize some of the things they do. But I think I look at them reasonably objectively. An objective look at Hezbollah and its power forces us at first to examine what groups like this represent. Why is it in a country like Lebanon, you can have this kind of group emerge and become so strong, or Hamas in Palestine, or other groups, Moqtada al-Sadr in Iraq? And there's groups like this all over the Middle East.

I think it's important to look at the lessons that they represent, which are lessons in credibility, efficacy, and legitimacy, in terms of how they respond to and are accountable to their constituents. The real question here is, how do you turn constituents into citizens? Their constituents are predominantly their own Shiite fellow citizens, but not only, because some of their services also serve other people who are not Shiites, who live in the areas where they predominate.

I would give you eight reasons why Hezbollah is powerful, credible, and seen to be, by its own people, very effective. These eight reasons are important to grasp as symptomatic of the rise of these kinds of parallel state actors or non-state actors alongside the weakness of the state. In the U.S., Hezbollah is seen predominantly as a terrorist organization. It's on the terrorist list. It's a bad guy. The reality from the ground in Lebanon and the Middle East is very different.

The reality is that Hezbollah is credible and powerful and effective, first of all, because it fought—successfully fought the Israeli occupation of South Lebanon and drove the Israelis out of most of South Lebanon. Second, it represents a very powerful reassertion of Shiite identity and a fight for Shiite citizen rights after the years and years of marginalization and discrimination. Third, they represent and are part of a broad pan-Islamic revival all across the Middle East. Fourth, they support the Palestinian cause, generally speaking, which is a very resonant cause with people all over the Arab world and much of the rest of the world. Fifth, they deliver key social services and other needs to their constituents: medical care, vocational training, unemployment assistance. Now they are doing reconstruction of destroyed areas from the war. Sixth, they fight corruption and inefficiency, and they provide a model of non-corrupt, efficient service delivery. Seventh, they promote a sense of pan-Arab sentiment. They mix their Islamism with their Lebanese identity with a pan-Arab identity in a very powerful combination that appeals to a lot of people, because the pan-Arab sentiment is still there at some level. And number eight, which is the most recent manifestation of the role they play, is that they present themselves as one of the actors in the region that is resisting American hegemonic aims. Those are their words, not mine. But that's how they present themselves, and that's how a lot of people see them. Those are issues that I think are important to note as reasons why Hezbollah is so strong. Those are also functions that you'd think the state should be carrying out. But it doesn't always do that.

If we're looking at this kind of context with all of these issues that I quickly tried to highlight, I think we have to ask ourselves—can we assess the quality and the depth of democracy in a place like Lebanon, or should we really be assessing the role of democracy as a valued condition or a goal for the Lebanese people, or the Arab people, vis-à-vis other goals of governance and communal life? Is it a question of "is democracy working?", or is it rather a question of, "should we talk about democracy and other things as well?"

I would say that, in fact, we should talk about other things as well, because you cannot just take democracy and measure it or assess it in the absence of the other issues. And the other issues are big-ticket items. We are talking of legitimacy. We are talking of efficacy of governance systems. We're talking of basic sovereignty, issues of fundamental sovereignty, of people in control of their lives, territory and destiny in the Arab world. Issues of identity; to reflect your identity, your individual, your communal, your national, your pan-Arab, your pan-Islamic identity are issues that people are concerned with every day, much more than democracy. Issues of nationalism: does your country make sense? Issues of stability and security, basic day-to-day stability and security. Issues of material well-being and survival. And finally, issues of religiosity versus secularism. These are really big. Every one of these is a big-ticket item. And collectively, they form that constellation of issues that ordinary Arabs and Lebanese and others deal with every day far more than they deal with democracy as a major issue that they're looking at.

I would say that the real issues we're looking at comprise a question of self-validation, countries and citizenries that have to validate themselves as countries and as nations. We have not had a single Arab citizenry or population that has truly had the opportunity to define itself in terms of its own government system, its own government officials, its relations with powers, foreign powers, its internal systems.

I think it's true to say that my children are addressing fundamentally the same issues that my grandparents addressed at the end of World War I. We've gone through a century without any significant change in addressing the fundamental public governance issues and identity and nationalism issues in most of the Arab countries, issues of secularism versus religiosity, relations between Zionism and Arabism, relations between the Arab world and Western powers, the relationship of a citizen to the state, the power of the central government, checks and balances on central authority, the role of the military services. The most fundamental issues of citizenship and statehood have not been fundamentally either studied or addressed or responded to, or decided by the citizens of the Arab countries themselves.

Consequently, we're seeing all these stresses all over the region. We're still seeing foreign armies coming into the region. We're still seeing Israeli occupation of Arab lands 40 years later. We're still seeing Arab regimes where fathers pass power to their sons, and where former army and air force generals become president and stay in power for 30 years or more. They also do so now with "democratic" elections. So the presidents of countries like Yemen, Tunisia, and Egypt are the leaders of political parties that have won elections and hold most of the seats in parliament. They're "democratically" elected leaders, but most of the time, "democratically" elected for life, and, in family terms, sometimes in perpetuity. And people don't want to put up with this very much. So this is why you are seeing these Islamist movements and some of these other movements coming up.

I'll finish by saying that we do need democracy in the Middle East. I know that most people in our region genuinely want democratic systems. They want good governance, accountability; they want justice and equality, and fair play. The analysis of global values surveys that has been done by serious American scholars shows that the convergence of commitment to values of equality, good governance, justice, and the rule of law are closest between the Arab-Islamic world and the U.S., among any other group of Western and non-Western countries or cultures around the world.

So it's not the values that are the problem. The real issue we have to address is the exercise of political power. Before looking much more deeply at issues of democracy in the Arab world or Lebanon, I think we really have to go back to the basics and look at the issues of self-determination, and whether these citizenries can finally be given an opportunity—for the first time ever—to actually decide questions about their own identity, governance, and political systems.

CONTRIBUTORS

Cynthia J. Arnson is Director of the Latin America Program at the Woodrow Wilson Center.

Gary Bland is Senior Governance Advisor at RTI International, an applied research institute based in Research Triangle Park, NC.

Michael Bratton is University Distinguished Professor of Political Science and African Studies at Michigan State University and Executive Director, Afrobarometer.

Luis A. Chirinos is Senior Local Governance Specialist at RTI International, an applied research institute based in Research Triangle Park, NC.

Phyllis Dininio is an independent consultant in international development who specializes in anticorruption with the U.S. Agency for International Development and the Department of State, among other organizations.

Larry P. Goodson holds the General Dwight D. Eisenhower Chair of National Security at the U.S. Army War College, where he is also Professor of Middle East Studies.

Patrick G. Heller is Associate Professor of Sociology and Co-Director of the Comparative Program in Development at Brown University.

Evelyne Huber is Morehead Alumni Distinguished Professor and Chair of the Department of Political Science, University of North Carolina at Chapel Hill.

Tim Judah is a freelance journalist who specializes in Balkan affairs for the *Economist* and the *New York Review of Books*, among other publications.

Rami G. Khouri is Director of the Issam Fares Institute for Public Policy and International Affairs at the American University of Beirut and editor-at-large of Beriut's *Daily Star* newspaper.

Brooke Larson is Professor of Latin American History at Stony Brook University in New York.

Michael S. Malley Michael S. Malley is Assistant Professor of Comparative Politics in the department of National Security Affairs at the Naval Postgraduate School in Monterey, CA.

Philippe C. Schmitter is a professorial fellow at the European University Institute in Florence and a recurring lecturer at the universities of Florence, Siena, and Trento and at the Central European University in Budapest.